Y0-ACG-763

Moral Complexity and The Holocaust

Marc Lee Fellman

WITHDRAWN
UTSA Libraries

University Press of America,® Inc.
Lanham · Boulder · New York · Toronto · Plymouth, UK

Library
University of Texas
at San Antonio

Copyright © 2009
Marc Lee Fellman

University Press of America,® Inc.
4501 Forbes Boulevard
Suite 200
Lanham, Maryland 20706
UPA Acquisitions Department (301) 459-3366

Estover Road
Plymouth PL6 7PY
United Kingdom

All rights reserved
Printed in the United States of America
British Library Cataloging in Publication Information Available

Library of Congress Control Number: 2009922307
ISBN-13: 978-0-7618-4443-3 (paperback : alk. paper)
ISBN-10: 0-7618-4443-0 (paperback : alk. paper)
eISBN-13: 978-0-7618-4444-0
eISBN-10: 0-7618-4444-9

Cover photo: Nazi soldiers evicting Jews from their hiding places.
Warsaw Ghetto, April 1943.
Source: Vad Vashem Archives.

♾™ The paper used in this publication meets the minimum
requirements of American National Standard for Information
Sciences—Permanence of Paper for Printed Library Materials,
ANSI Z39.48—1984

For

For Zsofia, Rupert & Nicholas

TABLE OF CONTENTS

Acknowledgements   vii

Chapter 1: A Topography of Moral Complexity   1

Chapter 2: Ordinary People in Extra-Ordinary Situations   19

Chapter 3: Dimensions of Moral Complexity   39

Chapter 4: Expanding on the Idea of a Weave of Responsibility   73

Chapter 5: Luck in Moral Experience   99

Chapter 6: Borderlines of Responsibility   115

Chapter 7: Listening to the Holocaust   149

Appendix   189

Bibliography   227

Index   233

ACKNOWLEDGEMENTS

This book is the product of research undertaken over the course of a number of years. In the writing it has been the cause of much self-reflection on the possibilities for moral life. So too it is also the product of the involvement of a number of significant people along the way. Among the many that I have had long conversations with I would like to make special mention of Peta Bowden who did much to sustain the original project. I also owe thanks to the Jewish synagogue in Budapest for permitting the use of testimonies which I originally sourced from the archive of the Jewish synagogue, Budapest. Thanks also to Murdoch University, Nagoya University of Commerce and Business and the University of Notre Dame Australia for support along the way. I would also like to thank my parents Lois and Fredrik for their enduring belief in me and lastly Midori for her unconditional love and support.

"The complete removal of Jews from Europe is not a question of morals, but of security for all states. Beetles that destroy potato crops must be destroyed. The Jews also destroy our crops and fields." (Attributed to Adolf Hitler) [1]

A TOPOGRAPHY OF MORAL COMPLEXITY

The continental philosopher Jean-Francois Lyotard has claimed that, in a sense, the Holocaust represents an obstacle to meaning. He has argued that the process of remembering the Holocaust entails a kind of forgetting.[2] I disagree with this argument but recognize the resistance engendered by Holocaust stories in their refusal to go the way of straightforward moral analyses. My argument is that the Holocaust constitutes a tension between moral complexity and moral enormity. I believe that it is this tension, in moral terms, that hinders understanding of Holocaust experiences. To this end I also argue that the difficulties associated with understanding the Holocaust in moral terms also presage new and fruitful interpretations.

It has been argued by many scholars that the Holocaust, in terms of the scale of the crimes perpetrated, is the paradigm case for moral enormity. Prima facie, the case for moral enormity in respect to the Holocaust seems strong. Of those who have argued in favour of the moral enormity of the Holocaust, most carry an echo of the philosopher John Dewey that certain historical events "in their production of good and evil . . . are so central, so strategic in position, that their urgency [demands] the most systematic reflective attention that can be given".[3]

I too, want to encompass the idea that what makes the Holocaust so distinctive is the scale of horror that was visited upon the landscape of Europe. Horror in all of its myriad manifestations was experienced in the course of the attempted destruction of European Jewry. My first point is that the Holocaust is a powerful symbol of moral enormity.

In addition, I argue that those aspects that we might associate, conceptually, with moral life, such as external circumstances, a person's individual dispositions and values, emotions and luck, in the context of the human experiences and events of the Holocaust, entail complexity, in the moral sense. That this is so is due in large part to the idea that careful examination of events reveals that the Holocaust is, in general terms, a geo-politically vast, complicated, 'modern', 'human' phenomenon. Put another way the Holocaust encompasses, on one level, an enormously diverse range of individual human experiences. By 'individual human experiences' I mean experiences that necessarily possess, at their core, a moral dimension. Thus I believe it is reasonable to suggest, that a phenomenon, with social and political parameters as broad and deep as those of the Holocaust, and encapsulating the range of human experiences that it does, will also be morally complex. When I speak of moral complexity I refer to the variety of factors characteristic of moral life in general that become amplified and intensified by experiences and events of the Holocaust. Factors that increase complexity include the way differing external circumstances affect how an individual might arrive at a moral decision, the nature and influence of what might be called internal factors or circumstances (such as a person's values, principles and loyalties); and the role of individual dispositions and predilections, emotions (such as a person's feelings of responsibility toward another) and even luck in the processes that impact upon motives, decisions, actions and their consequences. I shall argue that all of these components of moral life combine to provide the form and content of the moral complexity of the Holocaust.

The idea that an indispensable component to understanding the Holocaust morally is the moral complexity of the experiences that comprise it is given added weight by arguments contained within Philippe Burrin's important book *Hitler and the Jews, the Genesis of the Holocaust.*[4] According to Burrin historical investigation of the Final Solution is hampered by events that push comprehension to the limits of understanding. Burrin writes that:

> In the extent and forms of its carnage, in the circumstances and context of its accomplishment, the Final Solution forces the historian to acknowledge the limits of his understanding.[5]

I interpret Burrin here as referring to the way historical examination of the Holocaust struggles under the weight of a process that must include, as a core constitutive element, accounting for both scale and complexity of the moral dimensions of the Holocaust. It is because moral life can be complex and the Holocaust is morally enormous that historical narrative struggles under the burden of being able to take account of such complexity as is evinced by the experiences of the Holocaust itself.

In his exposition of how the Holocaust came to be, Burrin constructs an account that lays careful but persuasive emphasis on the complexities and difficulties inherent in being able to comprehend adequately the events in question. The difficulties and complexities raised by Burrin's account have an explicit moral dimension. In his assessment of differing and sometimes conflicting interpretations of the historical events, the sorts of questions that Burrin explores are deeply moral in their character. I interpret Burrin's questions as plumbing the depths of a moral abyss in the search for the reasons and motivations that lay behind the Final solution. The content of his investigation, though historical in both its orientation and its focus, is underpinned in a fundamental sense, by the practices and relations that characterise individual moral experiences. Whilst the task of reconstructing the event is shown to be difficult enough, he writes that "the event, in its enormity and diversity, remains largely unfathomable".[6] These terms 'enormity' and 'diversity', in the sense in which Burrin employs them, refer to both moral and historical scale and complexity. Elsewhere he uses language with a clear moral content. When he writes of the Holocaust as having "weighed on the European conscience"[7] there seems to be no doubt as to the moral importance he attaches to the Holocaust as an historical event. It is argued here that his book is not only a significant historical document but is a recognition of the complexity of events that he details. Indeed it could hardly be otherwise. Burrin's research shows that an event of the moral magnitude and complexity of the Holocaust necessarily involved millions of people and entailed a diverse range of moral behaviour from, in his words, "zeal" to "complicity" to "acquiescence" to "passivity"[8] and a myriad of other behaviours in between. On this basis it is claimed that Burrin's investigation is underpinned by what seems like the most elementary of questions but which in fact belies layers of complexity and which "historical investigation strains to comprehend."[9]

It could be argued that the knowledge of what was done, where it was done, how it was done, in what circumstances and on what scale it was done, whilst complex in its own right, may be less daunting than the attempt to understand the moral dimensions of the experiences of those involved. I propose that explanations like those of Raul Hilberg and Martin Gilbert, both of which I will take up later, and Burrin, in part because of the complex historical issues they explore, dredge up difficult and complex moral issues. The point is that the events of the Holocaust tested the parameters and indeed the limits of the moral sensibilities of millions of Europeans. Moreover, all of the above implies a note of caution against oversimplification of what was a complex phenomenon.

A most important element in the process of moving beyond the powerful though confining expression of horror is the ability to reflect on the different senses of historical complexity that comprise Holocaust events and experiences. I am not suggesting here a congruity between the Holocaust understood in terms of its historical significance and the Holocaust understood in terms of its moral significance. Rather the point I am making is that a connection exists between the way in which individuals live their lives and the historical circumstances that impact on those lives. I want to suggest that historical circumstances, external to the individual, can have the effect of contributing massively to the complexity that inheres in that individual's moral life. If the idea of a connection between historical circumstances and the way individuals order their lives, morally speaking, is plausible then it seems reasonable to further suppose that the more complex and attenuated the circumstances and interpersonal relations constituting a situation, then the more complex our moral analyses concerning the said situation are also likely to be.

In an effort to convey some of the nuances of the historical complexity of the Holocaust Ruth Linden writes:

> Dates . . . laws . . . military occupations . . . hundreds of transit, concentration, labour, and satellite camps ... millions of deportations and deaths. Scholars have constructed detailed historical narratives out of these fragments. As a concept, "Holocaust" permits us to recognize patterns amid the variations, similarities alongside uniqueness, and continuities among statistics of lives and communities destroyed. But the Holocaust was not a discrete event fixed in time with a beginning and an end. It is an analytic construct abstracted from lived experience.[10]

As Linden's passage suggests, the theme of complexity, as regards the Holocaust, functions on a number of different levels. On one level the Holocaust was a complex of events that took place over a long period of time, over a large and heavily populated geographic area, involving every state in Europe, overtly occupied or otherwise, and it impinged to some extent on the lives of nearly every person in Europe. On their own, though, these facts contribute little, in a direct way, to a sense of the tension between moral enormity and moral complexity. Linden's passage does, however, contain a very important clue to understanding the nature of the simultaneous presence of moral enormity and moral complexity with respect to the Holocaust. Her remarks suggest that overall understanding (moral or otherwise) of the Holocaust derives in a fundamental way from the texture of lived experiences. I believe that this is a crucial if problematic point. The recognition that the Holocaust is about lived experiences is problematic, on the one hand because of the sheer logistics of taking in the variety and volume of experiences. The sheer numbers of different lived experiences are one dimension of complexity. The question of logistics aside, however, there are also questions that relate to problems in evaluating experiences. Accounts of individual experiences all take the form of interpretations of events. And whether or not they are first hand, second hand or even more removed from the events by space and time they can only ever be representations of events. This makes the task of verification and substantiation very important in order that the representation in question is as accurate as possible. The focus on individual experiences is most important in terms of the questions it generates for attempts to evaluate the moral dimensions of the Holocaust. That the Holocaust is about lived experiences means that it is also about moral life. The one implies the other. For Linden individual experiences seem to represent a lowest common denominator. It was individual human beings who experienced, albeit in very different ways, the horrors of the Holocaust. It was individuals who were brutalized by events. It was individuals who witnessed events. It was individuals who had knowledge of events. It was individuals who were complicit in events. It was individuals who took responsibility and it was individuals who failed to take responsibility for events. In short it was individual human beings who responded to events in ways that are morally significant. It is individual human beings who comprised the 'flesh and bloodness' of the Holocaust.

Evidence for the veracity of the proposition concerning the importance of lived experiences is present in Norman Geras' paper titled 'Richard Rorty and the Righteous Among the Nations'.[11] In a critique of Rorty regarding the matter of the motives of individuals who risked their lives to rescue Jews, Geras concludes:

> The point is only that it is a complicated question just what combination of reasons, motives and other factors—temperamental, situational and so on—does, and just what combination does not, move people to act under risk for other people.[12]

I interpret Geras' comments as highlighting the complex causal conditions that are at play in moving people to particular actions. My point, though, is that it is the interpersonal relations in question that are the raw material of moral life. Geras' refutation of Rorty's position is grounded in the presentation and examination of the factors that underpin concrete individual experiences. His comments also contain a warning, however, that evaluations of a moral sort are always going to be contingent upon factors that will complicate rather than simplify matters. This warning also represents another dimension of complexity. For Geras, the motivations and situations of, in this instance, rescuers, are morally complex. Geras' account can be interpreted as amounting to a recognition of the complexity inherent in situations that require on the part of the agent, the ability to assimilate, prioritize and assess, on the basis of limited available data and time, complicated and morally significant outcomes. In short, moral complexity is an integral part of many Holocaust experiences. Moreover, the moral complexity present in Holocaust experiences, very often means that understanding their moral dimensions is a very difficult task.

Associated with the point above regarding relationships is the idea that individual experiences are woven together with the experiences of others. This is an inevitable part of the lived human life. It is the web of interpersonal relationships between individual lives that contributes significantly to morally complex situations and outcomes. A key point is that the moral complexity of the Holocaust derives, in some large part, from the way individuals understand their relations with others. Of greater significance, however, is the notion that those relationships entail moral responsibilities. Working with the same premise as Linden and Geras, that is, that it is the lived experiences of the Holocaust that provide the core ingredients of an enhanced understanding of the moral terrain of the Holocaust, this book will elaborate on the significance of Holocaust experiences, the nature of the relationships that constitute such experiences and the responsibilities implied by such relationships.

The importance I attach to lived experiences also foregrounds notions of particularity and historical locatedness as imperative for an adequate understanding of the moral dimensions of the Holocaust. Although I do not specifically pursue meta-ethical questions in this book, I believe that moral theories that rely on the application of universal moral principles organised according to certain general principles, are unable to provide determinate judgments concerning the sorts of complex moral questions that arise in the context of Holocaust experiences.[13] I contend that the moral complexity that inheres in Holocaust experiences is ethically irreducible. By this I mean that morally complex situations are not able to be reduced to, nor are they amenable to rule bound resolutions. In contrast to the tradition in moral thought that assumes that moral formulae can be imposed from the outside as it were, I believe that the outcome of questions concerning the moral life of individuals depends largely on a combination of factors that arise from the complicated overlay of experiences within concrete human contexts. With regard to the Holocaust this means paying careful attention to a complex array of motivational and situational factors in the evaluation of such problems as conflicting or dysfunctional values, extreme emotions, divided loyalties and the extra-ordinary nature of the situations people find themselves in. This is an important point because much Holocaust literature philosophically oriented or otherwise, brings with it a seemingly unnegotiable epistemological framework as regards what may be constituted as 'good' or 'evil'. Holocaust literature very often functions as if rules for judging individuals/groups, actions or decisions are able to be derived from a position independent of the situation in question. Through detailed and careful examination of actual events and experiences I will argue that accounts ascribing moral formulae to complex historical situations are deeply problematic. In one sense this book is a response to the attempted canonization of what counts as appropriate moral knowledge within Holocaust literature.

A good example of the complexities entailed in reducing human agency to morally distinct categories is evident in Hilberg's usage of the trichotomy 'victims, perpetrators and bystanders'.[14] The presentation of categories in this way needs to be mindful of the possibility that different categories are sometimes applicable to the same individual. Sometimes certain 'victims' seem to take on the role of 'perpetrators'; some 'perpetrators' are able to be interpreted as 'victims'; and some 'bystanders' also fulfil the requirements of, or are able to be perceived as 'victims' or 'perpetrators'. Differences and ambiguities within and between situations result in inevitable slippage as regards the establishment of moral categories such as those described by Hilberg. My point is that such slippage is often unable to be captured in generalised moral classifications. Millions of 'bystanders', for instance, were also witnesses of one sort or another. Thousands, perhaps hundreds of thousands, of people saw Jews being deported and millions of people knew of the brutalisation, deportation or extermination of Jews. Does this sense of 'witnessing' implicate them in some ethically significant sense? Does, for example, witnessing atrocities first hand entail some sense of moral culpability? Does the witnessing of such occurrences as the deportation of Jews indicate a certain sort of tacit complicity with that of more direct involvement? If not, then when exactly did an individual become implicated in the complex moral topography of the Holocaust? Does it depend on the certain knowledge of the fate of those deported? And if so, then what of the moral culpability of a Roosevelt or a Churchill, both of whom possessed knowledge of the fate of the Jews from an early stage in the war? Do the millions of witnesses, by virtue of their knowledge, their understanding, their silence, their possible indifference, fit somewhere within a schema of responsibility? Are those who witnessed or had knowledge of events at some level, also implicated somehow?

These are all difficult and unavoidably complex questions. The value of these and like questions lies in the way they draw attention to some of the difficulties associated with straightforward moral prescriptions with respect to the lived experiences of the Holocaust. Formulaic moral vision implies simplifications of a sort that are difficult if not impossible to sustain when pitted against the complicated schema of human relations that constituted the events. However, this is not to suggest anything like the homogenisation of distinctions. On the contrary I am saying that the role and status of some distinctions are in need of careful and critical reflection. I will argue, for example, that the sort of clarity in moral judgment suggested by Hilberg's distinctions is undermined somewhat given the recognition that actual lived experiences are a good deal more complex than such distinctions allow. I stress that this is not intended as a plea for a reduction of moral culpability in cases where such culpability is clearly established. The point that I seek to establish is that in order to extend understanding of such aspects of moral life as the nature of our responsibilities we need to move past simple expressions of blame and praise, and explore the complex interplay of factors that lead individuals to behave the way they do.

Hence the case for moral complexity that I have sketched complicates questions of moral judgment of the sort implied in clear cut moral categorisations. It might even be suggested that the tension between moral complexity and moral enormity has the effect of diluting the role and significance of judgment. This is not to say that moral clarity is necessarily unachievable, but rather that it is not simplistic. Questions surrounding the difficulties of judgment will be among those considered in this work.

By questioning moral ascriptions such as Hilberg's trichotomy I am not suggesting that 'ordinary people' are implicated in the same way as those who conceived and implemented the 'Final Solution', or those who staffed the killing camps, or even those 'bureaucrats' who participated, for example, in the organization of the rolling stock needed to transport those destined for the camps. A more difficult question, however, is whether or not the act of witnessing or the possession of certain knowledge entails some sense, and perhaps some significant sense, of moral responsibility. In my view the act of seeing itself is potentially morally perilous. To see is also to witness. Moreover, the act of witnessing may carry with it the implication that the agent in question is a participant as opposed to being merely an observer. Therefore, seeing, in the sense of witnessing an event contains a distinctly moral component. The act of witnessing entails a

level of involvement in the event that is being witnessed that possibly also erodes the witnessing individual's capacity to remain dispassionate. It may even be the case that the act of witnessing, in the sense that
I have described it, can sometimes lead to, or induce a decision to intervene to prevent or alleviate suffering. Another way of looking at this sense of seeing is to place it in the context of Sartre's maxim "L'enfer, c'est les autres (Hell is other people)".[15] As is the case for the character Garcin in Sartre's play 'No Exit', the mere presence of an agent at a particular place and time can entail moral responsibility.

Recapitulating here, I have indicated that among the difficulties inherent in understanding the parameters of moral life in the wake of opening a door onto a genocidal universe is the effect of the tension between enormity and complexity on the capacity for judgment. In other words, the Holocaust demands, yet possibly precludes certain sorts of moral judgments. As a result of the enormity of the evil involved, our capacity to appreciate the various facets of the moral terrain of the Holocaust has a tendency to be numbed. This reduction of the capacity to appreciate such a fundamental characteristic of the Holocaust as its moral complexity should alert us to the difficulties of exactitude and the need to remain open to new interpretations. So, whilst I'm not suggesting moving away from making moral judgments, I am expressing caution. A major theme of this project is that a careful appreciation of the complex range of factors, indicative of moral life, and that form a central component of the events of the Holocaust, is essential to understanding its broader parameters. A deeper comprehension of such questions as the nature of individual and group responsibility, with respect to the events of the Holocaust, and the range of possibilities for judgment that such understanding of responsibility may imply, requires extreme sensitivity to the particularity of concrete individual experiences. I will argue that it is on the basis of adequate assessments of contingencies specific to particular Holocaust experiences and events that moral understanding of such experiences and events is extended. For instance, in a given situation it may be necessary to consider the possibility of an individual's predilections to certain behaviour or the extent to which actions are influenced by particular external circumstances or even the role of moral luck on an agent's capacity to maintain personal moral integrity. My claim is that such considerations arise as a result of the tension between enormity and complexity. On the one hand enormity evaluations indicate the necessity for judgment, and indeed, it is in a sense unavoidable, imbedded as it is in our intellectual processes. However, complexity analyses require us to exercise care in the matter of how we exercise judgment.

The guiding argument of this book is that Holocaust experiences invoke a tension between moral complexity and moral enormity. Moreover, and in spite of a tendency toward an enormity analysis, moral understandings of Holocaust experiences are irrevocably caught up in this tension. One of the real difficulties lies in the idea that this tension itself hinders understanding, in moral terms, of Holocaust experiences. On the one hand, enormity presses us to judge and to ascribe responsibility. On the other hand, we need to understand the complexities entailed in ascribing and exercising responsibility if we are going to be able to forecast new interpretations that take understanding forward. Understanding, it should be noted, operates on two levels. There is the need to understand the tension and the difficulties it presents in moral terms. And there is also the need to understand the complexities of taking responsibility as a way of presaging as yet untested interpretations.

The above claim does, of course, require considerable fleshing out. In the first instance, the Holocaust, perhaps best symbolized by the idea of 'Auschwitz', was and is in the collective and individual mind's eye a powerful symbol of the potentialities for moral life generally. Alan Milchman and Alan Rosenberg have claimed that what Dan Diner has termed '*das Ereignis Auschwitz*' (the Auschwitz event) represents "a transformative event in human history", the likes of which "has the potential to radically alter the prevailing conditions in the historical world [and] reshape the human landscape in a decisive way".[16] Milchman and Rosenberg are making a strong claim here.[17] My point, in referring to it, is that the symbol of Auschwitz, also suggests a similarly radical questioning of the landscape of moral life. Holocaust experiences, by virtue of their depiction of the tension between moral enormity and moral complexity, are in my view demonstrative of the difficulties of charting this landscape.

In particular my questioning takes the form of seeking to understand the nature of moral responsibilities. It is my contention that attention to the nature of moral responsibilities is the key to working through the tension between enormity and complexity with regard analyses of Holocaust experiences. At the risk of stating the obvious I believe that such concepts and issues as guilt and innocence, blame and praise, the role of virtues and vices, and more generally, the grounds of our moral engagement with the world are, within the framework of the Holocaust, difficult issues. Understanding these concepts and issues requires understanding the conceptual fabric of our moral responsibilities. I base this last claim on the belief that the various aspects of moral responsibilities that I seek to examine indeed form the core of our moral engagement with the world.

Let me clarify here. Both moral enormity and moral complexity are integral to Holocaust experiences. Yet their simultaneous presence signifies a conceptual tension that threatens to seriously impede moral understandings of such experiences. Holocaust experiences themselves, and the responsibilities that define such experiences, are crucial to the attempt to understand the potential obstacle to meaning presented by the tension between enormity and complexity.

In the light of the case for both complexity and enormity it is surely noteworthy that philosophy, as an academic enterprise, has not for the most part engaged in systematic reflection on the possible moral meanings and implications of the Holocaust. It is philosophy's lack of attention to the Holocaust that has led Alan Rosenberg and Gerald Myers to write:

The murder of six million Jewish men, women, and children during World War

> II was of such barbarity that it constitutes one of the central events of our time; yet a list of the major concerns of professional philosophers since 1945 would exclude the Holocaust.[18]

Whilst this comment is now some two decades old it is not without continued relevance.[19] The reasons for this perceived inadequacy, whilst interesting in their own right, will not be the major concern of this book. What is important here is to seek ways to redress what Rosenberg suggests is a 'failure' on the part of contemporary philosophy. One possible line of argument for the lack of literature of a philosophical sort could be that the gap between experiences in the camps and 'ordinary' experience is too great to be able to reflect upon insightfully. It is even argued by some survivors of the camps that the exercise of rendering camp experiences in some way routinely knowable is itself a morally questionable exercise. Be that as it may, and despite certain epistemological difficulties, I argue that Holocaust experiences are an important source for verification of the tension between complexity and enormity. For this reason alone they warrant careful scrutiny and reflection.

A measure of the difficulties inherent in this task however can be understood from the opening remarks of Frances Degen Horowitz, to the conference titled *The Holocaust in Hungary: Fifty Years Later,* that whilst we can learn and remember we should resign ourselves "never to truly understand the enormity of the Shoah".[20] I interpret Horowitz's comments to mean that even such a basic association as that of extreme 'evil' with the Holocaust is far more widely acknowledged than understood. Given this powerful and entirely understandable association of moral enormity with the Holocaust I contend that what is required is more attention to the nature of the tension generated between the enormity referred to above, and the moral complexities also present. Difficult though this task may be, it is my view that it is best achieved using the evidence of the stories that have survived the Holocaust.

Something very important is at stake in this discussion of the Holocaust. I do not hold, for example, that it is possible to suppose that because the Holocaust is taken by many commentators to be the paradigm case of evil, it is therefore valid to proceed with straightforward judgments of condemnation or innocence on all levels. To follow this line would be to deny precisely what is at issue, namely the simultaneous occurrence of moral enormity and moral complexity. This combination, moral enormity and moral complexity, whilst not signifying a contradiction does point to a serious tension as regards the potential for understanding the moral dimensions of the Holocaust. The difficulty, in respect to the tension itself, lies in the attempt to do justice to both aspects of the tension. For example, the presence of moral enormity in many Holocaust experiences may well be overwhelming but this should not be allowed to obscure the fact that a vast number of Holocaust experiences and events contain clear evidence of the ambiguity, heterogeneity and sometimes conflicted nature of moral life. Put another way, the multiple (and multiple layers of) events, persons and experiences that comprise the Holocaust, entail a diverse range of moral values and responses. This brings me to my next point. Such aspects of moral complexity as responsibilities, circumstances, luck and so on are also multi-dimensional. They cannot be reduced to a single interpretation.

Concerning a more general question of how to interpret the Holocaust Lawrence Langer writes:

> Certain pivotal works on the Holocaust (or works accepted as pivotal) shape habits of mind that are difficult to dislodge, and I believe one of the main tasks of future historians and commentators is to identify such works and to subject them to a fresh scrutiny, so we can see whether the habits of mind they promote really provide greater insight into the issues we still need to investigate.[21]

If Langer's general observation about the habituating effect of established Holocaust studies texts is true, the same might also be true with respect to those interpretations that seek to extend understanding of the moral parameters of the Holocaust. Perhaps more importantly, however, investigations plumbing the moral depths of the Holocaust will almost certainly carry implications for the way we conceive the category of the 'moral'. For example, the capacity of the Holocaust to shock both individual and collective moral imagination might reasonably be supposed to have an effect on the way we understand a whole raft of aspects of moral life.

The almost mandatory expression of moral outrage with respect to the Holocaust is understandable and entirely justifiable. However, expressions of horror, as such, do little to carry forward our moral understanding of this complex of events. This is not to suggest that the expression of horror is unimportant because in a very simple sense the loss of the sorts of issues that that expression encompasses, like the ideas of prima facie judgment and accountability, would mean losing sight of the combination of enormity and complexity as a tension. On the enormity side of the quotient Kenneth Seeskin has written that "the Holocaust is unique in the sense that thought is overwhelmed by evil on this scale."[22] Whilst it should be borne in mind that Seeskin's comments are delivered in the context of a discussion on the limits of morality, it is also the case that his remarks seem to carry with them the demand that this sense of moral enormity be retained over and above all else that may be said about the Holocaust. In contrast I claim that in order to capture that which is morally significant in respect to the Holocaust there is a need to proceed beyond the 'mere' expression of horror. To collapse our understanding of the events and experiences of the Holocaust into an expression of overwhelming evil is to misunderstand the complexity of the dynamic within and between human relations and the situations moral agents find themselves in.

As a means of organizing the sorts of problems described above I propose the idea of a 'weave of responsibility'. My use of the metaphor of a 'weave' is intended to convey the very important sense of interconnectedness and density within and between the various factors that contribute to an understanding of moral responsibility whilst at the same time allowing for the equally important ability to discern, isolate and evaluate particular aspects of responsibility. I will employ the metaphor of a 'weave of responsibility' as distinct from say a 'chain of responsibility' as a means of conveying more fully the sense of overlap and proximity that I want to emphasise with regard to understanding the complexities of exercising responsibility. The term 'chain of responsibility', like 'chain of command', implies notions of hierarchy and the sorts of distinctions that I not only want to avoid, but intend to question. Moreover, by focussing on the factors that underpin the way in which individuals come to understand the moral dimensions of their experiences I hope to bring to life both the elements of moral complexity and of moral enormity that were a feature of their lives. I intend the idea of a weave of responsibility as the vehicle to demonstrate the different aspects of responsibility integral to the tension between enormity and complexity.

Among the benefits of conceptualising responsibility as analogous to a weave are the benefits it brings by way of a more structured understanding of the combination of moral complexity and moral enormity. Some strands of the weave are stronger, more visually arresting and stand in marked relief; and so pertain to that which signifies the presence of moral enormity, whilst others combine to form a complex pattern of interlacing threads, thereby suggesting that that which is morally significant is also compositionally complex.

At the heart of my explanation of the idea of a 'weave of responsibility', is an account of moral responsibilities developed in part from Christopher Gowans' text *Innocence Lost: An Examination of Inescapable Moral Wrongdoing*.[23] Where Gowans explores moral experience from the perspective of moral conflict and the claim that sometimes moral wrongdoing is inescapable, I extend his insight to develop an account of moral responsibility as derived from social relationships and social practices. This is because I am more interested in developing an understanding of moral responsibility within the social and political 'weave' of moral life, and less interested in the debates that place ideas of moral responsibility under the rubrics of free will or determinism. Hence, I incorporate Gowans' account of moral experience and the nature of moral conflict into a working definition of responsibility understood as responsibilities to persons within a web of social relations.

Underpinning my notion of a 'weave of responsibility' is the assumption that in 'normal' situations agents possess the capacity to choose from a range of options that will directly test their moral sensibilities. In other words, and speaking generally, individuals of sound mind possess an intrinsic capacity to choose good or bad. When it comes to Holocaust experiences however, it is apparent that there are situations where the extra-ordinary nature of the circumstances very often results in a gross impoverishment of the substance, quality and conceptual range of both agency and choice. That is to say, circumstances can massively affect how individuals are likely to choose. In fact, within the spectrum of Holocaust experiences there are some situations that by their very location at the extremes of moral experience effectively erase meaningful notions of choice and agency altogether. I argue that such experiences are also morally enormous in terms of their depiction of the extremes of moral life. My use of enormity in this respect requires some further explanation. Previously, I have intended enormity to entail cases where moral condemnation is indisputable. I believe such examples are, as I shall argue in the Chapter two, powerful instances of moral enormity. However, I also believe there to be a connection between enormity and extremity in cases where a lack of agency seems to be apparent.

The cases that most readily spring to mind here are what have become known as 'Sophie's choice' situations, or the 'choice less choice' situation, where all options are equally morally problematic. In such situations, examples of which will be examined in later chapters, the agents in question find their options so severely impoverished by conditions outside their control, that their very sense of agency may be placed into question. That is to say, the circumstances of such a situation so compress the range of ethically appropriate options that one of the key defining elements of agency, the self's sense of free will, is rendered meaningless. It is those sorts of situations that typify juridical understandings of a diminished sense of agency and choice. The Sophie's choice cases are also often remarkable for the way in which the individuals in question are seemingly able to continue on with their lives in spite of the choices they have had to make. That said the Sophie whose name is etched on the concept did eventually commit suicide.[24]

Not surprisingly it is the sorts of extreme examples exemplified by 'Sophie's choice' that are more able to be straightforwardly interpreted with respect to a moral weave of Holocaust experiences. This is largely because such examples suggest such an overt confinement of an agent's ability to exercise meaningful choices. More difficult to assess however are those examples (most especially those that entail some sort of witnessing), that whilst less visible within a 'weave of responsibility', nevertheless provide indispensable threads in the warp and woof of the moral fabric of the Holocaust. An important task of this book will be to more adequately comprehend the nature and content of these more morally problematic, and as I will argue, morally complex examples of Holocaust experiences, that give rise to differing ways of understanding responsibility.

To set the stage for the enquiry, Chapter two will entail an examination of Christopher Browning's text *Ordinary Men: Reserve Police Battalion 101 and the Final Solution in Poland*.[25] In addition to focussing on 'perpetrators',[26] the aim of this chapter will be to bring to life the sorts of philosophical issues of primary concern to this project. It will be argued that studies such as Browning's *Ordinary Men* provide a sound empirical background to the conceptual tension between the moral enormity and moral complexity that characterise Holocaust experiences.

In Chapters three and four I examine dimensions of moral complexity that, whilst they are a core feature of Holocaust experiences, are also a component of moral life more generally. Chapter three deals primarily with the formulation and development of the idea of a 'weave of responsibility' as an important means to extend understanding of the various aspects of responsibilities that I seek to convey. Structurally, the different aspects of responsibility that I examine all contribute to an enhanced understanding of the wider tension in question. Like Gowans, I will argue that responsibility is best understood in terms of ideas of concrete and specific responsibilities to particular persons as opposed to accounts in which responsibilities are derived from more juridical-like positions.[27] I will argue that an understanding of responsibility based on relations between particular agents, provides a conceptual ground for understanding the nature of the tension between enormity and complexity and hence the difficulties that such a tension presents for meaning.

I also evaluate other aspects of responsibility including responsibility understood as a certain kind of integrity, and as including the circumstances and the practices that bind moral life. I intend to show how all of these aspects contribute to an understanding of the complexities of exercising responsibility. My intention with the idea of a conceptual weave is to show how differing aspects of responsibility form the core component of an individual's moral engagement with the world, whilst at the same time providing a backdrop for the exploration of factors that constitute the tension.

In Chapter four I will also examine some of the factors that affect moral experience and moral analyses within an understanding of the Holocaust as morally complex. Some of the factors I will consider include: the influence of external circumstance on agency and choice, the sorts of problems associated with group ascriptions of responsibility, consideration of the difficulties in being able to clearly delineate complicated motivational forces and the possibility of moral failure as part of moral life. All of the above factors will be considered within the context of a discussion that focuses primarily on the category of 'bystanders'.

In the fifth chapter I will consider the role of luck in moral experience. As part of my examination of the place of luck in moral life I will also assess aspects of the debate surrounding akratic actions and the influence of emotions. Of importance here is the argument that moral luck features strongly in understanding how we exercise responsibility.

In Chapter six, I examine the moral implications of different understandings of the historical origins of the Holocaust as a European phenomenon. Not incommensurate with the notion of a complex 'weave of responsibility' is the idea of a particular understanding of responsibility that extends much farther than the borders of Germany. Extending understanding of responsibility in this way is compatible with a perspective of the Holocaust as historically but also morally complex, because responsibility, in the sense I intend is deepened rather than generalised. Put another way, empirical support for an extension of responsibility for the Holocaust beyond the geo-political borders of Germany represents a further complication of an already complex fabric. When the Holocaust is thought of in this way, European civilization, European culture and European people are implicated in its occurrence. In other words, the process of reinvigo-rating questions of responsibility has important ramifications as regards the nature of Western civilisation. Whilst it is true that the Holocaust fits 'our' strongest intuitions of extreme evil, it is also true that this complex of events did not occur in another world and its perpetrators were not devils. The Holocaust occurred in Europe at the hands of Europeans.

In a reference to the geographical, thematic, originary and ethical nature of Nazism (and thus the Holocaust) to 'the West', Jacques Derrida writes:

> What I am aiming at here is, obviously enough, anything but abstract. We are talking about past, present and future "events", a composition of forces and dis-courses which seem to have been waging merciless war on each other (for ex-ample from 1933 to our time). We have here a program and a combinatory whose power remains abysmal. In all rigour it exculpates none of the discourses which can thus exchange their power. It leaves no place open for any arbitrating authority. Nazism was not born in the desert. We all know this, but it has to be constantly recalled. And even if, far from any desert, it had grown like a mush-room in the silence of a European forest, it would have done so in the shadow of big trees, in the shelter of their silence or their indifference but in the same soil.[28]

The idea that the Holocaust was not an aberration in the moral topography of 'the West' but rather the outcome of a particular combination of ingredients in-trinsic to the socio-ethico-political culture of Europe is especially challenging. Peter Haas for example, has plausibly argued[29] that the Holocaust was the prod-uct of a 'Nazi ethic' but that this ethic in turn was derived from a more general Enlightenment tradition. I will examine Haas's thesis that the National Socialist (re)construction of the Jew-as-other was acted upon so successfully because of already entrenched, centuries old ideas of race and anti-Semitism and an ability to 'legitimately' utilise the well developed legal, moral, bureaucratic and techno-logical frameworks of modern society.

In addition to examining the Haas thesis I will consider aspects of the work of Berel Lang, Zygmunt Bauman and Philippe Burrin as a means of making ex-plicit the links between the Holocaust on the one hand and European culture, modernisation, rationality and moral consciousness on the other. In this way this study will question reductionist moral categorisations of the sort that tend to iso-late explanations from their encompassing cultural context. Utilising aspects of the work of these authors (particularly their understanding of the relationship be-tween modernity and the Holocaust) I intend to continue to develop the themes of the tension between complexity and enormity, and an understanding of the Holocaust as a complex of events informed by a more encompassing understand-ing of responsibility. It is the individual threads that comprise the factors affect-ing responsibility but it is only by standing back from the fabric that we can take in the context. I would point out here that my aim is to provide an understanding of responsibility in the context of the tension between complexity and enormity

analyses of the Holocaust. I do not seek to hold everyone individually culpable. I do wish to deepen what is understood by responsibility and the practices that sustain it. To this end, I include discussion
of the issues of praise and blame, and the degrees of mediation between conscious knowledge and the uses to which such knowledge is put.

With a view to further illustrating the tension between moral complexity and moral enormity, the final chapter points to the value of a return to particular concrete glimpses of the experiences of Holocaust survivors. The experience of survivors is examined because of the substance such experiences lends to my claim for the tension between enormity and complexity analyses of the Holocaust.

In response to Lawrence Langer's book, *Admitting the Holocaust,* I will argue that in spite of (or perhaps precisely because of) the difficulties of (re)presenting the Holocaust, it is essential that the testimonies of survivors are not excluded from academic considerations. My claim is that the testimonies of survivors are evidence of the survival of practices of responsibility. I demonstrate the notion that practices of taking responsibility for others were able to persist in the face of the terror of the Holocaust. If the aim of the Final Solution was total annihilation of the Jewish identity, then the testimonies of survivors are the material/discursive evidence of the failure of this aim. The intellectual, emotional and sometimes erotic vitality present in some survivor testimonies is evidence of not only the survival of notions of 'self', and of course the number of literal selves, but also the remains, in the face of moral tragedy, of practices of responsibility for others. I will argue that the evidence examined in this study of Holocaust experiences drawn largely from previously unpublished testimonies (see Appendix), by virtue of their specificity, contingency and particularity, personify both the moral complexity and moral enormity characteristic of the Holocaust.

The testimonies of Holocaust survivors tell concrete stories about particular experiences. Taken individually they represent discrete insights into the horror of a landscape that defies moral scale. Collectively, however, the testimonies mesh in intricate ways to serve as the basis for deepening understanding of the moral dimensions of the Holocaust. I would point out finally, that I am not implying some sort of identification with those who experienced the terrible events of the Holocaust. Rather I approach the Holocaust as Geoffrey Hartman suggests "not as something enclosed in the past but as a contemporary issue requiring an intensity of representation close to eyewitness report."[30] Thus my conviction is that the testimonies that I present and examine, though they do not convey the whole picture, represents valuable insights within what Maurice Blanchot, in his book *The Writing of Disaster*, has called an "impossible real".[31] In the final analysis I argue that the experiences examined, in their elaboration of the tension produced by the conceptual composite of complexity and enormity analyses, enhance our understanding of these very same experiences. Understanding how we ought to live depends very much on our understanding of how we do live.

Notes

1. Adolf Hitler, cited in a transcript of the subtitles of *"That was our War"*, SBS Television, Australia, 1995.

2. Jean-Francois Lyotard, *Heidegger and "the jews"*, (Minneapolis: University of Minnesota Press, 1990), 25-26.

3. John Dewey, *Problems of Men*, (New York: Philosophical Library, 1960), 11-12.

4. Philippe Burrin, *Hitler and the Jews, the Genesis of the Holocaust*, (London: Edward Arnold, 1994).

5. Burrin, 17.

6. Burrin, 149.

7. Burrin, 149.

8. Burrin, 149.

9. Philippe Burrin, *Hitler and the Jews*, 17.

10. Ruth Linden, *Making Stories, Making Selves, Feminist Reflections on the Holocaust*, (Colombus State University Press, 1993), 86.

11. Norman Geras, 'Richard Rorty and the Righteous Among the Nations', *Journal of Applied Philosophy*, 1986, vol.12, no.1, 151-173.

12. Geras, 167.

13. For an example of an attempt to apply a more 'formulaic' approach to the sorts of moral problems entailed in individual Holocaust experiences see Berel Lang, *Act and Idea in the Nazi Genocide*, (University of Chicago Press: Chicago, 1991). For an axample of an approach that seeks to convey both the sense of enormity with that of complexity in the context of a specific Holocaust event see Christopher Browning, *Ordinary Men: Reserve Police Battalion 101 and the Final Solution in Poland*, (New York: Harper Collins: 1993). And among those theorists that might embody a more particularist approach to moral experience see Margaret Walker, *Moral Understandings*, (London: Roultledge, 1998) and Lawrence Blum, *Moral Perception and Particularity*, (Cambridge: Cambridge University Press, 1994).

14. Raul Hilberg, *Pertpetrators, Victims, Bystanders*, (New York: Harper Perennial, 1993).

15. Jean Paul Sartre, 'No Exit' in Robert Solomon (ed.), *Existentialism*, (New York: Random House, 1974), 228.

16. Alan Milchman and Alan Rosenberg, *Martin Heidegger and the Holocaust*, (New Jersey: Humanities Press, 1996), x.

17. It is also worth noting that claims of this sort are distinctly Western in their conceptual orientation. This is not to say that the validity of the claims are in question by virtue of their cultural specificity. Rather that such claims are constructed within a certain cultural context and that this warrants acknowledgment.

18. Alan Rosenberg & Gerald Myers, *Echoes from the Holocaust: Philosophical Reflections on a dark Time*, (Philadelphia: Temple University Press, 1988), ix.

19. It also needs to be recognised that Rosenberg and Myer's claim should be tempered by recent additions to the field such as Eve Garrard & Geoffrey Scarre (eds.), *Moral Philosophy and the Holocaust*, (Aldershot: Ashgate, 2003).

20. These remarks are based on my own notes from this conference in Budapest in 1991.

21. Lawrence Langer, *Admitting the Holocaust*, (Oxford: Oxford University Press, 1995), 181.

22. Kenneth Seeskin, 'What Philosophy Can and Cannot Say About Evil', in Alan Rosenberg & Gerald Meyers (eds.), *Echoes From the Holocaust, Philosophical Reflections on a Dark Time*, (Philadelphia: Temple University Press, 1988), 93.

23. Christopher W. Gowans, *Innocence Lost: An Examination of Inescapable Moral Wrongdoing*, (New York: Oxford University Press, 1994).

24. See William Styron, *Sophie's Choice*, (New York: Bantam Doubleday Dell, 1985).

25. Christopher R. Browning, *Ordinary Men*.

26. I am comfortable using the categories that Hilberg employs as they are useful although, as I suggested earlier, I am not convinced that the distinctions they imply can always be sustained.

27. This latter conceptualization of responsibilities can in part be identified with the tradition in moral theory which lays emphasis on the primacy of the rule over the primacy of the particular.

28. Jacques Derrida, *Of Spirit, Heidegger and the Question*, (Chicago: The University of Chicago Press, 1991), 109.

29. Peter Haas, *Morality After Auschwitz: The Radical Challenge of the Nazi Ethic*, (Philadelphia: Fortress Press, 1988).

30. Geoffrey Hartman, 'Shoah and Intellectual Witness', *Partisan Review*, vol. 65, 1998, 38.

31. Maurice Blanchot, *The Writing of Disaster*, (Lincoln: University of Nebraska Press, 1986), 38.

ORDINARY PEOPLE IN EXTRA-ORDINARY SITUATIONS

In this chapter I will examine aspects of Christopher Browning's text *Ordinary Men: Reserve Police Battalion 101 and the Final Solution in Poland*. My intention will be to bring to life the moral philosophical issues of most concern in this book. More specifically, my reasons for initiating a discussion on the moral dimensions of the Holocaust by way of a consideration of Browning's text stem from a premise fundamental to the entire book, namely: concrete moral considerations are crucial to the veracity and cogency of an argument that seeks to elaborate on the simultaneous combination of moral enormity and moral complexity in accounts of the Holocaust. Whilst, on the one hand, we are required by enormity analyses to make judgments, we are also compelled, by complexity analyses, to recognize the difficulties and limits of such judgments. It is through examination of individual experiences that this tension between enormity and complexity can best be understood.

In the next chapter I will have more to say on the methodological underpinnings and implications of a focus on concrete moral experiences. For now it suffices to say that demonstration of the morally complex nature of the Holocaust, and the tension invoked by the combination of moral enormity and moral complexity, requires careful attention to the particularities and variations of individual moral experiences. In choosing to examine the experiences of the 'ordinary men' of Browning's work I will demonstrate the strengths of approaching moral philosophical problems from the perspective of a careful examination of concrete examples.

Browning's text, the outcome of research into a decade long (1962-1972) investigation conducted by the Office of the State Prosecutor in Hamburg, and the testimonies that formed its core, remains one of the most authoritive accounts of the role of the German Order Police in the execution of the genocide of European Jewry. The study itself is based on examination of the proceedings of trials in Germany in the 1960's into the wartime operations, in Poland, of Battalion 101 of the Order Police. My use of *Ordinary Men* focuses pointedly on elements of both Browning's evidence and his interpretation of individual police testimonies. Specifically I am interested in the circumstances surrounding and encompassing the initiation to mass murder for the 'ordinary men' of Reserve Battalion 101. When I refer to circumstances I mean the multiple social/political/cultural factors that make up a given situation at a given place and time. The place I want to first focus on is an area of occupied Poland. The date is July 13, 1942. It is this first 'action' and the circumstances preceding it that provide the descriptive background for an understanding of the presence of both moral enormity and moral complexity.

In order to understand the significance of this event in terms of the argument I seek to convey, some descriptive detail is required. As regards this first mass killing Browning writes:

> In the very early hours of July 13, 1942, the men of reserve Police Battalion 101 were roused from their bunks in the large brick school building that served as their barracks in the Polish town of Bilgoraj. They were middle-aged family men of working and lower middle-class background from the city of Hamburg. Considered too old to be of use to the German army, they had been drafted instead into the Order Police. Most were raw recruits with no previous experience in German occupied territory. They had arrived in Poland less than three weeks earlier. It was still quite dark as the men climbed into the waiting trucks. Each policeman had been given extra ammunition, and additional boxes had been loaded onto the trucks as well. They were headed for their first major action, though the men had not yet been told what to expect.[1]

A number of questions present themselves at this point. Foremost among them is how a battalion of middle-aged reserve policemen found themselves in a situation where they would be expected to carry out the task of shooting some 1,500 Jewish men, women and children? It is through attention to the detail of such questions that the importance of the context surrounding the first mass killing can be understood. Moreover, it is my view that this evidence demonstrates the tension between enormity and complexity analyses of the Holocaust. Especially relevant are the circumstances that led to the situation in question. On Browning's account the answer lies, in part, with the complex and diffused chain of command within which the 'Order Police' was enmeshed. As Browning explains,[2] the normal chain of command went from the Order Police battalions, to the permanent regimental commander (Kommandeur der Ordnungspolizei, or KdO), of which by 1941 there were five within the General Government in Poland. From the regimental commanders it went through to the overall commander of the Order Police in the General Government (Befehlshaber der Ordnungspolizei, or BdO), based in the capital city Kraków, and finally to the main office in Berlin under Kurt Daluege. The complexity of the situation was complicated further by another chain of command whenever operations entailed the joint action of the Order Police and the Security Police and other SS units. In fact it is this second chain of command that is the more fundamental in revealing the circumstances that lead up to the first 'action' of Reserve Battalion 101 in 1942. In the General Government Heinrich Himmler had established a command structure for the Security Police similar to that which existed for the Order Police with the exception that Security Police operations took precedence over 'normal' police duties. What this meant, in short, was that because of the influence of Himmler, and his desire to increase the manpower at his disposal for his ends, the Order Police would be lead to direct participation in the Final Solution.

It is possible that were it not for Himmler's ability to extend his personal power base to incorporate the Order Police into his sphere of influence, then the policemen of Reserve Battalion 101 may well not have found themselves confronted with the sorts of complex moral choices that they in fact did have to face. In addition to the question of Himmler and his influence on the role of the Order Police is the significance of the larger plan of the Final Solution itself. It is likely, although this is difficult to confirm from the available evidence,[3] that as early as the summer of 1941 Himmler informed the SS and Police leader in Lublin, Odilo Globocnik, of Hitler's intention to murder the Jews of all of Europe in addition to those of 'the East'. A key component of this larger plan entailed an alternative to the firing squad operations undertaken primarily by the *Einsatzgruppen* (mobile killing units of the SS). This alternative was to be extermination camps, the express purpose of which was the mass murder of Jews.

Aside from the obvious benefits of greater secrecy, and the alleviation of the psychological burden entailed by shooting, gassing was recognised as necessary if the larger plan of the total liquidation of European Jewry was to be achieved. In other words, Browning claims that by early 1941 it was recognised by the leadership of the R.S.H.A. (Head Office for Reich Security of the S.S.) that large-scale gassing would be the most efficient way of murdering the Jewish population of Europe on the scale intended.[4] .The Lublin district alone contained 300,000 Jews whilst in the General Government there were over 2,000,000. Browning also claims that it became increasingly clear to Himmler that if his ultimate goals were going to be able to be realised then he would have to incorporate within his command what would otherwise be considered inappropriate sources of labour. The task set by Hitler and Himmler and in the case of the General Government, passed onto Globocnik, would only be achievable, at a time when Germany's military commitment was approaching its limits, by drawing on all available sources.

Browning writes that for Globocnik the difficulty of the task lay not in the manning of the extermination camps themselves, but in the human resources required to clear the ghettos and round the Jews onto trains destined for the camps. In this task the Order Police battalions would be the obvious choice as they were the single largest source of uncommitted manpower. In addition to the Sonderdienst (Special Service), small units of ethnic Germans trained and mobilized after the German occupation and the specially trained 'Trawnikis', comprising Ukrainian, Latvian and Lithuanian 'volunteers' recruited from POW camps, the

Order Police would play a key part in both the shooting 'actions' and the deportation operations to the camps within the General Government.[5] All in all what I'm describing here is the evolution of a plan to exterminate millions of people. This must count as a morally enormous undertaking.

Given the scale and complexity of operations required for the overall implementation and execution of the Final Solution it is hardly surprising then that Reserve Police Battalion 101, although it was not explicitly formed for the purpose of the mass killing of Jews, would find itself called upon to perform its first mass murder on July 13, 1942. By the same token it is also important to note that the incorporation of the Order Police into the machinery of the Final Solution did in fact mark a considerable deviation from the battalion's legitimate and 'official' duties which would otherwise only have encompassed more routine elements of the administration of law and order in occupied Poland. It is also noteworthy that given the actual role played by the Order Police in the Final Solution, they were not, as an organisation, classified as 'criminal' during the Nuremberg Trials, alongside the SS, the Security Service and the Secret State Police. Thus, whilst the Order Police were not categorised among other criminal organizations at Nuremburg their role must nevertheless qualify as morally enormous.

On Browning's account the battalion's first mass killing (which he refers to as 'The Józefów Massacre' after the name of the village in which the massacre occurred) was substantively different from earlier activities in which the policemen had been involved. Previously the battalion had been involved in 'resettlement actions', guarding deportation trains and guard duty around the Lódz ghetto. Even so it is very likely that these activities would have contributed to the battalion's socialisation into the evolving framework of the 'Final Solution'. All of these activities were routinely brutal and would arguably have entailed an increased knowledge of the momentum that was building regarding the overall fate of Jews in the General Government. My point is that well prior to their specific initiation to mass murder it seems plausible that the deportation and guard duties of the policemen in question would have already placed serious pressures on their capacity to accommodate, morally speaking, the actions they were being called upon to perform. Or in other words, the sorts of duties the policemen were already performing prior to their first mass murder, although arguably not as morally repugnant, would in their own right probably have generated serious moral anxiety on the part of the policemen. The sorts of duties they were already performing would likely have entailed a complex configuration of elements we usually associate with moral life. That is to say, the policemen would have had to contend with the various aspects of taking responsibility for their actions such as issues of dignity of the person, integrity, guilt, moral dilemma, blame, obligations and duties. More discussion on the detail of such issues will be provided in subsequent chapters. Suffice to say here that the policemen in question faced situations that were, in addition to the presence of moral enormity, morally complex.

June 20, 1942, however, marks a particular turning point in the history of Reserve Battalion 101. During a period in which transports of Jews to extermination centres in the General Government was temporarily halted because of the shortage of rail stock and damage to rail lines, the battalion received orders, originating from Globocnik, for a 'special action' in Poland. It is noteworthy that the nature of the 'special action' was not specified in the written orders and that the rank and file of the battalion, that is, all but the officers and non-commissioned officers, were not officially informed of the nature of the action that was to take place. Note also the chain of command from the highest authority in the General Government. Although it is difficult, on Browning's account, to discern with certainty, it is likely that the large majority of the men of the battalion were unaware that this action was going to entail anything other than the relocation of Jews or that it would differ significantly from operations in which they had previously been involved. On arrival in the village of Józefów the commanding officer Major Trapp explained to the entire battalion that with the exception of male Jews of working age, who were to be sent to one of Globocnik's camps in Lublin, everybody else, the elderly, women and children, were to be taken a short distance to a forest and shot on the spot. On the basis of several testimonies, corroborated separately, it is clear that a very unusual offer was then made by Trapp. Any of the older men who did not feel capable of the task before them could step out and would be allocated assignments peripheral to the actual killing. Versions of this event in the testimonies cited by Browning vary, but in essence they remain the same. While the offer was directed at the older men, others from the rank and file were offered a choice whether to participate directly or not. It seems that only twelve or thirteen men out of a total of nearly 500 seized this moment to excuse themselves from the impending massacre. Browning points out that, as the real nature of the event had only just been made clear; reaction time to the extra-ordinary offer that followed was very short. The lack of time to reflect on what was actually about to happen must also be coupled with the difficulty of breaking rank in a battalion of 500 uniformed men. As research elsewhere has shown[6] the combination of the pressures associated with a lack of time to consider adequately the possibility of options or the implications of actions, and the power of rank and uniform, contribute significantly to conformity. Reinforcing this explanation Browning writes:

> As important as the lack of time for reflection was the pressure for conformity—the basic identification of men in uniform with their comrades and the strong urge not to separate themselves from the group by stepping out.[7]

At this point Browning's account of events raises an important question. How did the policemen in question react to their first killings? Browning's study shows that in the course of the day a significant number of those assigned to firing squads (in addition to the twelve or thirteen who initially refused to participate) either evaded shooting altogether or sought release from the firing squads. Of those who fell into this category Browning estimates that some ten or twenty percent either evaded shooting or were unable to continue after having begun the face-to-face process of killing the Jews that arrived from the village at the forest where they were shot. Of singular importance here is Browning's observation that:

> Even twenty or twenty five years later those who did quit shooting along the way overwhelmingly cited sheer physical revulsion against what they were doing as the prime motive but did not express any ethical or political principles behind this revulsion. Given the educational level of these reserve policemen, one should not expect a sophisticated articulation of abstract principles. The absence of such does not mean that their revulsion did not have its origins in the humane instincts that Nazism radically opposed and sought to overcome. But the men themselves did not seem to be conscious of the contradiction between their feelings and the essence of the regime they served.[8]

It is noteworthy that Browning seems to consider only as an aside the connection between the feelings of physical revulsion and how we might understand these feelings, in a moral sense. If Browning is correct and the men did experience strong feelings of physical revulsion then it is entirely possible that what they felt even if they were understandably reluctant to admit it were powerful emotions, deriving at least in part from the primary belief that the actions they were performing were indeed morally wrong. Browning himself is careful to point out that explanations in a study of this nature are hazardous if for no other reason than the fact that pre-trial and courtroom testimonies need to be interpreted with a large measure of caution. Apart from the knowledge that witnesses are being asked to recount events that occurred some twenty five years earlier, they are likely to be very guarded in relation to the possibility of self-incrimination and the incrimination of other defendants. On Browning's account, though, it is as if the feelings of physical revulsion experienced by the policemen might well be akin to the same sorts of feelings a vegetarian might feel at the sight of raw meat. I would claim, however, that in the case of the policemen, the nature of the situation itself would strongly suggest that the feelings described were morally significant in the sense that they conveyed both the moral enormity and the moral complexity of the situation faced by the policemen. Given the situation that the policemen found themselves in and the actions they were called upon to perform there would seem to be sound grounds for arguing that a clear link existed between the feelings of physical revulsion and the presence of a profound tension between the moral magnitude of the situation and the moral complexity and conflicted nature of the situation that the policemen were being forced to contend with.

Extrapolating from Browning's interpretation I claim that in light of the circumstances of the court it is hardly surprising that the policemen in question attempted to abstain from a clear ethical position. In the first and more obvious instance, admission of a moral position may have contributed to self incrimination. And in the second instance it is likely that there was a very strong need, on the part of the persons concerned to justify their actions morally within their own minds. If for no other reason the situation that the policemen found themselves in would almost certainly have required some sort of mental rationalisation in order to allay the quite certain contradiction involved in being ordered to kill innocent people. As regards Browning's comments concerning the lack of an ethical explanation I would contend that whilst most people may adhere to the principle of the sanctity of human life, they may have considerable difficulty in articulating carefully reasoned or argued grounds for such a belief. The absence of the ability to provide sustained reasons for such a belief in no way diminishes the extent to which that same belief may be deeply ingrained within a given individual's conception of morality. In this respect Browning does not, in my view, take sufficient account of the evidence that the policemen themselves provide suggesting a recognisable connection between the revulsion felt and the idea that the actions were morally repellent.

Evidence that what we might be dealing with here is at the very least a strong sense of moral unease is evident in a number of the testimonies. Browning reports that one policeman, in a description of the shooting of his first victim, said:

> I only reached the execution site when my comrades had already shot their Jews. At the sight of his countrymen who had been shot, my Jew threw himself on the ground and remained lying there. I then cocked my carbine and shot him through the back of the head. Because I was already very upset from the cruel treatment of the Jews during the clearing of the town and was completely in turmoil, I shot too high.[9]

This testimony clearly conveys the sense of moral distress felt by the given individual. In fact, this policeman, after having committed this murder became in his words 'so sick' that he requested that he be relieved from this 'work'.

Another policeman testified that he had been a member of a firing squad that had taken its victims to the woods and shot them in the back of the neck. After an attempt to shoot his fourth victim the policeman testified that

> The shooting of the men was so repugnant to me that I missed the fourth man. It was simply no longer possible for me to aim accurately. I suddenly felt nauseous and ran away from the shooting site. . . . Today I can say that my nerves were totally finished.[10]

In line with the previous account this testimony conveys the strength of the moral and emotional distress felt by the policeman in question. One policeman, who after killing as many as twenty Jews, is reported by Browning to have said:

> I thought that I could master the situation and that without me the Jews were not going to escape their fate anyway . . . Truthfully I must say that at the time we didn't reflect about it at all. Only years later did any of us become truly conscious of what had happened then . . . Only later did it first occur to me that had

not been right.[11]

What is it this policeman thought he would be able to master if not, in part, his feelings that his actions were morally wrong. Such evidence might also suggest that, at the time, the origins of this policeman's unease were not satisfactorily thought through. Many thoughts as regards the impending action were likely to have been going through the policeman's mind. For instance it is entirely possible that in the eyes of many of the policemen, participation in the killing could have appeared legitimate having been sanctioned, in a wartime situation, by the appropriate 'authority'. Moreover, as Browning describes it, it is also highly likely that there was little time for careful reflection and that an easier form of rationalisation was going to be the 'best' way of justifying their behaviour. In my view however, Browning's own evidence indicates extreme moral anxiety on the part of the policemen whose testimonies are cited. I suggest that the situation, as it must have presented itself to the policemen, would have required some sort of personal psychological accommodation of the serious moral conflicts generated within the minds of the policeman concerned. My point here is that the process of accommodating this behaviour in their own minds would, at least in the context of this first mass murder, have been no easy or straightforward process. The reported high incidence of psychological disturbances and breakdowns amongst the perpetrators of these actions is, I contend, testament to the high degree of difficulty in coming to terms, in an ethical sense, with such behaviour. In effect the high levels of moral anxiety witnessed are indicative of varying and overlapping combinations of mental processes, rationalisations and emotions in the minds of these policemen. I argue that Browning's documentation indicates the presence of the tension between the moral enormity and the moral complexity of the situation faced by the policemen in question. The moral enormity arose from having to kill innocent people and the moral complexity derived from a complex array of factors affecting the behaviour of the policemen, including issues of conformity, an absence of time for careful consideration, multiple and often contradictory emotions and intuitions, and individual histories and dispositions toward certain behaviour.

One potentially significant factor among the many and complicated feelings and thoughts likely to have been experienced by the policemen might have been the strength of anti-Semitic attitudes within the battalion. This is, however, a very difficult matter to gauge on the evidence. Browning reports that any discussion of anti-Semitism was universally absent from the testimonies. Whilst this is hardly surprising given the legally binding context within which the testimonies were produced, it is equally as clear that the then prevailing ideology of 'Jew-as-other' was present within the battalion. Browning writes:

> The Jews stood outside their circle of human obligation and responsibility. Such a polarization between "us" and "them", between one's comrades and the enemy, is of course standard in war. . . . It would seem that even if the men of Reserve Police Battalion 101 had not consciously adopted the anti-Semitic doc-

trines of the regime, they had at least accepted the assimilation of the Jews into the image of the enemy. Major Trapp appealed to this generalised notion of the Jews as part of the enemy in his early-morning speech. The men should remember, when shooting Jewish women and children, that the enemy was killing German women and children by bombing Germany.[12]

It has been argued elsewhere that there existed at the time of the Holocaust a prevailing ideology of 'Jew-as-enemy'. For instance, in his book *Hitler's Willing Executioners: Ordinary Germans and the Holocaust,*[13] Daniel Jonah Goldhagen, claims that the image of 'Jew' as enemy had become an integral part of the psyche of ordinary Germans. Goldhagen attempts to lend substance to this claim by tracing the origins of anti-Semitism back through Christian mythical beliefs. However, even if it is readily accepted that anti-Semitism contributed to the beliefs of many Germans and, as Browning claims, that this ideology of anti-Semitism was advanced by the officers as a rationalisation for the actions that were being demanded of the policemen, concerns with such explanations remain. In my view, the evidence of serious moral anxiety suggests that the existence of anti-Semitic attitudes was insufficient, in the eyes of the policemen themselves, to justify the mass killings. In this respect it is possible that the appeal to the imagery of 'Jew-as-enemy' would have served to exacerbate rather than ameliorate feelings of moral unease and repugnance when confronted with the actual acts themselves. Put another way, confronted with the faces of real children, women and the aged, it is unlikely that stereotypical images would have been sufficient to dispel conflicting and deeply held beliefs that the acts about to be performed were anything but deeply morally problematic if not profoundly morally flawed. As was the case with my earlier argument concerning the apprehensions faced by the policemen I argue here that the evidence of anti-Semitism would only have added to the tension between the enormity and the complexity of the situation.

Extrapolating further on what he argues was a generalisable absence of ethical considerations on the part of the policemen in question, Browning claims that in the aftermath of the Józefów massacre it was evident that the problem faced by Trapp and his immediate superiors was not opposition on ethical grounds but "the broad demoralization shared both by those who shot to the end and those who had not been able to continue."[14] Is Browning implying here that the policemen in question may have believed that what they were doing was somehow able to be construed as right but they nevertheless did not possess the strength of will to carry it through? Irrespective of how Browning is interpreted, on the evidence presented this is perhaps a difficult, though not inconceivable, conclusion to draw.

I further believe that the problem defined by Browning as 'demoralization' is not so readily distinguished from what can be termed the 'ethical'. Indeed the very word 'demoralization' implies, in my view, that the policemen had had their own sense of morality compromised. In other words, it is reasonable to suppose that it was the very horror of their initiation into mass murder, and the nature of the killing process, being so direct and face to face, that violated the perpetrator's deeply held feelings and beliefs of right and wrong. I contend that the demoralization referred to by Browning relates to the diminishment of integrity, sense of decency and self-esteem, which are very much moral issues. What demoralized the men involved in the killing seems to be very much ethical in its content. Again I refer to the evidence (previously cited) of moral anxiety contained in excerpts of the testimonies of the policemen.

The testimonies also detail attempts by some policemen to rationalise their actions in the midst of morally complex situations. I argue that the reason that rationalisation on the part of the participants was necessary was because of the need to make sense of the stark moral conflict entailed in the order to kill women, children and the aged for no other reason than the fact that they were Jews. More than this however, the very personal way in which the murders were meted out was particularly confronting for those involved in the killing. Constituting as it did a 'face to face' type of killing; moral sensibilities must have been intensely assaulted. It is my view that the behaviour of the policemen is difficult to understand, in a moral sense, because of the combination of moral incredulity and the complexity of the factors that arise as we seek to comprehend. The tension generated by this combination serves to foil attempts at rendering knowable, in a straightforward way, the events and behaviour in question.

Though the moral profundity of the behaviour of the policemen is readily demonstrated, the other side of the tension, namely the morally complex nature of the behaviour of the policemen, requires careful unpacking. In addition to the wealth of evidence from Browning's study of the Józefów massacre itself, the argument for the presence of the tension can also include subsequent events concerning the same policemen. Browning writes that on the basis of the severe psychological effects of the Józefów massacre, efforts were made to ensure that the future operations of Reserve Police Battalion 101 be restricted to what were referred to as clearing and deportation. Even with regard to these less ethically challenging actions it was to become standard procedure for the worst elements of the operation to be carried out by units of 'Trawnikis' (specially trained auxiliaries recruited from prisons and POW camps in the Soviet territories and trained by the SS). In addition to its careful reconstruction of the grim initiation to mass murder, Browning's study also details the continued descent of many of the members of this battalion of 'ordinary men' into mass killers. At the conclusion of the battalion's participation in the Final Solution, Browning reports:

> With a conservative estimate of 6,500 Jews shot at Józefów and Lomazy and 1,000 shot during the "Jew hunts", and a minimum estimate of 30,500 Jews shot at Majdanek and Poniatowa, the battalion had participated in the direct shooting deaths of at least 38,000 Jews. With the death camp deportation of at least 3,000 Jews from Miedzyrzec in early May 1943, the number of Jews they had placed on trains to Treblinka had risen to 45,000. For a battalion of less than 500 men, the ultimate body count was at least 83,000 Jews.[15]

These statistics are especially disquieting due to the fact that, in spite of the initial horror experienced in the woods outside Józefów, many of the battalion's members subsequently went on to become casualised and hardened participants in later killings, massacres and 'Jew hunts'. In an effort to explain this metamorphosis in the behaviour of the policemen Browning cites such factors as wartime brutalization, racism, the standardization, bureaucratization and routinization of tasks, special selection of perpetrators, careerism, obedience to orders, the legitimizing effect of authority, ideological indoctrination and general conformity to peer pressure as contributing to the process.

Finally, and recapitulating here, I argue that several points are striking about both the Józefów massacre and the events that followed as regards the policemen in question. Foremost among them is the graphic way Browning's study illustrates key elements of the tension between moral complexity and moral enormity. Browning's account of events also lends substance to this tension in the provision of a framework for some compelling questions. For instance, what was the nature of the moral choices for the policemen involved? Are the actions of the policemen morally puzzling or do their actions imply a straightforward moral explanation? Can the individual situations of the policemen be construed as morally complex? Or to put it another way, is it possible to understand the moral decisions that confronted the policemen as having derived from a complex combination of morally relevant factors? These are all difficult questions the unravelling of which suggests the need for a wider discussion on the nature of the relationship between enormity and complexity. One facet of such a discussion concerns the juxtaposition of extreme horror alongside so-called 'normal' day to day events, as they are perceived in the eyes of the perpetrators. It should be noted that revealing the mundane and routine aspects of the Nazi regime's policies of genocide is not the same as attempts to relativise or revise the legacy of the Third Reich. Browning's research, for instance, into the 'everyday life' of one single battalion demonstrates quite starkly the astounding ease with which mass murder can become routine; and how the 'abnormal' can become exceedingly 'normal'. However, rather than diverting attention away from the horror of such episodes of the Holocaust, Browning's study facilitates the task of understanding such horror. In order to account for the horror it is necessary to understand how such actions, as those performed by the police in question, can in some sense become normalised.

Hannah Arendt's interpretation of the Holocaust's extraordinary 'ordinariness' is a well known formulation of this idea of the combination of mundaneness with that which is horrific. In her book *Eichmann in Jerusalem*, [16]Arendt advances the thesis that Adolf Eichmann personified what she terms the 'banality of evil'. Arendt writes:

> The trouble with Eichmann was precisely that so many were like him, and that the many were neither perverted nor sadistic, that they were and still are, terribly and terrifyingly normal.[17]

Arendt's claim of the normalcy of Eichmann and the implications this claim possesses for attendant claims surrounding the question of whether or not the actions of such people constitutes intentional wrongdoing or inherent evil, remains controversial. Gertrud Ezorsky, in an article titled 'Hannah Arendt's view of Totalitarianism and the Holocaust', [18] is one writer to take issue with Arendt's claim of Eichmann's normalcy. Ezorsky argues that Arendt's portrayal of Eichmann as a normal person without an extreme hatred of the Jews is not supported by the evidence of Eichmann's background and role in the mass murder of the Jews or by the findings of the Eichmann trial. For example, Ezorsky claims that Arendt suppressed in her book important findings of psychiatric studies on the personality of Eichmann that point to an anti-semitic attitude. Ezorsky also points to numerous elements of Eichmann's biography, including his early membership in the Austrian Nazi Party, and his recruitment into the S.D. (the intelligence arm of the Nazi Party), as evidence that Eichmann would have had to have had what she refers to as a 'proper' attitude toward the Jews. In response to Arendt's use of Eichmann's own testimony Ezorsky points out, it was to be entirely expected that at the trial Eichmann would deny any anti-Semitic beliefs on his part. In fact, argues Ezorsky, such denials were consistent with the attempts of those accused at the earlier Nuremburg trials to defend themselves.

Furthermore, and in support of her argument that Eichmann was in fact a "sadistic, murderous psychopath",[19] Ezorsky asks the pertinent question: "If Eichmann had no fanatical hatred of Jews, what brought him to accept his role in their murder?"[20] On Arendt's account the answer to this vexed question lay in Eichmann's belief in his own conscience. Arendt writes:

> He [Eichmann] did not need to "close his ears to the voice of conscience", as the judgment has it, not because he had none, but because his conscience spoke with a "respectable voice," with the voice of respectable society around him.[21]

On Arendt's account, Eichmann himself believed he had a duty to remain loyal to the orders of the Führer. The examples that Arendt uses, most notably Eichmann's role in the deportation of Hungarian Jews in 1944, point to an interpretation suggesting that Eichmann had acted in line with what he believed was his duty to Hitler. On this point too, Ezorsky disputes Arendt's interpretation of events. Pointing to Arendt's selective use of Eichmann's correspondence on the issue of the deportation of Hungarian Jews, Ezorsky, in what is perhaps a more exhaustive examination of the same material, paints a more ambiguous picture of Eichmann's motives than one based on pure loyalty to Hitler. On Ezorsky's account it is likely that Eichmann had acted independently of either Hitler and Himmler and in a way that could well be interpreted as expressly anti-semitic. I believe that Ezorsky's commentary on Arendt does call her to task on a number of important details. Importantly however, none of what Ezorsky has to say seriously threatens Arendt's primary thesis combining banality with evil in the persona of Eichmann. In my view, Ezorsky's critique of Arendt's study of

Eichmann strays from the more primary issue. Arendt's insight concerns the way she connects banality with the radicalness that is more usually associated with evil. On Arendt's account the scale of the murder involved in the Holocaust would have been unachievable had the actual human and technical machinery needed for its implementation not included the mundaneness of rail transport and bureaucratic administrative details. It was precisely this sort of mundaneness, argues Arendt that allowed Eichmann to represent his actions to himself as the mere performance of quite respectable duties. From this perspective Ezorsky's criticism of Arendt's lack of attention to Eichmann's perceived anti-Semitism is of less relevance. The point is that even if it could be demonstrated that Eichmann's attitudes dove-tailed with those of the stereotypical anti-Semite, such a view doesn't seem to do justice to the way in which such attitudes can be combined with the idea of bureaucratic work to form a genocidal behavioural pattern.

There is another interesting interpretation that can be placed on Arendt's account. I believe that Arendt's formulation of the banality of evil contributes to an understanding of moral life in the midst of horror on the basis of the key recognition that such behaviour, whilst truly offensive, is also of greater complexity than more simple explanations can convey. Perhaps the real horror of the Holocaust, from the perspective of the Eichmann persona, lay in the way in which such actions as those performed by Eichmann-types are able to be, in their eyes, internalised as normal. That this is so is precisely because such behaviour entails a more complex composite of factors in addition to the morally enormous. My argument is that it is the tension thus created that makes such behaviour so difficult to explicate.

In the context of Browning's study it is worth noting the way in which he demonstrates the need to move beyond one-dimensional caricatures in particular of those who carried out the killings and deportations. Browning emphasises understanding rather than the provision of judgment or excuse. To this end, the recognition that the policemen involved in his study, both those who carried out the massacres and deportations and those who refused or somehow evaded, were all human beings, is crucial for analyses that seek to extend understanding beyond moral stereotypes. On the significance of this recognition Browning writes:

> I must recognize that in the same situation, I could have been either a killer or an evader—both were human—if I want to understand and explain the behaviour of both as best I can.[22]

I argue that the idea of a common humanity is so elementary that its significance, though difficult to articulate, is also easily passed by. Browning's study whilst pointing the way to a more complex understanding of the moral terrain of the Holocaust stops short of assessing the implications of the contentious issue of a common humanity.[23] Extrapolating further my argument would be that people, in a general sense, share the same basic moral potential. That is to say, people, by virtue of their humanity, share an equivalent potential for their actions to be, or to be judged, morally flawed, morally courageous or morally significant in some sense.[24] A decisive factor, however, conditioning the way in which an agent will eventually act concerns the circumstances that they find themselves in. It has already been established that the chain of events leading up to the Józefów massacre clearly entailed a large number of factors beyond the sphere of influence of any one individual policeman.

Browning's account of events also illustrates the way in which the massacre in question was a massive affront to the moral sensibilities to many involved. Thus, on the one hand, there is much to indicate the presence of moral enormity in the form of out of the ordinary moral demands. The evidence shows that moral capacities were tested well beyond the limits individuals ordinarily encounter. The real difficulty though, stems from the way such powerful demands upon moral bearing was rationalised by the policemen. I contend that such rationalisation would have entailed the factoring of a complex array of moral evaluations on the part of those involved. On the basis of their testimonies it can be deduced that the policemen involved were morally conflicted but not in ways that necessarily suggested the availability of clear and simple options. It is apparent from the testimonies of the policemen that a variety of relevant and sometimes contradicting factors needed to be accommodated in a short space of time. The policemen, confronted with a morally enormous situation had to cope with what they perceived as conflicting moral demands, severe emotional stress and for most involved, no real personal precedent for this sort of situation. I argue that they would have needed to have made some sort of sense of the combined presence, in varying measures and in respect to themselves, of their fellow policemen and those who were to be killed, of such morally relevant factors as duty, loyalty, fear, self-preservation, cowardice, intimidation, bravado, hatred, love, comradeship, loss of face, power, revulsion and possibly the exhilaration generated by the atmosphere that prevailed. In all, a complex mix of influences for any individual to internally organise into something approaching a morally cognisant and responsible decision. I further argue that examples such as those documented by Browning are evidence of the operations of the tension produced by the moral enormity of the events concerned and the complexity of the moral psychological deliberations experienced by the policemen. It is thus my contention that a direct correlation exists between the extreme nature of the circumstances in question and the way such circumstances contribute to the generation of complex moral landscapes.

It should also be stressed that this conclusion is not an attempt to establish a typology for diminished responsibility. Nor is it meant to imply that 'ordinary people' are all in some sense equally morally accountable. While the above might be relevant they are different matters. One point of emphasising the role and influence of circumstances is to recognise that it is the circumstances of a particular situation that contribute significantly to the shaping of individual moral character. In a given situation we are all vulnerable to the restricted range of choices generated by that situation. It follows that apportionment of responsibility and questions of judgment derive from how, in the end, an agent chooses to act. And the way an agent chooses to act depends, in large part, on the range of factors relevant to the particular situation. The intention here is to identify the basic links between the idea of a shared humanity, the role of circumstances in conditioning individual moral character and the way in which outcomes of actions are perceived. Moreover, understanding the nature of responsibility depends upon an understanding of the nature of the links between these different factors.

My claim is that in the situation detailed in Browning's study the circumstances were demonstrably important not only in affecting the way the policemen acted but also in regard to subsequent moral judgment of their behaviour. The process of discriminating between (and judging) different sorts of moral behaviour requires careful and measured assessment of the role of circumstances in the decisions that led to the particular behaviour in question. In the case of the policemen of Reserve Police Battalion 101, there is substantial testimonial evidence to indicate that the circumstances significantly conditioned the feelings, emotions, deliberations, judgments, actions and inactions of the men in question. The matter of how this evidence should affect subsequent moral judgment of these men is another issue although it is entirely possible that the sorts of moral conclusions able to be derived from research of the sort conducted by Browning are likely to be tempered by such factors as the extreme circumstances within which such events occurred. A more nuanced understanding of the reasons that led the policemen to commit mass murder does not of course lessen the moral enormity of such actions. The policemen of Reserve Police Battalion 101 who participated in the murder of Jews were morally flawed. Likewise those policemen who displayed moral fortitude in the face of the pressures described must also be recognised. The more fundamental point might be, though, and it is my view that Browning's study supports the claim, that faced with the sort of circumstances experienced by the policemen in question, most people possess a proclivity to act in ways that are morally flawed. This would seem to lend substance to the idea that it is circumstances external to the individual that feature large among the factors affecting a given individual's behaviour.

It needs to be said that I'm talking about the sort of demands placed upon a given individual's moral character. I want to establish the above claim as involving certain facts about the way humans function as moral individuals. In support of the claim that people are likely to behave in ways that are morally flawed if faced with the sort of circumstances in question, Stanley Milgram's oft cited 'obedience experiments' are an obvious point of reference. His primary finding: that people in a controlled environment are likely to harm others if asked to do so by someone who they believe has authority over them, resonates strongly with my claim concerning the importance of external circumstances upon the development of an individual's moral character.[25]

Milgram's experiments also provide a further clue to explain how most of the policemen in Browning's study were able to go on from their initiation to mass murder to become hardened killers. Milgram observed that "many subjects harshly devalue the victim *as a consequence* of acting against him."[26] It is difficult to say just what can be inferred from such observations but it is at least possible that the policemen who went on to participate in subsequent 'actions', may have been further morally desensitised by the initial killings themselves. It's noteworthy of course that not all of the policemen were affected in a way that degraded their moral sensibilities. In fact, Browning's documentation shows that some of the policemen, having been exposed to, or having themselves participated in the initial shootings, were then unable or refused, to continue. I would hold that my earlier general claim concerning the way people act, is supported by the evidence of Browning's study. Responsibility makes differing demands on us depending on how we are involved. And how we are involved, whilst it will depend to a significant extent upon our often complex individual moral histories that give meaning to our involvement, will also be structured by the circumstances that frame that involvement. All in all, the relationship between a person's behaviour and the variety of factors that may affect that behaviour and how that person's behaviour is subsequently to be judged is complex and requires that due consideration is given to the complex nature of such behaviour and the events surrounding said behaviour.

Finally, and given the evidence for the tension between both the enormity and the complexity of analyses of the behaviour of the policemen that Browning's study introduces, straightforward moral ascriptions are unlikely to be of much assistance in the task of understanding the situation and the behaviour it generated. It is true that the policemen in question faced choices that led many of them to commit heinous crimes. But it is also true that the perpetrators of these crimes were in many respects, ordinary people, perhaps only distinguishable from others by the fact that it was they who were in this terrible situation at this particular time. The fact that these policemen were ordinary people, and yet many of them committed serious crimes, requires, in my view, explanations of the sort that explore the nature of the tension between moral enormity and moral complexity. Moreover, such explorations would do well to avoid explanations of the sort that characterise those involved as one-dimensional caricatures of flesh and blood people.

The conclusion that the policemen of Browning's study were, in most instances, ordinary people faced with extra-ordinary situations, is convincing and accords with the evidence. I argue that it is not until the complex nature of the relation between agents, their moral histories and the circumstances in question is exhaustively examined that the full weight and meaning of human responsibility can be realised. The particular attention that Browning accords to the circumstances surrounding the actions of Reserve Police Battalion 101 is what makes this study so illuminating. However, his observations of ordinary humanity in an extra-ordinary situation contain insights of a most bleak kind. Browning's study shows that in circumstances of the sort depicted, people are more likely to be morally flawed than morally courageous.

I have consistently argued that the circumstances that individuals find themselves in represents a significant factor in the motivation of such individuals to behave the way they do. I believe that studies of the sort undertaken by Browning support this view. Further corroboration of my argument comes in the form of Inga Clendinnen's concluding remarks in her examination of the behaviour of the SS in Auschwitz in her book *Reading the Holocaust*[27] In a consideration of the role of circumstances and in words that resonate with my position, Clendinnen writes:

> When the work of the imagination is done, we ourselves remain the measure of plausibility. Tracing the experiences of a member of the Order Police set down outside that Polish village in that July dawn, *in his exact circumstances* [my emphasis], I can imagine—barely—how in the knowledge that my country was deep in war, in the strangeness of an unfamiliar place inhabited by people I cared nothing for, linked to familiar comrades by shared isolation and loyalty and a need for their respect, I might have tried to follow the orders given me by a trusted commander. I might have walked with a man, a woman, a child into the wood, and asked or forced them to lie down, so I could deliver the 'neck shot'. I also believe in the event that I could not, finally, have carried out that order.[28]

Whilst I respect Clendinnen's account she writes with the benefit of historical hindsight and I suggest that the conflict in the minds of the policemen generated by the situation described by Clendinnen is under-estimated. Especially in the absence of conclusive evidence of 'hard' anti-semitic views, I argue that, in some significant cases, a measure of caring, or some understanding of our responsibilities to others, accrues by virtue of being human and of living as a moral person among other moral people, if nothing else. To this extent the policemen in question were not exceptions. In short what is required is a more nuanced account.

Earlier I said that Browning's study showed, that in the circumstances depicted, people were more likely to act one way than another. This is not to say that in other circumstances different sorts of moral behaviour would not prevail. It is also the case that choices of the sort that confronted the policemen in Browning's study caused repeated instances of distress and revulsion in the extreme and in ways that seemed to violate basic feelings of right and wrong. What is especially alarming, in this regard, is the rapidity with which many of these same policemen were subsequently able to assimilate and submerge such strong feelings as those that were initially experienced. Browning's evidence shows that in future actions the ordinary men of Reserve Police Battalion 101 became key players in the mass murder of Polish Jews. With this in mind, I conclude that the challenge lies in being able to understand the nature of the tension that threatens to obfuscate moral meaning in the context of the Holocaust. In the next chapter I argue that the tension itself hinges on understanding the various aspects of the complex nature of moral life, and in particular the nature of responsibility.

Notes

1. Browning, 1-2.

2. Browning, 7-8.

3. The exact timing of Hitler's wider plan to exterminate the Jews of Europe continues to elude Holocaust historians. Philippe Burrin's research in his book *Hitler and the Jews* demonstrates that surviving documentation from the period of late July 1941 indicates intention if not an outright clear statement of a plan.

4. Browning, 49.

5. Browning, 51-53.

6. The most noteable of which are the Milgram experiments of the 1960's. See my discussion regarding these experiments later in this chapter for further details.

7. Browning, 71.

8. Browning, 74.

9. Browning, 66-67.

10. Browning, 67-68.

11. Browning, 72.

12. Browning, 73.

13. Daniel J. Goldhagen, *Hitler's Willing Executioners: Ordinary Germans and the Holocaust,* (New York: Vintage Books, 1997).

14. Browning, 76.

15. Browning, 142.

16. Hannah Arendt, *Eichmann in Jerusalem,* (London: Penguin Books, 1977).

17. Arendt, 276.

18. Gertrude Ezorsky, 'Hannah Arendt's view of totalitarianism and the Holocaust', *Philosophical Forum*, vol.XVI, nos.1-2, Fall-Winter 1985.

19. Ezorsky, 64.

20. Ezorsky, 67.

21. Arendt, 126.

22. Browning, xx.

23. I make mention of the question of a 'common humanity' as contentious in the light of contemporary anti-humanisms sceptical of this notion. I would note that I remain unconvinced of the veracity of postmodernist claims on this matter.

24. For an elaboration of this idea see Raimond Gaita, 'Remembering the Holocaust, Absolute Value and the Nature of Evil', *Quadrant,* December 1995.

25. Stanley Milgram, *Obedience to Authority,* (New York: Harper and Row, 1974).

26. Milgram, 10.

27. Inga Clendinnen, *Reading the Holocaust,* (Melbourne: The Text Publishing

Company, 1998).

28. Clendinnen, 180.

DIMENSIONS OF MORAL COMPLEXITY

A central claim of this book is that the Holocaust represents a genuine moral problem. On the one hand, the Holocaust appears to represent the paradigm case of evil while it is also the case that the Holocaust is a modern, human phenomenon, the very complexity of which has the effect of placing into question our capacity in such matters as judgment. Put another way, enormity analyses of the Holocaust demand that we judge and ascribe responsibility, yet, for equally urgent reasons, complexity analyses compel us to understand the whys and wherefores of human actions.

In this chapter I will expand on the form of the problem of the tension between enormity and complexity, whilst paying particular attention to establishing the presence and parameters of moral complexity within both individual moral experiences of the Holocaust and the Holocaust itself as a defining event in the moral topography of the twentieth century. Finally, and very importantly, I will argue that moral complexity is informed by a variety of understandings of responsibility. I will in fact contend that it is our understandings of responsibility that are a large factor in contributing to our understanding of the complexity of our moral lives. Thus it is the various understandings of, and issues arising from, responsibility, that are of prime importance to both understanding moral complexity itself and the tension that arises between complexity and enormity analyses. I will in this chapter elaborate on the ways of understanding responsibility that I think make significant contributions to the idea that accounts of the Holocaust are morally complex. To clarify here, I think that there are differing dimensions of responsibility that combine to give form to the discussion on a generalised conception of responsibility. Moreover, in the course of the chapter I introduce examples of expressions of particular individual's senses of responsibility that illustrate the various ways of understanding responsibility. The individual senses of responsibility inform the more generalised conceptualisation of responsibility.

As a means of conceptualising the relationship between moral complexity and responsibility I propose the idea of a 'weave' as the framework upon which to hang the various understandings of responsibility. In the next chapter I will expand on this idea of a weave by attaching other concepts that provide additional strength to the wider idea of moral complexity.

I justify my attention on complexity analyses of the Holocaust because this aspect of the tension seems more difficult to defend in the face of the moral horror that usually characterises the Holocaust. An invitation into the sort of general awe encountered in the face of the enormity evaluations of the Holocaust is conveyed when Douglas Lackey writes:

> The evils of the Jewish Holocaust are so numerous, so diverse, and so extreme that at first sight it seems presumptuous to judge them at all, much less to judge them by ordinary moral norms. Judgment requires comprehension and transcendence, and comprehension and transcendence of these events seems almost beyond human power. The ordinary moral categories feel too pale and narrow to do justice to our sense of condemnation. . . .[1]

The comprehension implied by Lackey is in itself a difficult enough proposition but when moral enormity is accompanied by moral complexity as a component of rendering morally intelligible, particular events and experiences, then the task is especially problematic. The combination of moral enormity and moral complexity with regard to the way the Holocaust was and continues to be understood, brings with it particular difficulties. The requirement for condemnation serves to restrict the capacity to comprehend the multiplicity of moral dimensions that are a feature of this complex of events. Or to put it another way, the sort of enormity analyses often associated with the Holocaust can have the effect of obscuring the ways in which this same phenomenon is also morally complex. Of course, the opposite can also be the case. Overblown attention to the presence of complexity analyses can have the effect of diluting the moral enormity of such experiences.

Part of the challenge lies in understanding the extent of the problem presented by the tension. Moral enormity, for instance, appears to imply straightforward accounts of the way moral life is assessed. Moral complexity, however, suggests that moral life is anything but amenable to straightforward ways of assessing what is at issue. I intend to demonstrate that this apparent incommensurability is both constitutive of, and explicable as a component of moral life generally and, moreover, that an important hurdle lies in the attempt to understand what the nature of the relationship between enormity and complexity may yield for an understanding of both Holocaust experiences and the Holocaust itself as an idea. One particularly sharp example of this aspect of the tension concerns the issue of recognizing the distinction between understanding and judgment. Mary Midgley, in her book *Wickedness,* [2] invites this distinction when she writes:

> Infection can bring on fever, but only in creatures with a suitable circulatory

system. Like fever, spite, resentment, envy, avarice, cruelty, meanness, hatred and the rest are themselves complex states, and they produce complex activities. Outside events may indeed bring them on, but, like other malfunctions, they would not develop if we were not prone to them.[3]

Midgley's analogy entices us to pursue its implications for what they may reveal about individual human behaviour and the factors influencing such behaviour. For Midgley, a key requirement of understanding why we act the way we do is being able to recognise that neither social nor individual causes are exclusive determinants of human behaviour. She contends that it is always going to be a matter of considering both aspects as supplementing rather than cancelling each other out. Midgley's aim is to enquire into the question as to why people treat others and sometimes even themselves abominably. She wants to be able to understand why, as she puts it "[people] constantly cause avoidable suffering".[4] As I indicated above this task is never going to be straightforward. One difficulty concerns the distinction between what she refers to as individual and public wickedness. The exact significance of the distinction becomes evident when the discussion moves to an examination of aspects of responsibility and, in particular, judgment. Midgley recognises that some actions are categorically wrong. But she is less clear about how the perpetrators of such actions are to be placed in a discussion of responsibility. The ambiguity Midgley displays here stems not so much from a concern over whether or not judgment is sometimes necessary as with recognition of the complexities and difficulties that judgment entails. She says as much when she refers to the way actions are spawned from 'complex activities'.[5] Such complexities very often render judgment problematic. Midgley's attempt at resolving the problem of judgment is interesting. She continues her discussion with the muted claim that moral judgments function to 'orient' us as we plot our way on the path that is moral life. In other words, moral judgments are a necessary pre—condition for making sense of our own behaviour as well as the behaviour of others. Midgley points out that the requirement to judge is not a licence, as she puts it, to stone people. Rather it is an important part of understanding the behaviour of others. This is not to say, that judgment and understanding are interchangeable here. While judgment is an important component of moral understanding, it is only one component among others. Whilst I find this facet of Midgley's argument plausible, it also seems to me there is enough prima facie evidence to indicate that in the collective psyche of 'modern' Western society, we are more likely to conceive of responsibility as a term prescribing the obligations for which a person is morally accountable. In this sense emphasis is on the fulfilment or violation of those responsibilities, praise and blame, rather than understanding what a particular individual might take to be his or her responsibility. The currency of such terms as 'retributive justice' and the proliferation in both Eastern and Western cultures of a mentality of harsher penalties, increasing incarceration rates and expanding police forces supports this view.

Midgley of course, is not unaware of the significance of judgment as a function of moral understanding. Midgley writes:

General scepticism about the possibility of moral judgment, though it may look like a piece of neutral, formal analysis, cannot fail to act as propaganda in this contest of attitudes. It must make us lose confidence in our power of thinking about moral issues involving individuals—including ourselves. Yet this power is absolutely necessary to us.[6]

She is claiming that judgment is a necessary part of what it means to be a 'responsible agent'. This is a significant point because, as I argue, moral judgments are a necessary part of the way we arrive at moral understandings. Many situations are not able to be reckoned with responsibly without incorporating matters of judgment. Discussions about the nature of judgment and its place within a more nuanced understanding of responsibility are important. More to the point, however, is the recognition that the significance of such discussions lies in their capacity to extend understanding of the reasons why people do wrong. In part this means that we need to move away from the traditional, reactionary and retributive understandings of the function of judgment and responsibility. Thus, my account of responsibility de-emphasises ideas of responsibility as accountability in favour of understandings that foreground responsibility as part of our engagement with others. In the latter case responsibility is understood as a forward looking idea in which one's commitments to others are followed through.

The benefits of a shift away from an understanding of responsibility as entailing too much of an emphasis on ideas of guilt, blame and punishment are tangible. Rather than necessarily focussing on some perceived imperative to mete out punishment or the idea that we treat individuals solely as responsible agents that must be held accountable, there is much to be gained by exploring more fruitful ways of understanding the dimensions of responsibility. In a broader context this also means maintaining a sense of the very centrality of responsibility in an understanding of the tension engendered by the combination of complexity and enormity. To this end, I return to the general point at issue here. On my account, responsibility is not exhausted by ascriptions of blame or praise. Understanding responsibility entails more than judgmental analyses. Instead I want to consider ways of understanding responsibility that extend to an elaboration of the case for complexity understandings. I contend that the key to understanding life as morally complex lies, in turn, with understanding various different but related conceptualisations of responsibility. It is the variety of aspects, or what may be termed understandings, of responsibility themselves that lends meaning to the ideas that moral life can be complex. I will consider the place of responsibility in moral life according to the different ways of understanding responsibility that I think are important. As such I believe that responsibility is best understood as a 'weave' comprised of differing threads. The different strands of this weave that I will consider include Margaret Walker's 'practices of responsibility',[7] Christopher Gowans' 'responsibilities to persons'[8], aspects of notions of a plurality of values, Mary Midgley's 'individual wickedness', Tzvetan Todorov's 'acts of ordinary virtue' and some of the issues surrounding integrity, judgment, blame and moral dilemma. All of the above are ways of understanding, or aspects of, responsibility that contribute to the complexity theme.

In the sense in which I intend it, moral responsibility comes to assume a central position with respect to the way the Holocaust might be understood as morally complex. I propose that careful examination of Holocaust experiences reveals understandings of moral responsibility the conceptual fabric of which is laced with folds and creases that testify to the moral complexity of the Holocaust. One of the core themes of my argument is the proposition that a careful understanding of moral life requires, in turn, a careful understanding of the significance of the various aspects of responsibility. To this end my argument will be structured according to how different understandings of responsibility come to bear on the way responsibility is expressed or neglected by moral agents, or even attributed to persons by others. In a nutshell I argue that responsibility represents the key to understanding the moral complexity of the Holocaust.

Primo Levi, a chronicler of life in the camps, has also chosen to place the question of responsibility to the forefront of his view of how the Holocaust might best be understood. For example, in the case of his friend Lorenzo, Levi's writing evokes a strong sense of how responsibility can manifest itself even in the most diminished of circumstances. In a discussion of the way camp life emptied people of their humanity Levi writes:

> I believe that it was really due to Lorenzo that I am alive today...for his having constantly reminded me by his presence, by his natural and plain manner of being good, that there still existed . . . a remote possibility of good . . . [and] for which it was worth surviving.[9]

This quotation suggests that even in the midst of a systematic attempt to degrade human values, a moral perspective, in the form of accepting responsibility for other persons, can not only exist, but can, in some sense, flourish. On Levi's account Lorenzo demonstrated the extreme importance of a belief in respect for self in the context of their relation to each other. In the midst of this relationship, of which little is known from the quotation, it seems that responsibility has a part to play. Levi claims that Lorenzo is in some measure responsible for his survival. Somehow Lorenzo enabled Levi to take responsibility for himself and so endure. Though it is difficult to articulate, examples like that of Levi's recollection of Lorenzo go to the heart of what I seek to convey in my understanding of responsibility as that which serves as the framework of our moral understanding of ourselves. That is to say, responsibility, in some sense, is a core component of our moral sensibility.

A strong sense of the moral significance of individual accounts of taking responsibility also pervades Jean-Francois Steiner's collection of reconstructed testimonies. Though there may be some doubt as to the veracity of the stories I would contend that they contain value as regards the claims they help to illustrate. Entitled *Treblinka*[10] Steiner's account challenges the claim that the Jews allowed themselves to be led like lambs to the slaughter. Noteworthy is his interpretation of the events leading up to, and including, the 1944 uprising at Treblinka led by the *Sonderkommando*.[11] Steiner makes the case that this event is testament to extra-ordinary acts of courage amidst a general atmosphere of helplessness. The Jews of the *Sonderkommando* were heroic individuals acting within extremely dangerous conditions. Complementing Steiner's account is Simone de Beauvoir's preface to the same book in which she foregrounds the importance of the circumstances that comprised the uprising. Beauvoir argues that resistance grew out of the presence of atrocity. Heroism, she writes:

> is not inherent in human nature. . . . What they passionately desired [the individuals involved in the uprising] by massacring the German 'masters' was to overcome their condition as slaves and so demonstrate to the world that the Jewish people had not allowed themselves to be led to the slaughterhouse like a flock of sheep.[12]

Beauvoir finds it astonishing that these individuals, given the circumstances, chose to rebel. Steiner locates what seemed to be a pivotal event that would serve as a catalyst for the decision to resist. He recounts how a particular act of individual resistance served to galvanise those working in the *Sonderkommando*. On Steiner's account, a Jew, whom he refers to as Langner is caught attempting to steal money in the process of sorting clothing and is summarily condemned to be hung by the feet and left to die an agonising death. It is the intention of the Germans to make an example of Langner. With the prisoners assembled in front of Langner, his body bloody and mutilated, it appears that both body and soul are broken. Langner himself begs to be put out of his misery. This of course is precisely what the German commanding Treblinka does not wish to do. Finally the prisoners are sent back to work though within sight and hearing range of the groans of Langner who hangs according to Steiner "bloody, mutilated, shapeless."[13] What happened next must have been quite unexpected for it apparently took everyone by surprise. Langner began calling the prisoners in Yiddish. Steiner, presumably on the basis of first hand testimonies of survivors reconstructs Langners final words. He writes that Langner purportedly called out:

> Yiden! Yiden! Jews, Jews my brothers! . . . Revolt! Revolt! Don't listen to their promises. You will all be killed. They can't let you leave this place after what you have seen . . . Avenge your fathers and your brothers, avenge yourselves. . . . Since you are going to die, die fighting! Long live Israel, long live the Jewish people![14]

After an initial stunned silence Steiner reports that Kurt Franz the German in command, though not having understood the speech nevertheless realised its significance and quickly ran to Langner and without hesitation smashed his skull with the butt of a rifle. According to Steiner's account Langner's speech had a powerful effect on the prisoners. In my view this episode demonstrates the intersection of different ways of understanding responsibility. There is Langner's expression of responsibility to his fellow prisoners. There is Franz's expression of responsibility as regards his position as the senior officer. There is also the prisoners' subsequent expression of responsibility to themselves in the form of a mass escape attempt. What I'm trying to suggest here is that there is in this story an inter-connected web of expressions of adoption of responsibility. And moreover, that this web of responsibility is central to understanding moral behaviour. The various players in Steiner's story all conveyed a keen sense of responsibility. Langner himself maintained an attitude toward death that ensured the survival of his dignity even in the most violent of circumstances. Key here is the way Langner, by taking responsibility for his own situation may well have served as a catalyst for other prisoners. There is also Kurt Franz, the German officer, who was unable to strip Langner of his dignity. There are also the circumstances of the event to factor in. In extremely diminished circumstances Langner not only took responsibility for his dignity but he re-affirmed to the other prisoners the degree to which they too were implicated in his understanding of what taking responsibility, under the circumstances meant. Indeed, Steiner argues that the later uprising in the Treblinka camp was due, in part, to Langner's actions. Like Levi's example, Steiner's too, demonstrates the significance of expressions of responsibility for understanding our moral behaviour.

Whilst I have been talking about taking responsibility for one's own situation it is also true that such situations are within the context of relations with others. To this I would add that the way in which we take responsibility, in our relations with others, is the way to map the complex byways of our moral relations. In conjunction with the view that moral life is interpersonal, that is that it is given meaning by virtue of our interactions with others, I want to introduce, as an aspect of responsibility, the idea that moral life is culturally situated and sustained by what Margaret Walker refers to as 'practices of responsibility'.[15] Elaborating on what she means Walker writes:

> morality consists in a family of practices that show what is valued by making people accountable to each other for it. Practices of making morally evaluative judgments are prominent among moral practices, but they do not exhaust them. There are also habits and practices of paying attention, imputing states of affairs to people's agency, interpreting and describing human actions, visiting blame, offering excuses, inflicting punishment, making amends, refining and inhibiting the experience or expression of feelings, and responding in thought, act, and feeling to any of the foregoing. In all of these ways we express our senses of responsibility.[16]

I believe that Walker has hit upon a very important aspect of responsibility. By linking responsibility to a variety of social practices, and indeed to morality itself, Walker introduces the idea that it is these practices themselves that play a large part in the expression of our sense of responsibility. And even more to the point, moral competency of the kind demanded by the sort of experiences that are a trademark of the Holocaust requires that we pull together and attempt to render morally intelligible this complex composite of practices. I contend that the focus of our investigations ought to be within individual histories as it is such histories that are the storage place of such practices. Daunting though this task of deriving moral meaning is, it is made more so by the added presence of moral enormity in regard to the experiences in question. The sorts of practices listed above by Walker, whilst not intended to be exhaustive, offer a sense of the intricacies entailed in living our lives as moral beings. In their own right they reflect something of the complexity that I contend is central to the moral lives of human beings. In other words they form part of what I term a complexity analysis of moral life. If, on the one hand, the sorts of moral practices described by Walker entail the ascription and/or the taking of responsibility they also strongly suggest that such analyses of moral life are going to be complex.

Another important theme connecting moral complexity to responsibility is Christopher Gowans' notion of 'inescapable wrongdoing'. I argue that Gowan's idea of 'inescapable wrong—doing' supports the notion that there is a plurality of values which is, in turn, why there are moral conflicts, why we are sometimes left feeling unsatisfied when we make moral decisions, and why moral evaluations are complex. In his book *Innocence Lost: An Examination of Inescapable Moral Wrongdoing,* Gowans explores moral experience from the perspective of moral conflict and the claim that sometimes moral wrongdoing is inescapable. In his introduction Gowans writes:

> Many philosophers maintain that in every moral conflict some course of action that is wholly free from wrongdoing is available to the agent (though it may be difficult, and perhaps in some cases virtually impossible, to know what this action is). In my view these philosophers are mistaken. We may find ourselves in moral conflicts in which, through no fault of our own we will do something morally wrong no matter what we do. In these situations we may choose the lesser of two evils and hence act for the best. But in acting for the best we still choose an evil, and in this sense we still do something wrong.[17]

By challenging the idea that it is possible to avoid moral wrongdoing Gowans is contributing to an old debate in Western philosophy over the status of moral dilemmas. He argues that although an agent may decide after careful deliberation that one of two conflicting responsibilities is more compelling than the other, the less compelling responsibility does not simply disappear. Instead the secondary responsibility is at best subordinated in the process of prioritising. A key factor in this grading of responsibilities is the idea that in situations that would typically constitute serious moral conflict the agent experiences, as a matter of course, various emotional responses to the process itself. Such emotions seem to be, at least for Gowans, prima facie litmus tests for the presence of moral conflict if not moral dilemmas. In other words, feelings such as anguish at the time of the decision and guilt after the decision, result from the recognition that the situation cannot be resolved in a way that avoids the feeling and knowledge of moral transgression. Perhaps not surprisingly, such outcomes have the potential to enrich our moral lives. Consistent with this, Gowans writes that it is important to recognise that "our affective moral responses [to certain situations] can be a source of moral understanding".[18] The emotions accordingly seem to play a necessary although insufficient role in the way we make sense of our lives.

As a means of tapping this potential for moral understanding in what he calls a 'logically consistent and systematic way' Gowans coins the term 'reflective intuitionism'. The term is derived from John Rawls' earlier conceptualisation of 'reflective equilibrium'. Rawls, in the tradition of social contract theorists, argued that members of a particular social group achieve reflective equilibrium if the principles agreed on in what Rawls calls the original position (Rawls adopts this term as the hypothetical place where people could deliberate on principles of justice in the absence of the sorts of prejudices we ordinarily acquire in the course of our lives) align with judgments and understanding acquired over time.[19] Irrespective of the veracity of the Rawlsian account, the important point here is the way in which Gowans adapts Rawls' understanding of the processes that lead to the accumulation of moral knowledge. With regard to the way in which agents acquire moral understanding Gowans writes:

> Since moral intuitions exclude judgments made under conditions likely to produce error, it might reasonably be supposed that moral beliefs brought into equilibrium would reflect moral reality.[20]

Gowans argues that moral understanding or 'moral judgments' as he calls them result in large part from processes that are more than mere gut reactions.[21] On Gowans' somewhat Aristotelian account, moral understanding comes about largely as the result of the acquisition and development of reflectively processed assessments of situations over time and handed down through successive generations. Furthermore Gowans writes:

> in some moral conflicts inescapable moral feelings of moral distress are natural.
> . . . In saying that these are natural responses I do not mean that every human being necessarily would have these feelings. Since our feelings are subject to variation on account of education, accidental circumstances, individual difference, and the like, none of them can be said to be universal and necessary.[22]

The following points in respect to Gowans' position are of interest. First, Gowans does not commit himself to saying that every moral conflict generates a moral dilemma or even makes moral distress appropriate. Rather he is saying that there are some situations where such feelings are appropriate and are felt intuitively. Second, Gowans' position would arguably allow the view that situations which do generate moral dilemmas do not necessarily entail great harm. However moral dilemmas where serious harm is entailed demonstrate that such situations are no trivial matter.

Some moral rationalists claim that the idea of a genuine moral dilemma defies rationality.[23] Gowans adopts the view, and one that I believe is supported by moral experience itself, that the tenets of rationality are insufficient to capture the complexity and ambiguity of moral life in situations of conflict. Very often it is the case that a so—called rational decision in a conflict situation is unable to convince people that all is right with their world. Such feelings as anguish, remorse, shame, regret and guilt as well as judgments of blame that often accompany rational decisions are evidence of the failure of moral life to fit into rational algorithms. Indeed the evidence of such failures are able to be witnessed in legacies of enduring moral remainders from these situations.[24]

Moreover commentators such as Ruth Barcan Marcus, Philippa Foot and Torbjörn Tännsjö have maintained that the existence of moral conflicts does not have to entail moral inconsistencies. Summarising these arguments Walter Sinnot-Armstrong has concluded that what he refers to as moral realism[25] , when it is pushed too far, "underestimates the complexity of moral life [by overlooking] the importance of individual choices and moral beliefs in moral dilemmas."[26] Regarding the specific criticisms of Alan Donagan, and in reference to the terms within which he defines the parameters of the debate[27] , it may be the case that moral systems that allow what Aquinas described as perplexity *simpliciter* (or conflicts of duties) are inconsistent. Donagan's statement that "moral agents will reject a moral system as ill constructed if there are situations to which its precepts apply, but in which their agglomeration would be invalid"[28] does not in my view always accord with the circumstances that individuals can and do find themselves in. Be that as it may there are nevertheless good reasons to suppose that there is still a need to factor in what Marcus refers to as "the contingencies of this world."[29] Donagan has tried to avoid the difficulty by making a distinction between moral and practical conflict. However, I find this distinction less than convincing. The sorts of conflicts experienced by the policemen in Browning's research demonstrated both moral and practical components. This I have already demonstrated with examples from Browning's study in which individuals were faced with a situation of considerably greater complexity, ambiguity and/or conflict than that able to be captured by a Donagan type account.

It is my view that Gowans' account of the factors at play in situations of moral conflict resonates strongly with the sort of understanding of responsibility that I am seeking to convey. I think that this is best demonstrated by considering the way in which he pulls his notion of inescapable conflict together with his understanding of responsibility. He says that our intuitions concerning feelings of moral anguish are best explained by the more fundamental proposition that in some situations moral wrongdoing is inescapable. He then proceeds to demonstrate that it is on the basis of responsibilities to specific persons that unavoidable feelings of moral distress are grounded. In regard to this important claim Gowans writes:

> an agent's moral responsibilities are based on recognition of the intrinsic and
> unique value of the particular persons (or social entities) with whom the agent

has, in various ways, established some connection. Hence, an agent's responsibilities are ultimately responsibilities to specific persons. The nature of these responsibilities is defined primarily by the agent's relationship with those persons to whom he or she is responsible and is not simply a function of the outcome of the agent's moral deliberations about what ought to be done in a given situation. For this reason responsibilities to persons may conflict. When they do, the fact that deliberation of necessity directs the agent to fulfil his or her responsibility to at most one person does not mean that the responsibility to the other person has in this situation been eliminated. There will thus be occasions of conflicting moral responsibilities when, whatever the agent does, he or she will fail to fulfil at least one of these responsibilities. It is with respect to moral wrongdoing in the sense of not fulfilling a moral responsibility so defined that I believe that moral wrongdoing is sometimes inescapable.[30]

Gowans' account of responsibilities to persons is worthwhile considering because of the way it resonates with the discussion of responsibility I am seeking to generate. It's worth stating here that I don't think that responsibility, as Gowans understands it can simply be collapsed to mean 'duty' or 'obligation'. That is to say I don't think Gowans is saying that responsibility to persons means solely the concerns one ought to have for others in virtue of one's relationships to those others. I think Gowans is pointing to a discussion of responsibility that is more conceptually complex than the language of duty or obligation usually allows. The example that Gowans' himself uses is Herman Melville's disturbing but compelling story *Billy Budd* .[31] It is a good example precisely because it brings to life the philosophical complexities germane to the moral wrong-doing and responsibilities to person's accounts Gowans seeks to establish. I believe that whilst our responsibilities might, and likely do, entail duties and obligations of one sort or another such categories are, on their own, insufficient as explanations as to how we arrive at the place where we are able to decide between one responsibility and another.[32] The reason that duties and obligations, by themselves, are insufficient as explanations of responsibilities, is because of the myriad other factors that additionally affect our responsibilities. Such factors as those discussed in this chapter, including the role of individual disposition, the influence of social practices and others, such as luck in one's circumstances, are pivotal to understanding how it is we arrive at our perceptions of our responsibilities.

It is because I believe that there are a number of significant conceptual and practical factors that should be considered when discussing what it is that enables us to understand our responsibilities that I also think that the idea of the analogy of a weave of responsibilities has merit. This is nowhere more evident than in respect to the wider attempt to understand the moral dimensions of the Holocaust. In the course of a person arriving at a decision with moral implications, a whole host of factors (including those mentioned above and elsewhere in this chapter), that relate to how that person understands their responsibilities to others, 'weave' their way into the decision making process. Given the complexity of the process itself, of factoring in that person's characteristics, the socio-cultural, economic and political aspects of their background circumstances, their overall emotional well—being and their sheer good or bad luck, it is hardly surprising that, there might be conflicted options. It should even be less surprising that because of the impact of the plurality of values that require consideration, after the decision has been made moral remainders remain. All of this points to a powerful conceptualization of a complex weave of inputs contributing, sometimes with conflicted results, to our understanding of our responsibilities.

In my view a large measure of the success of Gowans' account of responsibility rests on the nature of the claim of specific relationships between persons. For Gowans, relationships, and in turn the responsibilities that derive from these relationships stem from differing sorts of associations, primary and otherwise, between individuals. In other words, moral responsibilities derive from particular concrete relationships such as those typified by relations of kinship, friendship and love.[33] Additionally, I argue that it is on the basis of the sorts of intimate relations we build with those who are close to us that we develop standards for how we understand moral responsibilities in circumstances with others who are not so intimately connected to ourselves. This is admittedly a difficult argument to substantiate but one for which I think it is possible to locate support in studies of the sort undertaken by Browning. Browning's research showed how much more difficult it was for policemen to carry out murder when they personally knew or faced the victims.

To clarify here, I am saying that relations such as those between agents intimately involved, serve as exemplars for learning how to understand moral relations in circumstances such as those that may obtain between any two human beings. Gowans' account of responsibilities to specific persons as substantively informed by the nature of relationships between intimates represents an important insight into the way responsibilities are formed more generally. I think the value of Gowans' account lies in its ability to unravel aspects of the practical operations of our moral relations. By this I mean that Gowans' account is of most significance when the focus is maintained on aspects of the particularity of moral relations.

Gowans goes on to argue that persons, even if they are not intimately related, can still be regarded as valuable because of the intrinsic value that inheres in specific person to person relations themselves. The example[34] Gowans' uses is one based on the sort of intimate relationship between a parent and child. In this example he describes the responsibility of a parent to nurture his or her child. In the tradition of Kant such responsibility comes from a number of sources not least of which is the accepted knowledge that the infant in question is his or her child and as such would usually be regarded as intrinsically and uniquely valuable. Gowans' intent is to establish a connection between this primary relationship and the way we perceive the morality of our relations more generally. Gowans seems to be suggesting that the value we place on our relations with persons generally, and hence the value we place on persons themselves more generally, is informed to a large extent by our understanding of relations with intimates. Gowans also seems to be saying that our understanding of the intrinsic value of a person depends, in large part, on our understanding, more generally, of intimate relations with persons. Or to put it another way people with whom we do not share a close relation or even a distant relation may still be regarded as intrinsically valuable on the basis of the way we understand ideas of value and responsibility toward those with whom we are close. In this way Gowans builds an account of morality extrapolating from relations with intimates.

In this sense Gowans' position is closer to the Kantian notion of respecting persons as ends in themselves than the utilitarian subordination of specific persons to the 'greater good' of the wider social group. It is there that the similarity with Kant stalls, however, because for Gowans, motivation rightfully derives from our experience of intimacy as opposed to Kant's claim that it is consistency of reason that should be at the centre of our intent. Of more interest here, though, is Gowans' point that persons possess a unique value as opposed to a utilitarian 'equal' value. Gowans' emphasis on uniqueness points to the proposition that we ought to respond to different persons differently. For Gowans, although agents possess a unique value, they also need to be valued in recognition to the affinity that derives from the specific relationship. It might be objected that a focus on uniqueness might be construed as allowing for prejudicial treatment, and Gowans himself recognises and suggests a solution to this concern. He argues that emphasis on uniqueness will only be regarded as an avenue for prejudice if "we already think that the only alternative to regarding persons as equally important is to regard some as more important than others."[35] My point is that those who are prejudiced in the views they hold are not likely to be interested in the unique value of each individual in the first instance. Moreover some evidence seems to provide support for Gowans' claim as regards those who hold prejudicial views. Research has shown that typical patterns of prejudice project particular, though stereotypical features, as defining features. Daniel Pick, in his study of nineteenth century discourses of degeneration, *Faces of Degeneration*,[36] details numerous examples of the way in which nineteenth and early twentieth century 'social Darwinist' discourses manufactured a 'history' of racial degeneration (with attendant stereotypes) coupled with the need to eliminate inferior peoples on the basis of a hierarchy of 'uniqueness'. Such discourses, Pick argues, were typically legitimated by appeals to science. Pseudo-scientific language is also evident in a 1938 speech by Hans Frank, later Minister for Justice in the Third Reich and cited in Pick's *Faces of Degeneration*:

> National Socialism regards degeneracy as an immensely important source of criminal activity . . . in an individual, degeneracy signifies exclusion from the normal 'genus' of the decent nation. This state of being degenerate or egenerate, this different or alien quality, tends to be rooted in miscegenation between a decent representative of his race and an individual of inferior racial stock. To us National Socialists, criminal biology, or the theory of congenital criminality, connotes a link between racial decadence and criminal manifestations.[37]

Seeking to establish grounds for an agenda of discrimination, Frank claims a link between criminality and particular social groups. The sorts of features taken as defining are then universalised in a way that totally disregards the unique value of individuals. A prime example of this is the way Nazi propaganda constructed a certain image of 'the Jew' as universally applicable to the stereotype being sought. However, whilst it is possible to accept the trajectory of Gowans' argument in this instance, I am inclined to believe that a focus on uniqueness may also serve as a recipe for exploitation by those who would want to encourage prejudicial attitudes. Of course for Gowans the question of uniqueness is something that attaches to humans as opposed to that which is not human. Be that as it may, in my view, it needs to be remembered that the primary purpose of such examples as the Frank speech was to create a hierarchy of differentiation between what counted as human and what did not. Such 'intellectual' justification could then be applied as an explanation, and indeed impetus for, the coming 'solution' to the problem, as perceived by the Nazis, of the Jews and other inferior peoples.

I believe there is a wider importance as regards the idea of intrinsic and unique value of specific persons. The significance of an inherent value in specific persons lies in its ability to inform discussion of concrete responsibilities in encounters between persons. Gowans, whilst recognising that responsibilities vary substantively in scope, and as I mentioned earlier, perhaps including not only responsibilities to specific persons but also responsibilities to social entities or groups, nevertheless insists that a key factor in understanding the nature of moral responsibilities is our knowledge of responsibilities with intimates. Cognisance of responsibility to persons in the wider world depends to a large extent for Gowans on our previously established, although not always fully articulable, understanding of the 'other' within intimate relations. Summarising this aspect of moral responsibility Gowans writes:

> Constitutive of such [moral] relationships is an understanding of some form of responsibility by each person for the well-being of the other, though the nature and scope of these responsibilities, as well as the extent of their symmetry and the degree to which they are well defined, varies with the nature of the relationship.[38]

What I interpret Gowans to mean here is that an important part of the process of our moral response to a particular situation should be based around an understanding of the well-being of the other, whomever that other may be. In the process of deliberating about the nature of our responsibilities to a specific person in a specific situation one vital judgment will be the concerns necessary to maintain the well-being of the other. Of course, because of the wide variety of factors operating at the interface of deliberation and decision many different moral outcomes are possible. This is also why for Gowans, in concrete and often complex situations, responsibilities can, and do, emerge in ways that generate conflict.

I claim that it would seem to be the case that a further source of complexity other than that between responsibilities to differing people, is differing understandings of what it is that constitutes well-being in particular cases. For example, in the euthanasia debate, quality of life is often a central concern in deciding whether or not to allow an assisted termination of a person's life. In these sorts of contexts well-being itself turns out to be a contested term.

The key insight I think of Gowans' account is the notion that it is responsibilities to specific persons that are pivotal to our understanding of responsibilities generally. This is a difficult point to convey but it is of some significance as it carries with it powerful implications about the nature of moral agency itself. I want to provide this discussion on responsibility with more substance. Clearly there are some interpretations of responsibility that are morally unacceptable. For example, the Nazis may well have been responding to the Jews on the basis of a sense of responsibility to themselves. The understanding they used was clearly a morally bankrupt sense of responsibility. This is evidenced in my earlier example of Kurt Franz. My claim here is rather more subtle. As moral agents we do not, and indeed should not, only act in accord with some abstract set of guidelines but rather we should respond to every person we encounter and with whom we have some form of relation with some non-abstract sense of responsibility. This understanding of moral agency is important although, of course, it is also tempered by the recognition that just as some of our relations are more distant than others so the same is true as regards the intensity of our moral responsibilities. Let me clarify what I am trying to say here with an example. If indeed it is the case that moral responsibilities are, and should be, based around concrete responses to concrete individuals then this resonates strongly with the way we might best understand the feelings of the sort of distress evidently experienced by the policemen in Browning's study. Browning's research supports the claim that responsibilities, based on actual encounters, are mediated by the nature of the relationship in question. That this is so is evident in the reactions of policemen after encountering their victims. Thus Browning writes:

> Georg Kageler,* a thirty-seven year old tailor, made it through the first round before encountering difficulty. "After I had carried out the first shooting and at the unloading point was allotted a mother with daughter as victims for the next shooting, I began a conversation with them and learned that they were Germans from Kassel, and I took the decision not to participate further in the executions. The entire business was now so repugnant to me that I returned to my platoon leader and told him that I was still sick and asked for my release." Kageler was sent to guard the marketplace. Neither his pre-execution conversation with his victim nor his discovery that there were German Jews in Józefów was unique.[39]

The sentiment of this account strongly suggests that a conflict, and indeed, a change in prioritising different responsibilities developed in the mind of the individual in question. The policeman began by obeying orders and appears to have been able to proceed on that basis for some time. Once the policeman learnt that some of the victims were not just Jews but German Jews it seems that his understanding of his responsibility to them altered to a point beyond which he was unable to execute his orders and sought a way out of the situation that he henceforth found morally unacceptable. The conflict in responsibilities (as understood by the policeman) in this example is resolved as a result of a perceived change in the nature of the relationship, and hence the sorts of responsibilities that accrue, between the policeman and the victims. I argue that it is the case that the conversation that this policeman had with his victims brought more of their concrete uniqueness to the foreground, albeit in generalised terms. In spite of the pertinence of this example, however, some concerns remain. In many situations there is going to be the question of deciding where responsibilities to others end. There is also the difficulty of establishing the criteria for determining where responsibilities end. Be that as it may, the responsibility to specific persons account remains a strong one.

It might also be argued that the example above constituted, in the eyes of the policeman, a moral dilemma. That is to say, at least prior to his recognition of some of the Jews as German, the policeman may well have believed that he was faced with a situation in which an immoral outcome was the only possibility. It is possible that only after the policeman's conversation with his victims was he able to come to the view that a morally acceptable option was available after all. This is not to say that even in the event that the policeman came to the view that what he was doing was morally unacceptable he may still not have felt remorse at not being able fulfil his orders.

Other examples from Browning's study show that the case of the policeman Kageler was not unique. Conflicts between perceived differing responsibilities were apparent and suggest evidence of personal moral dilemmas between duty to the commanding officer and a recognition of a responsibility to a specific person(s) on the basis of a recognition of that other person as valuable in their own right. It is true that the value of the persons in the example in question was based upon a recognition by the policeman that these Jews were different from 'other' Jews. The point though is that, on the basis of this knowledge, the policeman was sufficiently morally conflicted to re-prioritise his understanding of his moral responsibilities and perhaps more importantly to act on this re-prioritisation.

There is one more clue in the testimony of this policeman, that eludes to yet another possibility in the complex moral jigsaw of this example. The policeman, having signalled the importance of his learning that the people were not only Jewish but also German, then indicated that the 'business', as he called it, henceforth became more repugnant than it had previously been. This raises the question as to whether or not the policeman had known all along what his real moral priorities were but had, in spite of this, succumbed to the pressures of such factors as obedience to authority. On the face of it this may seem to be the case but it would seem more evidence would be warranted for such a claim to be made with any conviction.

Finally, I want to make explicit the point that Gowans' assessment of the ways in which responsibilities to persons are formed foregrounds socio-cultural, economic and political circumstances as significant factors in understanding why it is that moral wrongdoing is sometimes understood to be inescapable.[40] As part of the explanation for how moral conflicts are generated and how responsibilities come to be shaped, the role of circumstances is an important factor. The significance of circumstance whilst it can be overstated remains a continuous thread in this book. I shall pick up this thread again in Chapter Five when I discuss the role of luck in moral life.

I now want to continue by taking up the link between individual disposition and responsibility. Hence I want to shift the focus of the discussion to the role of individual character. My view is that a person's personal moral fortitude has a part to play in terms of the way we as individuals take up issues of responsibility. I will examine the claim that responsibility, whilst it is in some important respects, subject to the force of external pressures, also derives from elements that are closely linked to features of our individual human natures. To this end I intend to show that a conception of responsibility that encompasses individual moral character can enhance our understandings of the form and content of responsibility more generally.

In her book *Wickedness,* Midgley considers the way in which contemporary thinking has weighed the debate surrounding human agency and the problem posed between an individual's autonomy and their position in the world. Her discussion is interesting therefore for what it contributes to my understanding of the role of individual disposition. Midgley argues against the tendency in current debates toward dichotomies that do little to illuminate the position of responsibility in moral life. Her concern is that debates become locked into the either/or of agents being at the whim of their environment or fully in command of their actions (as in the Sartrean dictum that 'Man is condemned to be free'). For Midgley there is much to be gained from each of these positions but little to be had by positioning these two extremes in opposition to one another.

She approaches the question of human autonomy via the problem of explaining individual wickedness. She canvasses the distinction between people of weak will, who do wrong against their real wishes and so-called vicious people who knowingly and maliciously commit wrongs. While Midgley does not directly engage with the question of weak will at length, her discussion is interesting, all the same, precisely because it broaches some important questions regarding individual behaviour. She admits that weak will is a problem but gives little indication as to whether what might be called genuine weakness of the will, that is when an agent knowingly does wrong, is actually possible. She does say that there may be uncertainty with regard to "the best way of describing the confused state in which people manage to do things which they admit to be wrong".[41] Midgley's example of Ernst Rohm (the Nazi S.A. leader depicted as someone who on face value at least seems to fit the criteria for akrasia) seems to match with her position on this matter. It may be true that Rohm's statement "Since I am an immature and bad man, war appeals to me more than peace"[42] might be nothing more than a 'passing mood' or a 'sarcastic joke' but this is not necessarily a reason for discounting out of hand the possibility that Rohm was of sound mind when he wrote this statement and that he meant what he said. She contends that a context, of the sort indicated above, within which to understand Rohm's statement, is required as such a statement could not be understood in the literal sense. To my mind, Midgley's account of the Rohm example does not offer sufficient allowance for the possibility that rational agents might knowingly do wrong. However, one of the strengths of her account lies in her insight into the problems associated with the reduction of wickedness to a form of madness. Extrapolating from the medical model of mental disorder Midgley argues that whilst madness counts as an excuse, calculated and deliberate criminal acts do not. Therefore to conflate wickedness with madness does not accord with what seems to be the case as regards much individual wickedness. That is to say, not all individual wickedness occurs as a result of the agent suffering from misfortunes that are able to be understood as some form of psychological disorder. Following this there seems to be no necessary inconsistency between maintaining that there are sometimes difficulties in rendering acts of wickedness intelligible but nevertheless that such acts are wrong. For this reason alone the view that wickedness is a form of madness seems to be implausible. Therefore there seems to be no real problem with the conclusion that, as a general rule, madness per se, and on its own, is insufficient reason to excuse wickedness.

Another very prominent aspect of Midgley's argument is her treatment of such emotional states as anger, fear and especially aggression, as necessary elements in the way we might understand motivations for action. For Midgley, aggression, like such emotions as fear, anger, sloth and greed, plays an important role among the range of necessary responses to what she terms evil. These emotions, she argues, form a necessary component of our relations with others and are essential to an individual's emotional processes. Midgley is not saying that all aggression is positive and in fact she stresses that, unchecked, aggression can lead to serious harm. Her point is that aggression is part of our being and is neither wholly bad or good. It can result in vice but it can also be conceived as a formidable weapon in our emotional armoury. As Midgley correctly points out, the world which we, as emotional creatures inhabit, is composed of experiences both pleasant and unpleasant.[43] In our pursuit of a good life, whatever that may be, we need to be able to respond appropriately to evil, whatever that may be, as there is no likelihood of exhausting the possibilities of its occurrence. Moreover, it is very much the case for Midgley that it is not until we come to terms with the role of such states of emotion as aggression, as a motive for iniquitous behaviour, that we can gain a deeper insight into the puzzle of individual wrongdoing more generally. The point I want to make here is that emotions, such as those mentioned here, clearly have a role to play in understanding how and why individuals commit acts of wrong-doing against other individuals. In other words, emotions which are a manifestation of our individual characters should be factored into understandings as to why we act the way we do and hence how we individually understand what our responsibilities are. If it is the case, as Midgley argues, that such emotions as aggression play a part in the configuration of behaviour then individual emotions need to be taken account of when we want to understand the source of acts of aggression in the context of people's responsibilities to others.

Gitta Sereny's book *Into that Darkness, From Mercy Killing to Mass Murder*, [44] an informative account of not only how individual dispositions affect our capacity to fulfil our own sense of our responsibilities to others but also of the way in which, as individuals, our actions express how we are enmeshed with those around us, provides support for Midgley's analysis. Sereny makes the large claim that her exhaustive investigation into Franz Stangl, the former commandant of Treblinka:

> aims to be a demonstration of the fatal interdependence of all human actions, and an affirmation of man's responsibility for his own acts and their consequences. [45]

In my view, Sereny's study directly reinforces Midgley's analysis of the derivation of wickedness in individuals. Sereny stresses the importance of not overlooking the fact that responsibility for the murder of millions of people lies, in some sense, with individual persons. This point needs to be fore grounded lest individual responsibility is trivialised. Significant here is Sereny's concern with the idea of the interdependence, via our actions, emotions, thoughts and desires, of individual human lives. Throughout the conversations with Sereny, Stangl constructed an image of himself as a victim of circumstances. As evidenced by the testimonies of defendants at Nuremberg and in the well documented trial of Adolf Eichmann, Stangl's self-construction has parallels elsewhere. Such rationalisations have been well documented by Robert Lifton.[46] In an attempt to explain the nature of his corruption by the machinery of the Final Solution and in response to Sereny's specific question concerning aspects of his close collaboration with his superior Globocnik, Stangl stated:

> All I was doing was to confirm to him [Globocnik] that I would be carrying out this assignment as a police officer under his command . . . It was a matter of survival—always of survival. What I had to do, while I continued my efforts to get out, was to limit my own actions.[47]

These and other conversations with Sereny suggest a situation in which Stangl wrestled with his conscience to the extent that he believed it was possible to live conscionably with his actions. I think it is possible to discern aspects of Stangl's personality in his comments about how he came to terms with his situation. As with many of the defendants at Nuremburg, Stangl showed complicity just by virtue of his confession of involvement. He showed that he was able to execute his 'assignment' however horrible and morally bankrupt it might be. He also showed an impotence in the face of the evil that was being perpetrated before his very eyes. On the face of it Stangl sold his soul to the devil even if he later showed remorse and guilt. In another example Stangl states that:

> I had heard that the new police chief of Warsaw was a man from my wife's home town in Austria. I went to see him as soon as I left Globocnik and I begged him to help me get a transfer. . . . Of course, any transfer required Globocnik's signature—without that it couldn't be done. And I know now it was stupid of me ever to hope. Globocnik would never have let me go.[48]

It is evident from these statements that Stangl's disposition to avoid standing up for what he knew to be wrong prevented him from avoiding the role he was to play in perpetrating horrible crimes. More generally, the example of Stangl, as confirmed by Midgley's account, demonstrates the significance of individual disposition upon a person's ability to perform moral actions.

The issue of the interdependence of one human with another is also significant, though in this case it is shown in sharpest relief in the context of Sereny's final and most difficult question to Thea Stangl, Franz Stangl's wife. In the form of a hypothetical that must have challenged the legitimacy of Thea's moral position Sereny asked:

> Would you tell me . . . what you think would have happened if at any time you had faced your husband with an absolute choice; if you had said to him: 'Here it is; I know it's terribly dangerous, but either you get out of this terrible thing, or else the children and I will leave you.' What I would like to know is: if you had confronted him with these alternatives which do you think he would have chosen?[49]

In my view Thea Stangl's answer strikes at the heart of the issues of interdependence, individual dispositions and our capacity to take responsibility for the situations we find ourselves in. In her reply to Sereny, Thea Stangl confronts her own inability to take responsibility for what happened. In the end Thea Stangl provided two interpretations as to how Franz Stangl would have chosen. In her first response over an hour after Sereny had put the question to her she is reported to have said that "if I had ever confronted Paul with the alternatives: Treblinka— or me; he would . . . yes, he would in the final analysis have chosen me."[50] Then on the next day, the last day of correspondence between Sereny and Thea Stangl, Thea Stangl, in a note wrote, that Franz Stangl:

> would never have destroyed himself or the family. And that is what I learned to understand in the critical month of July 1943.[51]

Both of these responses, if credible, and Sereny believes that they are truthful, are extremely revealing. The first response reveals the extent to which Sereny's question must have been a painful one for Thea Stangl. As Sereny recognises there is the clear implication in the first answer that had Thea Stangl displayed enough moral courage she might have saved him from moral turpitude even if they themselves would have ultimately perished as a result. In the first answer there is also a clear impression of compliance in what was happening. In what Thea later refers to as the critical month of 1943 lies a knowledge of what was happening within her husband's sphere of influence and with his consent. Thea's comments are a window into her personality. She was unable to stand up against what she knew was happening in Treblinka. In the second answer, there is evidence of the extent of moral anguish that Franz Stangl is likely to have felt in making the decisions that he did. Thea Stangl indicates that his decision might have been one where he would have been forced to choose between harming Thea and the children or continuing on the path of personal moral degradation.

As for Thea Stangl herself, I think that her comments display a feeling of impotence in the face of evil. More generally, I think that this example shows, within the terms of the relationship in question, the influence one individual can potentially wield over another. The example also shows how it might have been possible for someone of stronger moral fortitude to have made a difference to the direction of the events of Franz Stangl's life. And perhaps most significantly the example demonstrates how, in spite of the closeness of the relationship between Franz and Thea Stangl, neither of these people were able to find the courage within themselves to stand up against what they found themselves involved in. A final comment can be made with respect to Thea Stangl. Thea, like her husband, seems to have been a person of weak will. Whilst she or her husband may not have been in a position to have done very much the question remains as to what could have been done, at least in terms of responsibility for themselves not to mention their victims, had she put her foot down and demanded he refuse to take part in the mass murders. To recap, this example shows how recognition of personal disposition, in this instance a lack of moral courage, enables us to understand the complexity of the Stangl's experience of their moral responsibility and thus better understand the complexity of moral life more generally.

It could be claimed that the confessions contained in the statements above beg the question of the options that may have existed for resistance. Sereny herself does not explore this question. However, John K. Roth in 'On Losing Trust in the World',[52] does examine the possibilities for resistance. Roth considers Stangl's responses to the question of whether or not resistance would have made any difference and accepts that, on its own, the refusal of one individual would not have made any impression in the destruction process. This is not to say that Roth excuses Stangl's despair. Rather the opposite is the case. Roth argues that it is precisely Stangl's perception of his own hopelessness that foreshadowed situations within which heinous crimes were able to be committed. As individuals we need, claims Roth, to take account of not only our own actions, as important as they are, but also to take responsibility for the actions of others. Had more individuals assumed this kind of responsibility, that is to confront and question one another, Roth surmises that "the Holocaust need not have gone on

just the same."[53] Neither Thea nor Franz Stangl were exempt from the sort of responsibility that Roth identifies as an essential ingredient for a world in which
personal responsibility, that is owning up to one's choices, should entail responsibilities to others in the form of respecting, if not actually enhancing their well-
being. Though it is a tough line to take I agree wholeheartedly with the sentiments of Roth. I think that the example of Stangl highlights why it is imperative
that we adopt a more pro-active view of responsibility in spite of the potential
pressures and sanctions that may result. Our moral integrity and the well-being
of others depends on us holding firm. My wider point, however, is that the
Stangl example would seem to explain why it was that Stangl himself, because
of his personal disposition, was unable to challenge the authority of his superiors.

In her epilogue Sereny identifies a key issue of the interdependence between
actions and responsibility. It seems to me that there is a strong case to suggest
that our actions are very closely tied up with how we take up responsibility for
such actions. Our moral attitude or how we view ourselves in the light of our actions and our actions themselves, seem to be mutually dependent upon one another. Sereny sums up with the idea that individuals possess a moral essence but
that this core is "deeply vulnerable and profoundly dependent on a climate of
life."[54] In other words, individuals possess a sense of responsibility that includes
respect for others. What is interesting here is the way in which this essence is
deeply entangled with the moral lives of others. The testimonies of Thea and
Franz Stangl comprise particular pieces of evidence of the way ordinary individuals can become submerged within the processes of compliance imposed by a
state ideology. It is also clear that the sort of moral essence described by Sereny
is by necessity frail and subject to the lived parameters of our lives. Franz Stangl
himself came close to such a conclusion when in response to the question "Do
you think that that time in Poland taught you anything?", he included in his answer the words, "Yes, that everything human has its origin in human weakness."[55] Stangl's response to this question is in my view tantamount to an acceptance of personal responsibility for his actions. I also want to make the point that
Sereny's observations are entirely compatible with the sorts of claims that I am
proposing. That is to say, I think that Sereny's encounter with Franz and Thea
Stangl demonstrates the way in which individual moral personalities are comprised of dispositions of some complexity. There are many more examples
among Sereny's discussions with Franz and Thea to support this claim.

Her account also shows how individuals are powerfully affected by the myriad situations that operate to confer meaning on the processes of negotiating our
moral lives. Whilst conducted clinically and economically Sereny's questions
nevertheless foreground the effect of the particular circumstances that conspired
to strip both Franz and Thea of their humanity. It might be tempting to conclude
from these testimonies that, in the situations described, evil comes to reign in the
absence of a respect for the dignity and sacredness of human life. This, however,
would be a mistake. With the aid of Sereny's careful but persistent method of

questioning, Franz and Thea Stangl come to be revealed not as evil incarnate but as all too human and with all of the frailties that attach to what it means to be a human. It is true that Franz and Thea made moral decisions and compromises that placed them in positions for which the world would justifiably hold them accountable. But it is also true that events almost certainly conspired to diminish the possibility for the Stangls to have acted otherwise. Sereny's analysis provides us with some vital clues as to the way responsibilities, sometimes understood as calls upon people by themselves and sometimes by others, for concern for others, weave within and between situations and individuals with whom we are connected. In the examples examined here the calls to take responsibility were evidently heard by the Stangls, and were retrospectively manifest in the form of remorse and guilt. Sadly, however, both Franz and Thea were unable to meet this most difficult of tests upon their moral integrity. A combination of particular personalities, encounters with others and a specific set of circumstances conspired to overwhelm whatever moral fortitude the Stangls might have possessed.

I now want to consider another aspect of responsibility where responsibility to self is understood as a certain sort of integrity. In his book *History, Theory, Trauma: Representing the Holocaust*[56] Dominick LaCapra writes:

> It is . . . not a defence of a generalised "non-judgemental" attitude to observe that, in cases where one has not oneself been tested by comparable circumstances, one may be in no position to judge particular individuals. The judgments one seeks through an exchange with the past are related instead to more general questions of interpretation and argument that become specified not as one plays imaginary God or just judge vis-à-vis others in the past but as one confronts difficult challenges in the present and future.[57]

LaCapra's understanding of the role of judgment echoes that of Geoffrey Hartman, whom LaCapra also cites, as seeking a role for judgment that is primarily, in Hartman's words, 'forensic' rather than 'juridical'.[58] What are the implications of LaCapra's position as regards the matter of judgment? In my view the sort of account of judgment envisaged by LaCapra would be one where responsibility extends to all of 'us' including those who would claim the authority to judge. I think that what LaCapra is alluding to here, is a certain sort of integrity when it comes to the way we take account of ourselves in the situations we find ourselves in. I don't mean integrity in the sense of conjuring up images of purity of rightness or wholeness. Rather I envisage integrity in the sense that Cheshire Calhoun has explored as "the virtue of having the proper regard for one's own judgment as a deliberator among deliberators".[59] Or as Walker understands integrity, as something that relates directly to how people take up responsibility for their part in the collective project of working out how to live.[60] It is this sense of taking responsibility for one's place among overlapping relationships that I'm especially interested in.

Thus integrity relates more closely to responsibility to one's self as the self-conscious author of one's decisions and acts within a community of such authors, as opposed to responsibility to others. Sometimes integrity might take the form of sticking by principles. Other times it might take the form of owning responsibility for damage done. I venture to say that the onus is on every one to take moral account of themself and their own moral narrative to ensure that should they find themself in a situation where they might be held accountable by others, their integrity would not be threatened. Needless to say taking account of oneself in this way consists of a project of some complexity.

It is my contention that nowhere are the concerns of such a project more clearly identified than in Tzvetan Todorov's book *Facing the Extreme: Moral Life in the Concentration Camps*.[61] Perhaps Todorov's primary insight is the recognition that individual behaviour within the camps, whilst it produced examples of human vice of the most extreme kind, also evinced what he calls 'acts of ordinary virtues'.[62] I closely associate such acts with the sort of understanding of integrity I am seeking to elaborate. Todorov's examples show how these vices and these virtues manifest themselves in the networks of our responsibilities to others. He expressly highlights examples of 'ordinary virtues' as a means of stressing the survival of a morally courageous perspective *in extremis*. An important point here is that the death, destruction and degradation of human values that typified human relationships in the camps witnessed both vice and virtue in ways that defy simple explanations. The use of the word 'ordinary' is not incidental here. As my use of Todorov's examples will show, human individuals carry within them the potential for moral courage at one end of the spectrum, moral cowardice at the other, and everything in between. I will argue that, as moral beings, located somewhere in the spectrum, the potential to exhibit virtue and vice is a feature that we all share. One important difference though, when distinguishing between one moral being and another, in addition to their personal disposition, concerns the substance of their respective circumstances. There are many ways of underlining this argument. One way is to point out, as Terence de Pres does that "the state of nature, as it turns out, is not natural. A war of everyone against everyone must be imposed by force".[63] What de Pres is saying is that camp life, as hellish as it was, was an artificial creation of the totalitarian regime of Nazi Germany. So whilst survivor Levi may have been correct in his comparison of camp life with Hobbes' view of society in the absence of absolute monarchy,[64] there was nothing natural about such a life. It was an imposed situation.

Todorov's study, like Sereny's, also supports my claim that individual lives, the acts that mark them out and the circumstances that surround them, are interdependent. In Todorov's account of moral life in the camps, the theme of responsibility is ever present. In his account of the Warsaw Uprising of 1944 Todorov arrives at a distinction between actions that might be equally virtuous but nevertheless require different ways to describe them. Todorov recounts the heroic actions of Colonel Okuliki, Mark Edelman and Michael Klepfisz among others as illustrating what he identifies as 'heroic virtues'.[65] Citing Edelman, however, Todorov also draws attention to the particularly edifying story of a young girl named Pola Lifszyc. Though Edelman does not state when Pola's story took place it must have been during the late stages of the so called first 'action' in August or September of 1942. Any earlier than this and Pola would not have known about the death camps. Edelman writes that Pola

> went to her house and . . . saw that her mother wasn't there . . . Her mother was already in a column marching toward the *Umschlagplatz*. Pola ran after the column alone, from Leszno Street to Stawki Street. . . . At the last minute, she managed to merge into the crowd so as to be able to get on the train with her mother.[66]

For Todorov the story of Pola constitutes an act of what he terms 'ordinary virtue'.[67] This act and acts like it, I would argue, leave a powerful impression on not only Edelman and Todorov but on the moral imagination of most who happen to encounter such accounts. For Todorov such acts embody the core virtues of integrity and a caring for others. Pola acted with integrity inasmuch as she displayed, in Todorov's words, "the capacity of the individual to remain a subject with a will" [and moreover that] "that fact, by itself, is enough to ensure membership in the human race."[68] The point to recounting Pola's story, and one of the reasons I draw attention to it here is to raise the question of the difference between choosing death and submitting to it. It seems to me that to choose one's death is to take responsibility for one's actions, to own one's actions. Choosing death is an affirmation of the power of taking responsibility. The act of choosing serves also to enable more careful discrimination between the overly used and simple categories of victims and perpetrators. So whilst in a simplistic sense, it is possible to view Pola as a 'victim', it seems to me that she epitomises what Claudia Card refers to as someone who chooses "forward looking responsibility".[69] Pola's action, in my view, subverts simple understandings of victim hood. The implications of Pola's act of 'merging into the crowd' also show just how strongly interconnected individual lives are with one another. This relates to my earlier point concerning the connection between our personalities, our relations with others and the circumstances we find ourselves in. Whatever else might be able to be said of this situation and the sense of futility it may engender, for Pola, while she made her choice she also maintained the integrity of the relationship between herself and her mother.

Moreover, I believe that her decision could well have entailed a complex interplay of moral deliberations. She would very likely, for example, have been considering her responsibilities to her mother. She would almost certainly have feared for the safety of her own and her mother's life. She might have wondered at the brutality of those who had forced such actions upon her. She might have wondered about the consequences of not choosing to attempt to find her mother and join her. In his personal recollection of events Edelman himself comments that Pola "could easily have crossed to the Aryan side because she was young, pretty, she didn't look Jewish, and she'd have had a hundred times better chance."[70]

She might also have felt hatred or even pity for those who had forced such actions upon her. She might even have experienced some exhilaration at having managed to merge un—noticed into the crowd at the last moment. She would likely have needed to rally all of her courage to join her mother. She would almost certainly have felt fear generated by the circumstances. I argue that, in spite of the obvious fact that we shall never know with any certainty, all of these hypotheses were at least possible and maybe even likely. My point is, irrespective of whether or not the above considerations were part of Pola's deliberations, it is alternatives of this sort that represent the very source of morality. Deliberations of the sort listed above are part of the complex interplay of emotions, loyalties and responsibilities, moral agents grapple with both in terms of self and relations with others. If the choice in the end was simple for Pola, it is at least possible that the ingredients that led to such a choice were not.

Todorov also writes of an additional, and in his estimation, necessary piece in the composition of acts of ordinary virtue. Todorov calls this simply, a caring for others and thereby identifies how it is that acts of ordinary virtue are different in their essence from acts of heroic virtue. Acts of ordinary virtue, he writes, are always undertaken as part of a genuine concern for another individual human being. Todorov contrasts such acts with those which might be undertaken on behalf of an ideal or a nation. Probably, Pola's action took the form of an act of ordinary virtue. Pola took control of her destiny but it was also an action that would seem to have been directed toward, and out of love and concern for, another human being.

It might be argued that actions of the sort epitomised by Pola are counterintuitive in that they run against notions of self preservation. My argument, however, is that the structures of individual moral lives are never as simple as claims of self preservation on their own. I am not suggesting that the drive for self preservation lacks significance in accounts of what motivates people to action. Rather it is accounts like that of the story of Pola that show that, although self preservation is a factor, it is but one factor among others including the complex interplay of moral deliberations that comprise moral life. Stories like Pola's contribute to the view that understanding such behaviour requires careful attention to the complex intersection of individual dispositional and contextual coordinates that combine to produce narratives of this sort. Todorov, citing elements of the work of Viktor Frankl and Jean Amery,[71] argues that the sorts of stories he recounts, as examples of ordinary virtue, go to the core of what it means to retain one's humanity in the face of situations designed to obliterate that humanity. Todorov thereby adds dignity and caring for others to his analysis of the way individuals take, maintain and retain responsibility for their attitude toward life. It might be argued that Todorov's understanding of dignity translates as an affirmation of the freedom of the will. I am also of the view that Pola's story invites claims of dignity in the form of a sort of bravery in the face of adversity. Edelman too, seems to be of the same view when he says more generally that:

Those people went quietly and with dignity. It is a horrendous thing, when one is going so quietly to one's death. It is infinitely more difficult than to go out shooting. After all it is much easier to die firing—for us it was much easier to die than it was for someone who first boarded a train car, then rode the train, then dug a hole, then undressed naked. . . . Do you understand now?[72]

The understanding of dignity and integrity conveyed here by Edelman also bears on an interesting connection and contrast between the earlier example of Franz Stangl and that of Pola. Pola, as I've conjectured, chose a particular moral path and in so doing, maintained, in the sense that Todorov intends, her sense of self worth. The connection concerns this sense of dignity and the way Pola's integrity, by virtue of the choices she made, was also preserved. On the other hand the story of Pola contrasts with the way Stangl seems to have submitted to the position he found himself in. The story of Stangl seems to represent the antithesis of 'forward looking responsibility'. The two stories together confound stereotypes of the powerless victim and the powerful perpetrator. In all Todorov's account of integrity, dignity and caring for others represent an important aspect of the understanding of responsibility I am seeking to develop.

What is also interesting about Todorov's sense of dignity is the way it is able to be maintained under the most extreme of situations. This is not to discount the place of circumstances within an understanding of responsibility and the complexity of moral life. Rather I am seeking to give due recognition to the ability of particular individuals to maintain their dignity in the face of situations that would powerfully test most people's capacity to make decisions affirming their understanding of their responsibilities to others.

It might also be of interest to ask the question what if Pola had chosen instead to try to escape. In this instance would she have been able to maintain the security of her dignity? Or was her dignity tied to respecting the dignity of others? In my view had Pola chosen to escape few would argue such a choice would have tainted Pola's dignity. The point is, that in either instance Pola would have been engaged in taking responsibility for her actions as opposed to any attempt to pass that responsibility onto others. Alternately, passively allowing herself to be taken by the Germans might have constituted a situation which arguably showed a lack of responsibility.

Even in regard to what might be described as a minimalist form of dignity there are enough examples of individuals securing responsibility for their own attitude to the circumstances they find themselves in to lend credibility to the importance of dignity in the explanation of moral responsibility that I'm seeking to convey. The story of Pola is one such example. Another similar example is recounted by Tadeusz Borowski in *This Way for the Gas, Ladies and Gentlemen*, where he writes of a young woman, who once becoming aware of the fate that eventually awaited her, decided nevertheless to board the transport of new arrivals on their way to the gas chambers.[73] The point here is that this person exercised choice in a way that preserved her dignity. It was not the choice itself that was significant but the choosing. In situations of this sort the objective of the Nazis was to strip the Jews of any last vestiges of dignity through ill-treatment and brutality. In the case of the young woman in question, I think that choosing certain death was a form of resistance to the attempts of the Nazis to violate her self respect.

Amongst such testimonial literature and accounts of camp life as Borowski's, there are many examples of individual experiences that testify to the sense of dignity that Todorov speaks about. Perhaps not surprisingly, as is the case with other virtues, Todorov also recognises what he refers to as ambiguities that arise in the context of particular aspects of dignity. He says that not all dignity is morally defensible and cites examples where doing the job well was not necessarily a virtuous quality. Whether it be a prisoner who would build a sound wall around the camp, or the guard who would take pride in the work they performed in the camps, not all examples indicating the appearance of dignity are able to be credited as virtuous. The point is that whilst dignity is a virtue it is contestable whether a particular act is one of dignity. So, whilst it can be argued that by keeping his shoes clean Levi was able to maintain a semblance of self-respect and thus of dignity, it is more difficult to hold that the same can be said to apply to those guarding Levi. Todorov considers the moral ambiguity evident in the virtue of dignity when he cites Fania Fenelon in her book *Playing for Time*. Fenelon writes:

> I don't know whether this concern for appearance was part of Nazi ideology but it certainly occupied a key position in their lives. Furthermore, their shoes and boots always shone and smelled; I shall never forget the smell of German leather.[74]

Of course the sense of pride Fenelon is referring to is something that stands in contrast to that which Levi was seeking to maintain. The point here is that the Germans in question emphasised pride in their appearance in order to accentuate the degradation they were seeking to impose on those like Fenelon.

Another of the virtues that Todorov singles out for attention is that of caring. As with the virtue of dignity he cites many examples of caring. In the case of caring, though, the instances cited are marked out by the fact that the acts are directed toward other human beings. This is a significant if complicated point to make with respect to my understanding of responsibility. As is the case with dignity, many instances of caring entailed taking responsibility for one's destiny. My point here is that instances of acts of caring might sometimes entail the presence of a tension between the requirement to take responsibility for oneself, and to care for another. It seems to me that such a tension might signify the presence of moral conflict. I argue that such conflict is further evidence of the case for moral complexity I'm constructing.

I think that it is also worth pointing out that the sorts of situations that I'm referring to here include those that would probably have entailed decisions of the gravest sort. In some situations such decisions would have meant taking responsibility for something as difficult as the personal attitude able to be adopted toward an imminent death. In some instances it might have meant the difference between the maintenance of a genuine concern for the well-being of another and an inability to sustain that concern. The sorts of examples cited by Todorov include instances ranging from the more tangible sharing of food or other basics necessary for survival to a mere look of compassion for another human being. Some acts of caring were more dangerous than others while some meant certain death as in the example of Pola.

Also not unlike dignity, the virtue of caring is, as Todorov explains, able to be distinguished from acts more properly understood as acts solidarity, charity or sacrifice. Sometimes it is exceedingly difficult to separate out an act of caring from one of solidarity, charity or sacrifice and it may be the case that in some instances two or more of these possibilities overlap. In the story of Pola for example, it is not absolutely clear whether her actions were born from sacrifice or caring concern for her mother or solidarity with the deportees. It does seem to be the case, however, that most acts of a sacrificial kind stem from heroic virtues. The much cited case of Father Kolbe giving his life to save another springs to mind.[75] With the example of Pola, though, it is not difficult to imagine that she may have thought that both she and her mother stood a better chance if they remained together. It seems to me that acts of caring are also closely linked to retaining, and indeed the future flourishing of, one's own well-being. It may well have been the case that, for Pola, understanding life lived in accordance with a balanced, if complicated sense of responsibility, meant remaining with her mother. In this way her own well-being may well have been linked with the responsibility she felt for her mother.

It is my view that Todorov's examples of 'acts of ordinary virtue' are continuous with what I'm seeking to convey with my understanding of integrity as an aspect of responsibility. As I understand it the maintenance of integrity depends on how a person takes up responsibility for themselves and others. The taking up of responsibility is a result of the way their character interacts with their context. Thus such 'acts' provide the substance of, and serve as a means for the individual to make sense of, the moral dimensions of their existence.

Referring once again to the example of Pola, her decision to remain with her mother ties in with the strength of her dignity. In turn, the survival of her dignity can be understood as an expression of her responsibility to her mother and may have been a result of her loyalty in the face of the oppressive situation. Taking responsibility for others, understood in the context of such 'acts', can then be recognised, in part, as something that structures our own moral frame of reference. For example, and in reference to my discussion of Gowans, individuals are able to come to understand their morality in terms of the way they understand their responsibilities to others. The point that I am seeking to make is that understanding our responsibilities to others is linked to our responsibility to self.

Another study to demonstrate something of the complexity of the way responsibility to others is able to be manifest is Gunnar S. Paulsson's book *Secret City, The Hidden Jews of Warsaw 1940—1945*.[76] In this very carefully documented account of how a large number of the Jews of Warsaw were able to hide outside the ghetto or escape from it, Paulsson shows the extent to which the assistance of Poles and others effectively enabled so many Jews to survive. Paulsson convincingly reinstates the notion of evasion as a noteworthy Jewish response to the Holocaust entailing what he describes as large-scale "initiative, ingenuity, courage and perseverance"[77] on the part of the Jews themselves. Significantly, the survival of some 11,500[78] Warsaw Jews owes its success, in large part, to the courage exhibited by many non-Jews. Paulsson's account, however, demonstrates the complex nature of the story of the Jews of Warsaw. It is my view that the persuasiveness of Paulsson's documentation, his interpretation of events, use of testimonies, diaries, memoirs and records all help to convey an argument of necessary depth and complexity. In what I believe amounts to a recognition of the complexities of Polish responses to the plight of Warsaw's Jews, Paulsson writes, perhaps somewhat surprisingly, that whilst

> The Jews faced numerous threats and problems on the Aryan side . . . survival was not only possible but actually not unlikely, despite the gauntlet that all the Jewish fugitives had to run. Above all, survival on the Aryan side would not have been possible without an army of Poles and also some Germans, who actively took Jews under their protection at the risk of their lives. I have estimated the numbers of these helpers at 70,000 and 90,000, or about one-twelfth of the city's population.[79]

Importantly, Paulsson's observations do not convey a straightforward picture of Poles helping Jews or indeed, the opposite, an image of Poles as predominantly anti-semitic collaborators. Rather what emerges from the evidence he presents of the networks of people who helped Jews, both Jews and non-Jews, concerns a wide range of individuals who were in Paulsson's words "mainly decent and honest people".[80] My point is that Paulsson's observations of Jews and Non-Jews has some parallels with Todorov's 'acts of ordinary virtues' and my idea that such acts are encompassed, in large part, by the moral complexities inherent in the way in which individuals understand their responsibilities to others and to themselves .

Let me recapitulate here on the various understandings of responsibility that I have thus far canvassed. In this chapter I began with a discussion of the presence of the tension between enormity and complexity analyses of the Holocaust. I then continued with an elaboration of the relationship between this tension and various ways of understanding moral responsibility. I argued that these different ways of understanding responsibility, given the level of complexity that such discussion generates, can be fruitfully structured according to the metaphor of a 'weave'. I also sought to illustrate these ways of thinking about responsibility with examples of people's own senses of their responsibilities. The idea here is to show how the conceptual variations of responsibility are embodied in people's actions and decisions. As I have previously stated I am particularly interested in how the combination of complexity and enormity analyses is expressed in respect to the Holocaust and how this can be understood according to various intersecting aspects of responsibility. The idea of a weave of responsibility is designed to lend further substance to this account. I then examined an account of responsibility as integral to what Walker refers to as the practices that bind moral life. Next I sought to link responsibility, understood as integrated with various social practices, to a discussion of Gowans' idea of responsibilities to persons. My account included the idea that responsibility entails the sort of concerns that one should have as regards what one should do for others on the basis of one's relationships to others. Following Gowans I argued that our understanding of our responsibilities to others is grounded in our understanding of our relations with those with whom we are intimate. I then looked at aspects of the connection between actions and responsibility in terms of the way circumstance impacts upon personal dispositions. I wanted to demonstrate the significance of individual disposition upon actions. In the context of the work of Todorov, I connected responsibility to a certain way of thinking about the place of dignity and integrity in our moral relations . Finally, with respect to the observations of Paulsson I sought to demonstrate something of the complexities of how responsibility to others was understood in the case of the Jews of Warsaw and those who helped and those who harmed them.

By focusing on these differing 'threads' of the weave my intention has been to extend the argument that the Holocaust is morally complex. In the next chapter I both broaden and deepen my discussion of responsibility. I broaden it by considering individual moral experiences of those who witnessed the Holocaust and I deepen it in an examination of the limits of our understanding of responsibility.

Notes

1. Douglas P. Lackey, 'Extraordinary Evil or Common Malevolence: Evaluating the Jewish Holocaust' in Brenda Almond & Donald Hill (eds.), *Applied Philosophy, Morals and Metaphysics in Contemporary Debates*, (London: Routledge, 1991), 141.

2. Mary Midgley, *Wickedness*, (London: Routledge & Kegan Paul, 1985).

3. Midgley, 3.

4. Midgley, 2.

5. Midgley, 3.

6. Midgley, 71.

7. Margaret Walker, *Moral Understandings, A Feminist Study in Ethics*, (London: Routledge, 1998), 9.

8. Gowans, 122.

9. Primo Levi, *If this is a Man* and *The Truce*, trans. Stuart Wolf, (London: Abacus, 1987), 127.

10. J.F. Steiner, *Treblinka*, (London: Weidenfield and Nicholson, 1967).

11. The *Sonderkommando* were those Jews conscripted from within the camp to carry out the physical work of extermination.

12. Simone de Beauvoir, 'Preface' in J.F. Steiner, *Treblinka*, xi-xii.

13. Steiner, 137.

14. Steiner, 138.

15. Walker, 201.

16. Walker, 10.

17. Gowans, 3.

18. Gowans, 19.

19. See John Rawls, *A Theory of Justice*, (London: Oxford University Press, 1973), 48-51.

20. Gowans, 38.

21. I would also want to make the point that my understanding of judgment seems to differ from Gowans' understanding inasmuch as I understand judgment to be only one aspect of moral understanding.

22. Gowans, *Innocence Lost*, 100-101.

23. Alan Donagan presents this view in 'Consistency in Rationalist Moral Systems', *The Journal of Philosophy*, LXXXI, 6, June 1984.

24. Both Margaret Walker and Martha Nussbaum have also argued extensively in support of a more nuanced understanding of moral life.

25. For his purposes Sinnot-Armstrong defines the term 'moral realism' as primarily entailing the claim that moral judgments and especially their truth value, are independent from certain mental states. In other words, according to this common-usage definition, a moral realist might claim that the truth conditions of moral judgments are independent of changes in certain mental states.

26. W. Sinnot-Armstrong, 'Moral Realisms and Moral Dilemmas' in *The Journal of Philosophy*, 1987, 276.

27. Alan Donagan bases his critique of the commentary on moral conflict of Ruth Barcan Marcus, according to a particular distinction in the work of Aquinas between two kinds of conflict of duties, 'perplexity *simpliciter*' and 'perplexity *secundum quid*'.

28. Donagan, 300.

29. Ruth Barcan Marcus, 'Moral Dilemmas and Consistency', *The Journal of Philosophy*, LXXVII, March 1980, 135.

30. Gowans, 19-20.

31. Gowans, 3-24.

32. By duties and obligations I mean what our moral consciousness might ordinarily dictate to us.

33. In a similar vein to Christopher Gowans, Margaret Walker in her book *Moral Understandings* develops the idea of a 'geography of responsibility' to explain the way moral responsibilities develop. See especially 107-109.

34. See Gowans, 122-123.

35. Gowans, *Innocence Lost*, 125.

36. Daniel Pick, *Faces of Degeneration: A European Disorder, c. 1848-c.1918*, (Cambridge: Cambridge University Press, 1993).

37. Hans Frank, '*Nationalsozialistische Strafrechtspolitik*', Munich 1938 in Pick, *Faces of degeneration*, 28.

38. Gowans, 127.

39. Browning, .67.

40. See especially 117-128 of *Innocence Lost* and Gowans' discussion of responsibilites to persons in the context of the significance of circumstances on the way we understand our responsibilites.

41. Midgley, 59.

42. Midgley, 59.

43. For my part I am not affirming aggression but rather recognizing its existence entwined in the various social practices that comprise, in part, our relations with others.

44. Gitta Sereny, *Into that Darkness, From Mercy Killing to Mass Murder*, (London: Pimlico, 1995).

45. Sereny, 15.

46. See Robert Jay Lifton, *The Nazi Doctors: Medical Killing and the Psychology of Genocide*, (New York: Basic Books, 1986).

47. Sereny, 163-164.

48. Sereny, 160.

49. Sereny, 361.

50. Sereny, 361.

51. Sereny, 362.

52. John K. Roth, 'On Losing Trust in the World' in Gerald Myers & Alan Rosenberg (eds.), *Echoes from the Holocaust, Philosophical Reflections on a Dark Time*, (Philadelphia: Temple University Press, 1988), 163-180.

53. Roth, 172.

54. Sereny, 367.

55. Sereny, 363.

56. Dominick LaCapra, *History, Theory, Trauma: Representing the Holocaust*, (London: Cornell University Press, 1994).

57. LaCapra, 11.

58. See Geoffrey Hartman, 'Judging Paul de Man', in *Minor Prophecies: The Literary Essay in the Culture Wars*, (Cambridge: Harvard University Press, 1991).

59. Cheshire Calhoun, 'Standing for Something', *Journal of Philosophy*, 1995, 259.

60. Walker, 116-118.

61. Tzvetan Todorov, *Facing the Extreme: Moral Life in the Concentration Camps*, (New York: Henry Holt, 1996).

62. Todorov, 59.

63. Terence de Pres, *The Survivor*, (New York: Oxford University Press, 1976), 28.

64. Primo Levi, *If this is a Man.*

65. Todorov, 15.

66. Todorov, 17-18.

67. Todorov, 15.

68. Todorov, 16.

69. Claudia Card, 'Living with Evils', Joram Haber & Mark Halfon (eds.), *Norms and Values: Essays on the Work of Virginia Held*, (Lanham: Rowman & Littlefield, 1998), 125-139.

70. Marek Edelman in Hanna Krall, Joanna Stasinska and Lawrence Weschler (trans.), *Shielding the Flame*, (New York: Henry Holt, 1986), 45.

71. See Victor Frankl, *Man's Search for Meaning*, trans. Ilse Lasch, (Washington: Washington Square Press, 1997) and Jean Emery, *At the Mind's Limits*, trans. Sidney Rosenfeld and Stella P. Rosenfeld, (New York: Schocken, 1986).

72. Marek Edelman in Hanna Krall, 37.

73. Tadeusz Borowski, *This Way for the Gas, Ladies and Gentleman*, trans. Barbara Vedder, (New York: Penguin, 1976).

74. Fania Fenelon, *Playing for Time*, trans. J. Landry, (New York: Atheneum, 1977), 96.

75. Todorov, 55-56.

76. Gunnar S. Paulsson, *Secret City, The Hidden Jews of Warsaw*, (New Haven: Yale University Press, 2002).

77. Paulsson, 247.

78. Paulsson, 231.

79. Paulsson, 162-163.

80. Paulsson, 164.

EXPANDING ON THE IDEA OF A WEAVE OF RESPONSIBILITY

In this chapter I expand on the idea of a weave of responsibility within the wider context of elaborating upon the moral complexity of Holocaust experiences. My broad aim will be to consolidate the claim for the significance of the complexity of moral life within the context of accounts of the Holocaust. In the previous chapter I sought to establish the case that it is primarily our understandings of responsibility that are the basis for the moral complexity of Holocaust accounts. In this chapter I seek to incorporate the idea of people's own senses of responsibility as metaphorically representing the fibres of the weave of the various aspects of responsibility that I seek to convey. Thus the metaphor of the weave is a vehicle of some considerable complexity in itself. I envisage the weave as a tool that can be used to structure, not only the various understandings of responsibility, but also the many individual experiences that I examine, as expressions of individual understandings of responsibility. And as will become apparent the weave can also be used to arrange other issues that contribute directly to the view that complexity analyses are a core component of the tension underpinning Holocaust experiences.

Quite deliberately, the examples that I choose for this chapter are from the experiences of those who are conventionally described as bystanders. I have chosen this category of experiences as distinct from those of perpetrators or victims precisely because the examples in this category are very often more problematic. They are more problematic because the examples are less black and white, and more ambiguous in respect to the sort of moral assessment they in-

vite. However they also have, from my perspective, more illustrative impact because they sharpen the tension between complexity and enormity evaluations.
The cases of perpetrators and victims are considered separately elsewhere, most
notably in Chapters One and Seven.

Whilst understandings of responsibility remain core elements to the case for
complexity evaluations I will also examine other issues that arise from the bystander accounts that directly contribute to the idea of moral complexity. Foremost among these issues is the influence of circumstance. I examine the way
people come to terms, morally, with the difficult situations they find themselves
in. My claim will be that people's responses depend, to some extent on the different situations they find themselves in. In particular I will consider how it is
that that which was initially experienced as an extra-ordinary shock to people's
sensibilities is able to be rendered somehow acceptable.

Let me begin, however, with a quote from another context that resonates
strongly with what I want to argue, from Holocaust victim Etty Hillesum, in a
letter dated 1942 from Westerbork, the deportation assembly depot for Dutch
Jews. She wrote:

> What is going on, what mysteries are these; in what sort of fatal mechanism
> have we become enmeshed? The answer cannot simply be that we are all cow-
> ards. We're not that bad. We stand before a much deeper question.[1]

By identifying and unpacking what I interpret Hillesum as having referred to as
this 'deeper question', I intend to show that an adequate map of the moral topography of the Holocaust must somehow account for and comprehend evidence revealing the deeper fact that there was a time when 'we' came to inhabit, and
perhaps still inhabit, a world where in the words of Ernst Klee, Willi Dressen
and Volker Riess, "Jewish citizens could be beaten to death with iron bars in the
street in broad daylight without anyone intervening to protect them".[2] In fact, in
order to make some sense of Hillesum's question I believe there is a need to examine the circumstances that surrounded particular Holocaust experiences.

It might almost go without saying that the way in which moral choice comes
about differs sharply, although in no less complex a fashion, in accord with who
it is that is confronted with the particular situation in question. I think it needs to
be said, however, that in order to incorporate the experience of the many millions who witnessed the events of the Holocaust into accounts of the morality of
the Holocaust, it needs to be recognised that those individuals were forced to
make moral choices. Those who knew of and or witnessed the events, large and
small, were faced with moral choices. This is true irrespective of whether or not
they were involved in a more overt sense. As bystanders, I argue that those who
were aware, or who saw what was occurring, or more problematically, those
who were more closely implicated although at some remove from actual involvement in the deportations and murder of Jewish people, bear some measure
of moral responsibility. By this I mean in part that such people, as bystanders,

were also witnesses. The mere fact of their presence, as witnesses, means that they would have had to make, for themselves, moral choices as regards the sort of action or inaction they would take. The sorts of action I refer to here might range from contempt, indifference or silence, to various forms of intervention on behalf of those in peril. As the examples that follow demonstrate, the category of bystanders/witnesses is difficult to place in the overall fabric of Holocaust experiences. Adam Lebor and Roger Boyes make exactly this point in their consideration of the differences between the ethical choices on offer to victims and bystanders. Making this general comparison they write that:

> In the camps the imbalance between crime and consequence was such that it was difficult to compare the ethical dilemma of ordinary Germans with those facing ordinary Jews. The moral maze is almost too complex for modern minds but we try nevertheless to chart a way through it.[3]

Lebor and Boyes correctly identify a key element that faced victims and ordinary Germans alike, that choices were available. Of course the sorts of choices facing victims and ordinary Germans were different. The role and motivation of bystanders in ignoring or even cooperating in the events of the Holocaust is, in itself, complex. First of all, bystanders are in my view, necessarily involved. And how we understand this involvement varies. On this question Geoffrey Hartman, in his discussion of intellectuals as witnesses writes that:

> While writers, journalists and academics in Nazi-occupied Europe were often active accomplices, there was also a larger group who waited it out as bystanders. The very concept, therefore, of bystander seems tainted.[4]

Further on in the same discussion he continues his assessment with the supposition that: The category is somewhat vague and confronts us with the ambiguities of Primo Levi's "grey zone", in which the demarcation between victim and collaborator remains unclear.[5]

Hartman also recognises the significance of the difficulty of the bystanders' situations. He identifies the tension between knowing and not knowing, and such issues as guilt and deliberate forgetting. He discusses the complexities that arise in efforts to think about the moral status of bystanders including accounting for their feelings of misery, anxiety, relief, gratitude as we try to understand questions of culpability, insensitivity and guilt or innocence. Following Hartman, I suggest that the experiences of bystanders are of a more morally ambiguous kind than other categories and as such are more difficult to comprehend. All the same such examples represent further evidence of that aspect of a weave of responsibility that emphasises the interdependence of individual moral lives and the significance of a moral attitude toward the events as they were witnessed. To clarify here I am not saying that any moral attitude will do. In line with my discussions on responsibility thus far I understand it to encompass an attitude that entails concern for others within a family of practices of responsibility. The examples that follow are intended to illustrate the ways of understanding responsibility that I am weaving together. In turn, I hope to shed further light on the content of the complexity of moral lives faced with morally enormous situations. Specifically, I examine the evidence of bystanders as witnesses.

The following extract refers to a conversation between Claude Lanzmann, creator of the film *Shoah* and Walter Stier, ex Chief of the Traffic Planning Office in Warsaw from 1943 who was responsible for eastbound traffic. In the course of the interview Lanzmann asked Stier:

> *Why were there more special trains during the war than before or after?*
> I see what you're getting at. You're referring to the so-called resettlement trains. *"Resettlement."*
> *That's it.*
> That's what they were called. Those trains were ordered by the Ministry of Transport of the Reich. You needed an order from the Ministry.
> *In Berlin?*
> Correct. And as for the implementation of those orders, the Head Office of Eastbound Traffic in Berlin dealt with it.
> *Yes, I understand.*
> Is that clear?
> *Perfectly. But mostly, at that time, who was being "resettled"?*
> No! We didn't know that. Only when we were fleeing from Warsaw ourselves, did we learn that they could have been Jews, or criminals, or similar people . . .
> *Did you know that Treblinka meant extermination?*
> Of course not!
> *You didn't know?*
> Good God no! How could we know? I never went to Treblinka. I stayed in Krakow, in Warsaw, glued to my desk.
> *You were a...*
> I was strictly a bureaucrat!
> *I see. But it's astonishing that people in the department for special trains never knew about the "final solution."*
> We were at war.
> *Because there were others who worked for the railroads who knew. Like the train conductors.*
> Yes, they saw it. They did. But as to what happened I didn't.[6]

In response to Lanzmann's questions the interviewee, Stier, first of all attempts to deny responsibility by distancing himself from the chain of authority and then proceeds to deny knowledge of the mass murders until after their occurrence. In this example it is true that Stier is, as he stresses a bureaucrat and that he may never have personally seen what happened to the human cargo of the special trains. But it is also entirely possible that someone of Stier's seniority would have been privy to knowledge about the fate of the Jews upon their arrival at the extermination camps. In the context of Stier's occupational proximity to events as they were occurring, and the fact that verified testimony and documentation has established that among those in related positions of authority, the fate of the

Jews was often known, it seems that his claims of ignorance are dubious. I would at this point call into question his personal integrity. Moreover, if it was the case that he did know, it seems reasonable to suppose that he would have had to accommodate and somehow rationalise the knowledge of his participation in the killings with his personal conscience. In short, Stier would almost certainly have had to come to terms with the ethical conflicts that arose with his participation in the genocide of the Jews. Stier would have had to make a moral choice and adopt a particular moral attitude with regard to his understanding of the fate of those on the trains, and even more problematically, the degree to which he bore some measure of responsibility within his sphere of influence.

Such possibilities as discussed above indicate problematic expressions of responsibility. In particular I argue that the person in question, Stier, failed in the sense of taking responsibility for himself and others. In other words, he neglected his basic responsibilities to others and in so doing might be said to have diminished his responsibility to himself. In fact, even his self respect is on the line. By not seeking the necessary knowledge of what was happening to the Jews passing through his hands, assuming that he didn't indeed know, he places himself in a position where he didn't want to know. I think the interview reflects this sentiment in the way Stier pointedly avoids knowledge of events and direct responsibility as he goes to considerable lengths to distance himself from the chain of command. This idea is further evidenced by Stier's use of euphemisms and categories of people that are tangential to the discussion. For instance, the transports are referred to as 'resettlement' trains and Jews are grouped together with so called 'criminals' and 'similar' people as if to say such categories are all tarred with the same brush.

Another eyewitness account, that of Franciszek Zabecki, provides a telling contrast to the interview with Stier, especially as regards the moral attitude expressed and the sense of responsibility conveyed. Zabecki is altogether more frank concerning what he understood was occurring at the time and the effect this had on himself and the people who witnessed the events in question. As reported by Gitta Sereny in her account of her interviews with Franz Stangl, Zabecki worked as a traffic supervisor during the war for the Polish underground. In this capacity Zabecki occupied a unique position as an eye witness during the entire existence of the Teblinka camp. On the question of knowledge of what was occurring in the camp, and describing the day of the arrival of the first train, Sereny, quoting Zabecki, writes:

> "But that first day—as I said before, it happened I was not on duty, and I wanted to know what was going on. We had been warned that the approaches to the camp were strictly off-limits and guarded. But actually there was a road of sorts that passed the perimeter of the camp—you see, there were fields all around it belonging to peasants who . . . oh yes . . . continued to work their fields throughout the existence of the camp. . . . " "Anyway", Zabecki went on, "I took a bicycle and cycled a stretch up the road and then got off, pretending that my chain had slipped, in case somebody saw me. I heard machine guns,

and I heard people screaming, praying to God and—yes—to the Holy Virgin. . .
. I cycled back and I wrote a message to my [Home Army] section chief . . . I
informed my chief that some disaster was happening in my district".[7]

Then, regarding the effect on those who came to know what was happening in
the camp, Zabecki continues:

> "When people realised that not only adults but babies were being killed," Pan
> Zabecki said, "they felt pity . . . The population was horrified not only because
> of what they saw; they were paralysed with fear and horror, and then quite soon
> they became physically ill from the terrible smell that began to emanate from
> the camp. But then too, you see, everybody became terrified for themselves;
> they were *seeing* [my italics] all this . . . There was a period—in the begin-
> ning—when my wife could no longer function at all; she could no longer do
> anything around the house; she couldn't cook, she couldn't play with the boy,
> she couldn't eat and hardly slept. . . . This extreme condition she was in lasted
> for about three weeks, then she became pathologically indifferent; she did her
> work, moved, ate, slept, talked—but all of it like an automaton".[8]

Both of these passages give an indication of the powerful effect that knowledge
of what was occurring in the camps had on those who made the attempt to try to
work through all of the implications, including the moral implications, of this
knowledge. Zabecki attempts, in hindsight, to clarify and justify the reactions of
the German and Polish witnesses to the killings in Treblinka. There is also a
sense in which he recounts these events with a clear conscience. Zabecki states
that there was nothing that he could do to help the Jews because of the risk that
this would entail to his work for the underground. In other words, in Zabecki's
mind, the wider war effort of the Allied powers against the Axis powers justifiably took precedence over any possible action to help the Jews who were arriving
at Treblinka. The issue of where Zabecki's responsibilities lay is a difficult one.
It might be argued that he had parallel, and perhaps conflicting, responsibilities.
That is to say, responsibilities, as he says, to the wider war effort and to safe-
guard his family, but also very immediate responsibilities to the Jews going to a
certain death. What is apparent in reading Sereny's account of Zabecki's story is
that he was able to maintain both his integrity and his dignity in so far as his efforts helped to make a difference.

Other reactions to what was occurring in Treblinka, however, convey, in my
view, a different understanding of responsibility to that evident in Zabecki's
story. In an interview in present-day Treblinka with a Pole named Czeslaw
Borowi an interpreter reports:

> *While all this was happening before their eyes, normal life went on? They
> worked their fields?*
> Certainly they worked, but not as willingly as usual. They had to work, but
> when they saw all this, they thought: "Our house may be surrounded. We may
> be arrested too!"

Were they afraid for the Jews too?
Well, he says, it's this way: if I cut my finger, it doesn't hurt him. They knew about the Jews: the convoys came in here, and then went to the camp, and the people vanished.[9]

This example differs, in my view, from both the account of Stier and Zabecki. First, the interviewer seems to want to build a case for the existence of a prevailing sense of indifference to the fate of the Jews. The interviewee, Borowi, conveys by his choice of words an absence of feeling or emotion for the fate of the Jews who were sent to Treblinka. The sense of indifference that is present in the sentiment of Borowi certainly seems to lack any sign of compassion for the terrible fate of the people who were sent to their death in Treblinka, and may even be attributable to a deeper anti-semitic belief. Indeed it could be argued that the attitude conveyed by Borowi might have been a component of, what were at the time, quite accepted social practices or expressions of anti-Semitism.

More significantly, however, I want to argue that this sense of indifference represents a moral attitude of a particular sort. Borowi's attitude conveys neither a sense of moral outrage nor moral approval. The person in question failed to take up the challenge presented by the situation. In so much as it can be said that he is responding in thought and feeling to what happened it can be argued that he made choices based around the understanding of responsibility he possessed. It would also be true to say that I am implying that 'choice' on its own fails to capture all that is of significance in this example. As I have previously argued, responsibility entails a composite of factors among which is a concern for others and a recognition of the need to sustain a semblance of our integrity that broadly matches Walker's 'family of practices'[10] that make people accountable to one another. Thus, and in spite of the possibility of the presence of anti-semitic attitudes embedded in various social practices, Borowi would also have been aware of responsibilities entailing certain ways of behaving, of particular sorts of attitudes to others. As Walker has argued, society possesses what might be termed a sort of moral capital:

> . . . as culturally situated and socially sustained practices of responsibility that are taught and defended as "how to live". . . . this system provides us with a medium for expressing our identities, relationships and values through our senses of responsibility, and it *requires of us that we do so* [my italics].[11]

Borowi, however seems to possess a depleted moral capital in the sense that his understanding of responsibility for the Jews who went to their deaths stopped short of an attitude of caring from one human being to another. This may raise the question as to why his sense of responsibility was or had become so diminished with respect to the Jews in his midst. Possibly practices of anti-Semitism within the social fabric would have played a part in Borowi's moral understanding.

I also argue though, that Borowi seemed to have opted for a moral attitude that was casual and perhaps callous in terms of the indifference displayed. It is also possible that other factors, like fear or self-preservation, played an important part in the mix of elements in his personal disposition. Even so, indifference seems to have been present. If this is so,[12] moral indifference can be taken to mean a failure to take responsibility. The interviewee in this example, who had been present as a first hand witness, adopted a moral attitude that not only allowed him to pass over the inhumanity being perpetrated against the prisoners in Treblinka but also, by virtue of this very process severely diminished his own humanity. His diminished humanity can be seen to be the result of moral indifference to the suffering of fellow human beings. I want to make the point here again that I'm not interested in ascribing guilt. I am interested in working through examples that can contribute to the ways of understanding responsibility I am seeking to establish. I want to distinguish, for instance, between individual moral attitudes, aided and abetted by some measure of moral luck,[13] and those that constitute more deliberate acts of wrong—doing, and those that form part of the evils of structural racial discrimination and acts of genocide. This is not to say, however, that any of the above is mutually exclusive. It is conceivable that there were individuals whose moral situation included both bad luck and racially motivated patterns of discriminatory behaviour.

Also of interest here is the way in which the example of Borowi provides a powerful comparative counterpoint with a recent example of an attitude expressed by individuals of the local Polish population of the town of Jedwabne, during and following the consecration in 2001 of a new memorial to mark the pogrom against the Jewish inhabitants of the village sixty years ago.[14] The journalist Imre Karacs, attending the village for the ceremony writes that whilst the President of Poland formally apologised on behalf of the nation, the Catholic Church shunned the ceremony. Karacs quotes the village priest, Father Edward Orlowski as saying that "Germans are responsible. Why should we apologise".[15] Such sentiment is all the more surprising given the presence of strong evidence that attributes most of the killing to local Poles.[16] Karacs also noted ominously a sign on the door of a grocery store in the village which read "We do not apologise". The exact circumstances of what happened in Jedwabne on the 10th of July aside; this would seem to constitute evidence, similar to that of the earlier example of Borowi, of a moral attitude that is at the very least grossly insensitive and at worst deliberately callous.

The above examples also highlight the way in which choice and moral dilemma manifest themselves differently for those directly implicated in the implementation of mass murder and those who witnessed or participated in some sense on the periphery. I argue that in order to understand the nature of the differences between those confronted with more difficult moral choices and those who were not; the role of circumstance is of crucial significance. From the examples of Stier and Borowi it is surely noteworthy that some of those who 'merely' witnessed the events described do not convey the impression that they themselves were also participants in this moral drama. As bystanders who may not have been confronted with such difficult decisions as were those with their fingers on the triggers or even those among the victims who may have been in the position to make good an escape but who chose to remain with infants or the elderly and so sealed their fate,[17] the responses of these bystanders indicates an impoverished moral attitude. In the first instance, they chose to erode regard for their moral self worth. And in the second instance, by acting either with indifference or with disdain toward those, whose fate they knew of, the interviewees convey a compromised integrity. I would like to cite another example to provide more substance for this claim.

Claude Lanzmann interviewing a group of Polish villagers in the village of Grabow, twelve miles from Chelmno where some four hundred thousand Jews were killed cites an interview with an unidentified man:

> *Are they glad there are no more Jews here, or sad?*
> It doesn't bother them. As you know, Jews and Germans ran all Polish industry before the war.
> *Did they like them on the whole?*
> Not much. Above all they were dishonest.
> *Was life in Grabow more fun when the Jews were here?*
> He'd rather not say.
> *Why does he call them dishonest?*
> They exploited the Poles. That's what they lived on.
> *How did they exploit them?*
> By imposing their prices.[18]

The responses to this set of questions indicate not only a failure to take responsibility for what happened in their presence but also the palpable presence of antisemitic sentiment some fifty years after the events, and the sorts of stereotypical explanations used to justify such feelings. The sentiments contained in these responses seem to parallel those reported earlier by Karacs within contemporary Poland. From the same group of interviewees an unidentified woman responds to a question:

> *Are they sorry the Jews are no longer here, or pleased?* How can I tell? I never went to school. I can only think of how I am now. Now I'm fine.[19]

Consistent with the sentiment of the earlier examples of Borowi, the unidentified man and the report of Karacs, this response also contains evidence of a certain sort of moral attitude. Not only does it represent an abdication of responsibility in the sense that she fails to acknowledge the enormity of the crime committed or feelings of sorrow that might ordinarily be attached to such a crime. The comment "Now I'm fine" could be interpreted as meaning that life is indeed better now in the absence of Jews.[20]

I argue that the moral attitude present in the examples of Borowi, the unidentified man, the Karacs report and the unidentified woman, is highlighted even further when contrasted with the recollections of those individuals who went to the aid of those in peril. Norman Geras, in his article 'Richard Rorty and the Righteous Among the Nations', examines the accounts of rescuers from a range of countries across what was at the time occupied Europe. In his account Geras identifies evidence of the importance of what he calls shared ideas of "a common capacity for suffering",[21] a "feeling for justice",[22] and generalisable "humanitarian motives".[23] However, he also identifies more concrete motives for the actions of rescuers such as familiarity and friendship. Geras cites repeated instances where moral commitments resulted in moral courage. For example he writes:

> Opdyke was a student nurse at the time of the invasion of Poland. . . . Running an errand one day in the nearby ghetto she witnessed scenes of great brutality. . . . Opdyke decided that 'if the opportunity arrived I would help these people.' She subsequently befriended twelve Jews employed in the laundry at her place of work. . . . When she learned of a move impending to liquidate the ghetto, she managed to hide and finally save these friends, at a not insignificant personal cost to herself.[24]

The significance of such evidence cannot be overstated. In the case of the earlier example of the unidentified man, the Jews in question were known personally either as friends, acquaintances, neighbours or members of the same community. In the earlier example the unidentified man had feelings, reasons, justifications and values that led to an attitude of moral indifference as regards the Jews he knew were going to their death. In the case of Opdyke, she also had feelings, reasons, justifications and values engendered by a particular situation but which in her case led her to act in a morally courageous way. Contrasting the example of the unidentified man with the story of Opdyke, it is evident that while circumstance has a key role to play in the development of an individual's moral schema other factors also feature. My point is that it seems, on the basis of the evidence presented, that it would be unwise to lay too much emphasis on circumstance. Whilst circumstance is significant, other factors like individual disposition, luck and so forth have a place within the panoply of reasons explaining our understandings of responsibility, moral attitudes and behaviour.

Another issue that arises from the abovementioned examples concerns, in a direct way, the difficulty of anti-Semitism as a mitigating factor in the behaviour of people who witnessed Holocaust events. I argue that it is conceivable that recognition of the presence of anti-Semitism as a socio-cultural aspect of European civilisation assists in no small way in understanding the sentiments of the interviewees in question. In *The Catholic Church and Anti-Semitism: Poland, 1933—1939* [25] Ronald Modras examines the evidence of anti-Semitism within the institution of the Polish Catholic Church and Catholic Poland more generally, in the years preceding the Second World War. In Modras' assessment there was no other institution more influential in the formation of popular attitudes on the subject of the 'Jewish Question' in Poland than the Polish Catholic Church. Moreover, Modras, in a summary of the assessments of prominent Polish writers, writes:

> these authors still acknowledge that they feel a certain amount of shame and guilt—not that Poles participated in the murder or withheld reasonable assistance, but that they were widely indifferent to the crime perpetrated before their eyes. Their criticism of the Polish response to the Shoah is that Poles held back.[26]

And as regards the more specific link between the Catholic Church and the Holocaust Modras writes:

> there was an indirect connection between Christian, including Catholic, anti-Semitism and the Holocaust. . . . The Holocaust would have been inconceivable without the prior history of alienation and hostility which divided Christians and Jews. It was an alienation for which the Church was not wholly but greatly responsible.[27]

These conclusions are, not surprisingly, somewhat controversial. Whilst those interviewed by Lanzmann did not in any obvious way express either Polish or Catholic shame it needs to be borne in mind that the first conclusion refers to the self-assessment of individual Poles themselves. It is also true that in the case of both conclusions the empirical evidence that Modras provides is as exhaustive as it is convincing and serves to lend credibility to his conclusions.[28]

Among the examples of bystanders reported in this chapter, and indeed, the perpetrators (Stangl and the individuals of Reserve Police Battalion 101) and victims[29] (Levi, Fenelon and Pola), that I have used in earlier chapters, it is evident that the decisions and choices made were arrived at in the most appalling and diminished of circumstances. Significantly, however, these decisions invariably contained distinctive moral dimensions. When it comes to the sorts of choices demanded by Holocaust events, it becomes apparent that moral responsibility itself is implicit in what it means to be a human. That is to say, human agents find meaning in the context of individual struggles to understand the moral dimensions of a given situation. In this sense feelings such as guilt can be interpreted as positive signs inasmuch as they can be seen as efforts to internalise and organise social ideas regarding right and wrong. Alternatively, the absence of such feelings as guilt could be interpreted as a failure to develop and nurture moral understanding. My claim here is that the choices and attitudes of the bystanders of the Holocaust, like those of the victims and perpetrators, can be understood according to the various notions of responsibility that their actions express and that these notions of responsibility in turn can be understood as constituting the threads of a weave of responsibility.

I have been drawing attention here to the idea of a weave of responsibility at the level of individual moral experiences. It is also the case, however that such experiences collectively form an important component of the complex of events that comprise the genocide of European Jewry. I have been stressing a methodological approach to understanding the moral dimensions of the Holocaust based around particular ways of understanding responsibility as entwined with moral agency, choice and significantly, circumstance. Further to this I have claimed that understanding the Holocaust in this way is most satisfactorily captured by a focus on particular concrete examples within the range of possible Holocaust experiences. It is of course possible to argue that to focus too much on individual experiences diminishes other important issues. A. H. Lesser makes just this case when he writes that:

> Essentially the mistake has been to see the issue of the Holocaust too much in personal moral terms, to see it in terms of individuals either resisting evil or failing to resist it. But this is to ignore the whole political dimension of what was happening.[30]

I do not want to dispute what Lesser is saying here. In a general sense, it is clear that the Holocaust entailed among other elements the subversion of the legal, educational and political systems, and the explicit manufacture of social conditions conducive to the deterioration of a sense of moral responsibility. My point though, is that the Holocaust is also about particular individuals behaving in particular ways to other individuals. Importantly the two ways of understanding are not incompatible. In fact, they are closely linked. Understanding such basic moral acts as individuals killing other individuals requires an account that will be informed in part by such macro factors as indicated by Lesser. Indeed, such information is essential to the task of understanding the moral dimensions of the Holocaust.

It is also particularly important to note that my decision to emphasise the concrete, the particular and the individual, is in part a response to those narratives within Holocaust literature that seek to justify guilt in a collective or national sense. I argue that in the case of the Holocaust such attempts are seriously flawed, both conceptually and empirically. This said, I am also aware of, and find value in, the sort of distinction indicated by Jürgen Habermas who writes:

> There is no collective guilt. Anyone who is guilty has to answer for it as an individual. At the same time there is something like a collective responsibility for the intellectual and cultural situation in which mass crimes became possible.[31]

It seems to me that emphasis on ideas of collective guilt misses the target. Such ideas avoid the issue of how we might understand how individuals take, or fail to take responsibility for situations and their place in such situations. Moreover, it seems to me that little constructive purpose is served in the attempt to apportion guilt. Guilt may well be a legitimate feeling but on its own it doesn't carry forward our comprehension of the situations individuals find themselves in. My primary point, though, as argued in Chapter Three, is that the moral dimensions of the Holocaust are best supported in terms of an explanation of responsibility that focuses on specific individual relations between agents. It is on the basis of relations among and between individuals that moral life is best understood. In this context there is no necessary incompatibility between my focus on responsibility understood at the level of individual agency and Habermas' understanding of a collective climate of responsibility within which individual responsibilities become manifest. This latter claim is founded on the premise that responsibility is understood as something we take, whether it be at the level of the individual or collectively, as opposed to something we ascribe and use as a means to judge others.

Holocaust experiences in a general sense, invoke both diversity and repetition, extremity and the mundane. It is also true, however, that the vast majority of Holocaust experiences are of those who witnessed events as opposed to those individuals who were more directly implicated. It seems to be the case that the largest category of expressions of responsibility concerns the vast numbers of those who knew of, or were able to attest to events encompassing the Holocaust. I say this in spite of the fact of the millions of victims. I contend that most Holocaust experiences concern individuals who had some knowledge of, and perhaps witnessed its occurrence but who might ordinarily not be considered as crucial to how we might best be able to comprehend how the Holocaust was able to occur.

One noteworthy contribution to the discussion on this sort of experience is Karl Jaspers' treatment of what he identifies as 'active' and 'passive' forms of guilt. Focusing on the idea of 'moral guilt' Jaspers writes:

> There is a difference between *activity* and *passivity*. The political performers and executors, the leaders and propagandists are guilty. If they did not become criminals, they still have, by their activity, incurred a positively determinable guilt. But each one of us is guilty insofar as he remained inactive. The guilt of passivity is different. Impotence excuses; no normal law demands a spectacular death. Plato already deemed it a matter of course to go into hiding in desperate times of calamity, and to survive. But passivity knows itself morally guilty of every failure, every neglect to act whenever possible, to shield the imperilled, to relieve wrong, to countervail. . . . Blindness for the misfortune of others, lack of imagination of the heart, inner indifference toward the witnessed evil—that is moral guilt.[32]

In this passage I take Jaspers to mean that a potential for guilt exists or is latent in and integral to moral agency and is inversely proportional to the degree to which the individual in question, in this case the witness to the persecution, mistreatment or murder of victims of the Holocaust, acted to prevent wrong—doing. What is important here is the distinction Jaspers proposes between active participation and passivity or indifference. Perhaps the key problem to overcome, if this distinction is to be useful, is being able to work out lines of demarcation between what he terms activity and passivity. There seem to be difficulties in separating out active from passive 'guilt'. Passivity itself represents a choice not to act and in this sense might be considered to be an active decision. Jaspers however, argues that a distinction is not only possible but necessary. For my part, I am not convinced of the significance of such a distinction. It is readily accepted, for example, that some individuals do need to be held accountable for criminal actions but it is also clear that not everybody can be guilty. Maybe the problem lies, in part, with the term 'guilty'. Guilt and responsibility are clearly not the same. In my view, guilt implies the need for a moral judgment and judgment is of less value in terms of the process of understanding the 'how' and 'why' questions. For Jaspers, however, the point is that there is a difference between active and passive guilt and that this difference makes all the difference. My point here, and the reason I consider Jasper's account of guilt is to draw attention to the fact that the bulk of Holocaust experiences might be considered as examples of passive guilt.

Some commentators have argued that responsibility, with regard to the Holocaust, needs to be understood as something ascribed in a collective sense. In an article titled 'Measuring Responsibility',[33] A. Zvie Bar-On argues in the affirmative the case for collective responsibility. I argue here that Zvie Bar-On's account is paradigmatic of those interpretations that seek to ascribe guilt in a generalised, over-simplified and indemonstrable manner. In order to establish the case for collective German guilt/responsibility Zvie Bar-On makes a number of strong claims. Firstly, he claims that the 'Nazi crime' against the Jews was historically unique. He then extends the claim of historical uniqueness to argue that this crime was a uniquely German crime. Zvie Bar-On writes:

> The crime is exceptional, entirely new, without precedent in the history of mankind, and this fact justifies the use of the concept of collective guilt when trying to measure the responsibility for the crime.[34]

and elsewhere:

> . . . the question has to be formulated in terms of collective guilt: are the whole German people guilty, and if so, what is the nature of that guilt?[35]

The connections that Zvie Bar-On is attempting to make seem to be, in some important respects, questionable. First, as debate within the literature has demonstrated,[36] the claim that the Holocaust is historically unique is a very difficult claim to support, except in the trivial sense that every event is unique. There also seems to be no necessary link between the Holocaust, as unique in history, and the Holocaust being an especially/uniquely German crime. The Holocaust was a European event, undertaken on European soil, by the hands of Europeans in most of the countries of Europe. To sum up here, I want to say that there may be a case to argue for the idea of collective guilt as a concept. However, when it is invoked as a reason to attach blame to the German people for the Holocaust, as it seems to be in the example above, I believe it is fatally flawed.

Elaborating further Zvie Bar-On discusses three variations of the theme of collective German guilt. These themes comprise interpretations of accounts by Adolf Eichmann, Günter Grass and Karl Jaspers respectively. Zvie Bar-On seems to seek to align his interpretation with Jaspers' understanding of the different types of guilt that form the argument for collective responsibility. Jaspers' explanation turns on the attempt to confine the Holocaust to a uniquely German crime. That this is so is evident in his 1965 interview in the German weekly *Der Spiegel*. The interviewer questioned the 'moral' validity of the argument that by excluding only German war crimes from coming under the twenty year Statute of limitations, non-Germans who committed similar crimes would escape prosecution whilst Germans would still be punishable. Jaspers is quoted as responding that:

> This argument would not have been unwelcome if it were correct. But it ignores the radical difference between war crimes and crimes against mankind. War crimes are not against humanity (die Menschlichkeit) . . . The pretension to decide which communities and nations are allowed to live on this Earth and which are not, and to materialize this decision by extermination is a crime against mankind (die Menschheit). . . . Such actions were done to Jews, Gypsies, the mentally ill.[37]

On the face of it Jaspers' distinction is less than clear. If I interpret Jaspers correctly, however, he is attempting to sustain a distinction between what would pass as the responsibility of Germans alone and what other Europeans could be held accountable for. In my view this is unsustainable especially in the particular context of attempts to bring to justice individuals (irrespective of nationality) responsible for the perpetration of crimes against humanity. I would maintain that even if Jaspers is correct in claiming that the Holocaust was different to the extent that it presupposes what he calls "a state of a new type—the state of criminals",[38] it does not necessarily follow that responsibility for the Holocaust is uniquely that of the German people.

Following Jaspers, Zvie Bar-On seems to be arguing that the guilt of 'the Germans' was of a different kind from that of other nationalities. Zvie Bar-On claims that the guilt generated by the Holocaust is a 'metaphysical' guilt. In his first public address after the war Jaspers wrote:

> We, the survivors, did not seek death. When our Jewish friends were taken away, we did not go into the streets and shout until we had been exterminated as well. We preferred to stay alive for a weak though correct reason that our death cannot possibly help. That we are alive is our guilt.[39]

Zvie Bar-On interprets this passage as a confession of what Jaspers means by the metaphysical guilt that all Germans share. My claim is that the 'we' of this passage is legitimately open to differing interpretations. Witness, for example, Jaspers' discussion of guilt in *The Question of German Guilt* where he writes:

> There exists a solidarity among men as human beings that makes each responsible for every wrong and every injustice in the world. . . . If I fail to do whatever I can to prevent them, I too am guilty. If I was present at the murder of

others, without risking my life to prevent it, I feel guilty in a way not adequately conceivable either legally, politically or morally.[40]

Zvie Bar-On interprets the guilt referred to by Jaspers as a metaphysical guilt.
Be that as it may, I believe that Jaspers is also referring in a specific way to the
content of individual moral responsibility and in a way that refuses to limit this
responsibility to geo-political borders. Moreover, I interpret Jaspers' understanding of 'co-responsibility' as a particular mode of comportment such that guilt in
the metaphysical sense may even be a necessary predicate of the human condition. In conclusion Zvie Bar-On writes:

> If the guilt imputed to every German who did not do his utmost to save his fel-
> low man from destruction did not follow from his moral duty, there is an alter-
> native way of proving it real—by making it follow from the metaphysical fact
> of human solidarity. Nevertheless, the overall result of Jasper's argument is un-
> equivocal: every German who lived in Germany during the Nazi rule and did
> not actively oppose the regime, bears responsibility for the lot of the victims of
> that regime.[41]

On my account the phrase 'persons living in Europe' could as well be substituted
for the word 'German'. On the other hand, I propose that Jaspers' understanding
of responsibility need not be extrapolated to convey a simplified and morally
comforting, collective German guilt that seems to imply the exclusion of Europe
more generally from participation in the Holocaust. Sometimes Jaspers seems to
be arguing for a distinction between German and non-German responsibility
while at others his discussion supports an altogether more complex picture of
how responsibility ought to be understood.

In support of this last point, I argue that the historical evidence clearly demonstrates how attempts to couch discussion of responsibility in terms of 'the
Germans' is seriously flawed. The exhaustive historical studies, implicating
other nationals in the extermination of Jews, of Martin Gilbert,[42] Raul Hilberg,
Jean Ancel,[43] Randolph Braham,[44] Susan Zuccotti,[45] Jan Gross, Tzvetan Todorov[46] and others all demonstrate the flaws associated with claims of collective
German responsibility. On the other hand, this is not to say that the idea of collective or group responsibility as such, is without foundation. Rather, in the case
of the Holocaust, it is more a matter of grounding the idea in terms of specific
groups. For example it can be argued that group responsibility makes more sense
with regard to those groups of individuals who volunteered to be Nazis and
thereby actively identified with a common ideology or political platform. On this
theory, 'Germans' as a nation are unable to be classified as belonging to such a
group but Nazi ideologues, for example, are. Likewise it could be argued that
not all Germans were responsible in a collective sense. Admittedly, however, it
might also be able to be argued that many more Germans were responsible, to
varying degrees, than those who would generally be prepared to admit it. That
this is the case is supported by the fact that a large number of war criminals were

able to live undisturbed after the war in their home towns and even under their own names and in spite of local knowledge of their crimes. It can also be argued that the Holocaust was only possible in conjunction with the tacit cooperation and knowledge of many within Germany who acquiesced in the face of the unfolding horror of the war against the Jews. Another order of responsibility might be said to apply to the populations and institutions (both government and non-government) of other countries within and beyond Europe. Thus there are some good reasons to entertain a certain sense of collective responsibility but always in a qualified sense.

Finally I want to make the point that although it is the case that certain specific groups like the core of the Nazi party, both within Germany and within occupied Europe, can and should be held responsible, it is also the case that the events that comprise the Holocaust, were in the last instance committed by individuals. In other words, the Holocaust was perpetrated by individual agents making individual choices with specific consequences. In a very real sense the Holocaust was not committed by abstractions, whether 'German' or 'Nazi'. This is not to say, that an organisation such as the Nazi party does not represent a culpable group. Rather it is to make the point that individuals made individual choices of one sort or another and as such bear individual responsibility of some sort or another, irrespective of whether they belonged to a specific group or not. I believe that in the final instance it is the individual and not the group that is the most elementary moral unit.

Returning to my earlier discussion on the active/passive distinction, Judith Shklar, in her book *The Faces of Injustice* [47] argues that this is an important conceptual distinction in terms of understanding our moral responsibilities. In a discussion of the difference between active and passive injustice Shklar argues that refusal to prevent wrongdoing when we can and should do so, is in effect contributing further to that injustice. Shklar is careful to note that the possibilities for preventing injustice are naturally greater in 'free' societies than within those that existed, for example, in Nazi Germany and the occupied countries. A sense of the difficulties involved in attempts to give meaning to some of the more ambiguous examples of moral responsibility is apparent in Shklar's examination of the lack of clear moral boundaries between injustice and misfortune. Shklar writes that:

> the difference between misfortune and injustice frequently involves our willingness and our capacity to act or not to act on behalf of the victims, to blame or to absolve, to help, mitigate, and compensate, or to just turn away. The notion that there is a simple and stable rule to separate the two is a demand for a moral security, which like so many others, cannot be satisfied. [48]

Shklar is, however, quick to point out that this lack of clarity does not mean that we should give up distinctions of this sort. Rather there are very good reasons why we need to retain such differences, not the least of which is in order to continue to make sense of our experiences so that we can more adequately understand what it is that is conducive to the maintenance of just social systems. Additionally, Shklar argues that the absence of simple rules to guide us will invariably mean that moral responsibility is going to be a matter of what she calls 'political choice'. In other words, the difficulty for Shklar is, in the absence of an overarching moral code, more a question of finding ways to negotiate the lines of difference between, for example, active and passive complicity or active and passive resistance toward injustice. I take Shklar to mean that although distinctions of the sort described above are a part of moral experience they are likely to be more complex than they might appear.

In both Jaspers' discussion of moral guilt and Shklar's account of the differences between active and passive injustices the individual is a common reference point. An emphasis on the individual, together with the proposition that moral evaluations are always situation specific, point to the value of evaluating questions of moral responsibility on a case by case, example by example, basis. One critical assumption, however, concerns the idea that individuals possess freedom of will. Associated with this assumption is the idea that it is always the case that individuals operate within the confines of a social context with all the attitudes, values and levels of conformity that this situation entails. In perhaps what is the most well known 20th century statement regarding the implications of the assumption of free will, Jean-Paul Sartre, in his essay 'Existentialism Is a Humanism writes:

> And when we speak of "abandonment"—a favourite word of Heidegger—we only mean to say that God does not exist, and that it is necessary to draw the consequences of his absence right to the end. . . . We are left alone without excuse. That is what I mean when I say that man is condemned to be free. Condemned because he did not create himself, yet is nevertheless at liberty, and from the moment he is thrown into this world he is responsible for everything he does.[49]

Some measure of the importance that Sartre attaches to both the individual and individual responsibility is apparent in this passage. The point that I want to make here, however, is that whilst the Holocaust was, in terms of its inception and implementation, of German origin, this does not mean that it can, as a complex amalgam of events, be primarily understood in accordance with one particular national culture or group. I want to recognise the significance of what Sartre has to say whilst at the same time holding onto the view that responsibility can admit both collective and individual dimensions. Sometimes it will make more sense to focus on responsibility understood on a case by case basis and sometimes there will be sound reasons to justify responsibility as it pertains to a group. Moreover, it will sometimes be the case that group influence will be a factor in understanding individual behaviour and vice versa. For example, a group case might be constructed on the basis of the national responsibility of states toward indigenous or minority peoples. My wider point, though, is that I see no incompatibility between this sense of 'group' responsibility and the sort of individual responsibility that I want to propose with respect to the Holocaust. I argue that there is a distinct problem in the attempt to attribute, for example, group responsibility for the Holocaust to 'the German people'. My assertion is that individual people chose to support Nazism but they didn't choose, for example, to be Germans. In fact it makes little sense to ask whether or not they could have chosen not to have been Germans. Similarly, there were people in every country in Europe who chose to support Nazism.

In an extension of Sartre's passage I propose that a key condition for an action to be subject to moral consideration is that it be the product of a conscious intention and therefore a conscious mind. If it is the case that only individuals have minds then only individuals can formulate conscious intentions and only individuals can bear moral responsibility.[50] This is not to suggest that such factors as the outcome of events, ignorance or non-voluntary obligations and duties are not part of the process of evaluating responsibility. In particular I recognise that responsibility, accrued in virtue of one's involuntary associations, is a very prominent strand in the complex weave of our responsibilities. Rather there is a need to continue to attach importance to individual moral agency in the way in which choices are determined. If what Sartre says is of some significance and the individual does exist in some sense in a 'state of abandonment', with the freedom to choose that this conjures up, then the case for emphasising individual moral responsibility remains strong.

Moreover, and notwithstanding the difficulties that accounts that unproblematically assume an unbridled sense of free will present,[51] Sartre's formulation that 'existence precedes essence'[52] resonates strongly with the way many individuals make sense of their interaction with the world. I want to illustrate this point with some examples that point to the way in which it is sometimes inappropriate to categorise responsibility in terms of 'groups'. In regard to the Holocaust, assigning responsibility to the German nation is, in one sense, more than inappropriate, it is misleading. In seeking to work through the moral implications of the Holocaust there is far more at stake than those attempts to confine questions of responsibility within the borders of Germany. The question of responsibility figures prominently, for instance, with regard to the active participation of individuals of certain European governments in the mass murder of Jews. One noteworthy example concerns individuals in the Antonescu regime of Romania (questions of responsibility might also be asked of Antonescu himself). Members of the Antonescu regime needed no prompting and even managed to surprise the Nazis with the vehemence of their programme of eradication of Romanian Jewry. Elsewhere in occupied Europe individuals of native military, para-military and civilian governments in Italy, Bulgaria, Hungary, Croatia, Norway, France, Finland, Slovakia, Serbia, Greece and Denmark all participated in measures against the Jews.

Questions of individual responsibility might also include individuals from Western nations and their failure to assist in averting the destruction of European Jewry during the period of, and from an early stage in, the war.[53] This category of responsibility extends even to elements of Western Jewish leadership. Then there are those who, whilst not responsible for the wholesale validation of National Socialist ideology, are nevertheless culpable for having willingly collaborated with the Nazi regime. Examples in this category include individuals in the Vichy government in France.

There is also a large number of individuals who may be defined by their distinctive indifference to the way the 'Jewish problem' was being resolved. They include large segments of Europe's general population and reflect, in part, the ebb and flow of anti-semitic feeling over the preceding centuries. In this category it may be possible to include individuals within the ranks of the Catholic Church in Europe and members of the Swiss government among other neutral states and churches. I want to make the distinction again between assigning guilt, in which I am not so interested, and the sorts of situations where individuals were required to make decisions about whether or not to become complicit in, actively or passively, the unfolding disaster confronting European Jewry. In other words, I am seeking to make some sense of the sorts of moral options that existed for individuals in terms of the way in which they took or failed to take responsibility for their lives and the lives of others.

There are also other 'ordinary' people of Europe who witnessed events but remained silent for whatever reason. This is surely a difficult category of responsibility to interpret. It is unclear in what sense, if any, these millions of so-called bystanders are somehow implicated in this complex of events. Could the Holocaust have occurred without their silence, without their knowledge of events as they unfolded? What factors are relevant when considering the position of those people who witnessed in silence particular episodes of the Holocaust? Fear is almost certainly a factor but could ignorance also be a factor? And there is also the question of what constitutes reasonable human actions in such circumstances. The question remains whether or not the passivity of the 'ordinary' people of Europe is morally significant within the moral topography of the Holocaust.

Different again are individuals who displayed the sort of characteristics that allowed them to go beyond fear and attempt to save Jews and others, often with marked success. Examples of such individuals are to be found in every country in Europe including Germany. The choices they made, and the moral courage they displayed deserve special attention as real if isolated instances of a particular expression of individual moral responsibility in extremely difficult situations.[54]

Finally, I want to turn to an examination of an account of an atrocity which, whilst containing many examples of perpetrator and victim behaviour also reinforces the special place bystander accounts hold in the depiction of the presence of moral complexity in the face of moral enormity. I intend to use the bystander examples as evidence of how comprehension is stalled in the tension between complexity and enormity analyses. I argue that these examples show not only how our capacity for sound moral judgments is compromised by the presence of this tension but also how our understanding is enriched upon comprehension of the implications of the tension.

In a book titled *Neighbours*,[55] Jan Gross tells the story, mentioned earlier, of a day in July of 1941 when half the population of a small Eastern European town murdered the other half, some 1600 men, women and children. Gross discusses the murder of the Jews of the town of Jedwabne in the context of a number of themes but I want to concentrate here on accounts of eye witnesses contained in various court depositions obtained by Gross in the course of his research.

Not surprisingly, the massacre of Jews at Jedwabne is not an isolated event. On 24 June, 1941 in the village of Radzilow hundreds of Jews were murdered. An eyewitness, Menachem Finkelsztajn, who managed to survive reported:

> On the 24th Germans ordered all males to assemble near the synagogue. Immediately people knew what that meant . . . Only a few managed to escape, including myself and my father. In the meantime German soldiers proceeded to give lessons of "good manners" toward the Jews. These "lessons" took place in the presence of many assembled Poles. . . . On the very next day squads of young Polish sons were organised: The Kosmaczewski brothers, Jozef Anton, and Leon, Feliks Mordaszewicz . . . and others who inflicted terrible moral and physical pain on frightened and miserable Jews. From morning till night they led old Jews, laden with sacred books, to a nearby river. They were sent on their march by crowds of Christian women, children and men.[56]

Like many of the bystander accounts I have previously discussed there is the sense that the arrival of the Germans acted as a catalyst for an already present sentiment of anti-semitic feeling. And, if the report is to be accepted as credible, anti-semitic attitudes seem to have been widely-dispersed through the populations of such villages as Radzilow. The scenes described must have been hideous to behold, perhaps also serving to further habituate anti-Semitism in the children of parents involved in some way. As has been exhaustively documented elsewhere[57] a long history of periodic if discontinuous anti-semitic behaviour can explain, in part, the raft of social practices manifest in the behaviour of those involved in the violence toward the Jews in question. However, I hold to the view that such behaviour remains startling in its absence of a sense of responsibility to others.

It is with respect to accounts of the massacre of the Jews of Jedwabne, however, that Gross's research is most thorough. Clearly this is because the Jews of Jedwabne are the focus of his book. Whilst it was the case that there was no shortage of willing participants in the pogrom in Jedwabne there were also those who were apparently badly affected by what occurred though the day. On the question of who participated Gross writes that:

> The crowd of perpetrators swelled somehow as Jews were being herded toward the barn where they were incinerated. . . . The accused, who all resided in Jedwabne during the war, could not identify many participants, because a large number of these were peasants who flocked into town from neighbouring ham-

lets.[58]

Citing court sources Gross quotes one of the accused, a Mr Miciura, who reportedly said that:

> There were many peasants from hamlets whom I didn't know . . . These were
> for the most part young men who enjoyed this catching of the Jews, and they
> tortured them.[59]

And elsewhere Gross cites the testimony of one of the participants, Boleslaw Ramotowski, who recalls that:

> when we were chasing them to the barn, I couldn't see, because it was very
> crowded.[60]

These examples are particularly interesting because they suggest a blurring of the boundaries between bystanders and participants. Is it possible that in this atmosphere of shouting, beating, screaming, running, knifing, clubbing, watching, stoning, seeing, crying, hearing, burning, ordering, resisting and smelling that some bystanders, in the confusion and climate of heightened feelings, crossed the line to become perpetrators? I think it is very possible.

On the question of those who were affected adversely there is evidence that some of those who witnessed, without participating were troubled by the level of brutality. Gross again citing someone who heard second-hand from a witness, reports:

> A certain gentleman told me about this, Mr. Kozlowski, who is no longer alive.
> He was a butcher. Very decent man. His son-in-law was a prosecutor before the
> war. From a very good family. And he told me that one could not look at what
> was going on.[61]

And further on an elderly Polish woman in an interview with a journalist, whilst distancing herself personally from the act of witnessing, talked of her mother's sister's reactions. Gross writes that she reportedly said that:

> I was not present when they were beheading Jews, or piercing them to death
> with sharp spikes. I also did not see how *our* [my italics] people ordered young
> Jewesses to drown in a pond. My mother's sister saw it. She was all in tears
> when she came to tell us about this.[62]

The evidence of these accounts shows that some individuals were clearly distressed. As well as being distressed they would almost certainly also have been fearful of what might have happened to them if they intervened. Gross elsewhere writes about a nightwatchman, one Wincenty Goscicki, who upon returning home from work was confronted by his wife who told him that:

> bad things were going on. Near our house people were beating Jews with clubs[63].

Goscicki reportedly said that:

> I got up then and went outside the house. Then I was called by Urbanowski who told me, "Look what is going on", and showed me four Jewish corpses. . . . I then hid in the house.[64]

Gross also recounts how another man, Karol Bardon, came across the Pole, Wisniewski and two others. As the story is reported:

> they were bringing another man of Mosaic persuasion, a married owner of the mechanical mill where I had been employed till March 1939, called Hersh Zdrojewicz. They held him under the arms and blood was flowing from his head and onto his torso. Zdrojewicz said to me, Save me, Mister Bardon. Being afraid of these murderers, I replied, I cannot help you with anything, and I passed them by.[65]

In regard to this last example, it should be remembered that as Karol Bardon was later convicted as a perpetrator it is difficult to accept his claims on face value. However, these examples show that among those who were bystanders, some may have joined the perpetrators, others clearly felt distress at what they saw or heard about and yet others were fearful for their own personal safety. All exhibit particular expressions of responsibility, or the lack thereof. Worthy of mention would have been certain social practices characterised by anti-semitic attitudes, notions of certain responsibilities to others, character traits peculiar to the individuals in question and responsibility understood as expressions of integrity and dignity. All of these aspects of responsibility would have combined to form the moral dimension of the relationships between those individuals involved. My claim is that the examples exhibit, quite starkly the juxtaposition of moral enormity and moral complexity: enormity, in terms of the moral extremity of the choices made and behaviour exhibited, whether heroic, indifferent or cowardly; complexity, in terms of the various understandings of responsibility that are required to be accounted for. In this chapter I have focused on bystander experiences tested against the various ways of understanding responsibility I consider to be important. In this way I hope to have demonstrated how individual expressions of responsibility illustrate the various notions of responsibility within the weave. The aim has been to further reinforce the case for moral complexity within moral accounts of the Holocaust. In the next chapter the argument for moral complexity is further explored by way of a consideration of the role of luck in understanding responsibility.

Notes

1. Etty Hillesum, *Letters From Westerbork*, A.J. Pomerans (trans.), (New York: Pantheon Books, 1986), 126.

2. Ernst Klee, Willi Dressen and Volker Riess (eds.), D. Burnstone, *"The Good Old Days": The Holocaust As Seen By Its Perpetrators and Bystanders*, (New York: The Free Press, 1991), xvii.

3. Adam Lebor and Roger Boyes, *Surviving Hitler, Corruption and Compromise in the Third Reich*, (London: Simon & Schuster Inc., 2002), 8-9.

4. Geoffrey Hartman, 'Shoah and Intellectual Witness', *Partisan Review*, vol. 65, 1988, 44.

5. Hartman, 45.

6. Claude Lanzmann, *Shoah: An Oral History of the Holocaust*, (New York: Pantheon Books, 1985), 134-136.

7. Sereny, 152.

8. Sereny, 154-155.

9. Lanzmann, 24-25.

10. See the discussion of Margret Walker's account of how responsibility evolves in Chapter Three.

11. Walker, 201.

12. See also the discussion of Jaspers and Sartre on failures of responsibility later in this chapter.

13. See my extended discussion of moral luck in the next chapter.

14. Imre Karacs, 'Poland apologises 60 years after Nazi massacre', *The Daily Yomiuri*, Sept. 2001, 15.

15. Karacs, 15.

16. See Jan Gross' insightful and compelling account of the experience of Jews at the hands of Poles in his book *Neighbours, The Destruction of the Jewish Community in Jedwabne, Poland*, (Princcton: Princeton University Press, 2001). Gross' example will be discussed later in this chapter.

17. The young woman named Pola whom I mentioned earlier is a good example of this latter group.

18. Lanzmann, 89-90.

19. Lanzmann, 91.

20. I want to note and recognize that there is some controversy surrounding the reliability of Lanzmann's interviews. In particular, Lanzmann's procedure when interviewing poles is to record his conversation with his interpreter as opposed to the actual words of the witnesses. There is also some errors in some of the translations. These concerns notwithstanding I believe that the interviews remain important evidence of certain moral attitudes.

21. Geras, 170.

22. Geras, 169.

23. Geras, 153.

24. Geras, 164.

25. Ronald Modras, *The Catholic Church and Antisemitism in Poland, 1933-1939*, (Chur: Harwood Academic Publishers, 1994).

26. Modras, 405.

27. Modras, 405.

28. The evidence that Modras presents is drawn from thousands of pages of Polish Catholic periodical literature sourced from a wide range of institutions.

29. This is not to suggest that the victims are to be judged or held responsible in any sense, but rather that as moral agents in this human drama, the victims of the Holocaust, like the bystanders and perpetrators, faced moral quandries in the very midst of the actualisation of the 'Final Solution'. As moral agents such people were confronted with having to take account of not only their own personal predicament but also the general moral and social malaise that surrounded them.

30. A.H. Lesser, 'The Holocaust: Moral and Political Lessons', *Journal of Applied Philosophy*, vol.12, no.1, 1986, 149.

31. Jurgen Habermas, 'More Humilty, Fewer Illusions—A Talk Between Adam Michnik and Jurgen Habermas', *The New York Review of Books*, March 21, 1994, 25.

32. Karl Jaspers, *The Question of German Guilt*, (Fordham: Fordham University Press, 2002).

33. A. Zvie Bar-On, 'Measuring Responsibility', *The Philosophical Forum*, vol.XVI, nos. 1-2, 1984-85.

34. Zvie Bar-On, 106.

35. Zvie Bar-ON, 95.

36. See Philippe Burrin, *Hitler and the Jews, The Genesis of the Holocaust*, (London: Edward Arnold, 1994.

37. Karl Jaspers, *Der Spiegal*, March 10, 1965, p.57.

38. Jaspers, *Der Spiegal*, 57.

39. Jaspers in Zvie Bar-On, 106.

40. Jaspers, *The Question of German Guilt*, 32.

41. Zvie Bar-On, 109.

42. Martin Gilbert, *The Holocaust: The Jewish Tradegy*, (London: Fontana Press, 1987).

43. Jean Ancel (ed.), *Bibliography of the Jews in Romania*, (Diaspora Research Institute: Tel Aviv University, 1986).

44. Randolph Braham, *The Holocaust in Hungary*, (New York: East European Monographs, 2002).

45. Susan Zuccotti, *The Italians and the Holocaust: Persecution, Rescue and Survival*, (Lincoln: The University of Nebraska Press, 1987)

46. Tzvetan Todorov, *The Fragility of Goodness: Why Bulgaria's Jews Survived the Holocaust*, (New York: Princeton University Press, 2000).

47. Judith Shklar, *The Faces of Injustice*, (London: Yale University Press, 1990).

48. Shklar, 2.

49. Jean-Paul Sartre, 'Existentialism Is a Humanism', in Robert Solomon (ed.), *Existentialism*, (New York: Random House, 1974), 201-202.

50. I also recognise the idea of corporate responsibility where it is claimed there is a group internal decision making structure equivalent to that of a single mind.

51. Following Marion Smiley's excellent account of responsibility in *Moral Responsibility and the Boundaries of Community: Power and Accountability from a Pragmatic Point of View*, (Chicago: The Universit of Chicago, 1992) as very often deriving from social practices I believe that any careful account of responsibility needs to factor in the way individuals are always embedded in, and influenced by, the social relations that comprise the edifices of society.

52. Jean-Paul Sartre, 'Existentialism Is a Humanism', 198.

53. I recognize that the issue of responsibility with regard to Western governments is

a complex matter that has brought about considerable controversy.

54. For an excellent account of the extent to which assistance to Jews was afforded in Poland see Gunnar S. Paulsson's book *Secret City, The Hidden Jews of Warsaw 1940-1945*, (London: Yale University Press, 2002).

55. Gross, *Neighbours*.

56. Gross, *Neighbours*, 61-63.

57. See Ronald Modras' excellent study, *The Catholic Church and Anti-semitism in Poland, 1933-1939*.

58. Gross, *Neighbours*, 86-87.

59. Gross, 87.

60. Gross, 86-87.

61. Gross, 88.

62. Gross, 88.

63. Gross, 93.

64. Gross, 93.

65. Gross, 95.

LUCK IN MORAL EXPERIENCE

Fundamental to an understanding of the nature of moral responsibility and indeed questions related to the conceptual uneasiness between moral enormity and moral complexity, are the various points of intersection between the factors of individual agency, circumstance and choice. Principally, understanding the nature of the relationship between these categories entails examining the extent to which external circumstances affect and alter individual agency, choices, intentions, actions and outcomes. In other words, what is most important here is the role and significance of circumstances in affecting the way people reason, choose and subsequently act. In this chapter therefore, the focus is on circumstance in order that more light might be shed on understanding the conjunction of moral enormity and complexity in evaluations of the Holocaust.

One of the more challenging aspects of this question of the importance of circumstance is to consider the possibility of luck as it relates to morality. I intend to examine the way luck, in connection with morality, connects with responsibility. If there was a case where, prior to reflection, we would want to make morality immune to luck then the Holocaust would be just such a case. Any claim that appears to confound the primary intuition that the Holocaust is the paradigm case of evil appears, on the face of it, to run the risk of placing into jeopardy the notion of the 'moral' itself. By the same token, however, if moral luck can be demonstrated to play a substantial role in the determination of moral responsibility then its existence might be argued to exacerbate further still the problem of understanding the complex conceptual coordinates of the moral landscape of the Holocaust.

Within contemporary moral philosophy the significance of the role of luck with respect to morality has been persuasively argued by such leading commentators as Bernard Williams and Thomas Nagel.[1] The concept of moral luck itself derives in principle from the idea that morality is no more immune from the influences of luck than any other aspect of human life. Within the broad tradition of Western moral philosophy there is a deeply held assumption that morality is, and ought to be, impervious to luck. Following Kant, this assumption has become more deeply embedded in mainstream moral theory. This is demonstrated by the fact that standard objections to the idea of moral luck are now mostly regarded as having been signposted by Kant's view expressed in the opening passage of the *Groundwork*. Kant writes:

> The good will is not good because of what it affects or accomplishes or because of its adequacy to achieve some proposed end; it is good only because of its willing, it is good of itself. And, regarded for itself, it is to be esteemed incomparably higher than anything which could be brought about by it in favour of any inclination or even of the sum total of all inclinations. Even if it should happen that, by a particularly unfortunate fate or by the niggardly provision of a step motherly nature, this will should be wholly lacking in power to accomplish its purpose, and even if the greatest effort should not avail it to achieve anything of its end, and if there remained only the good will (not as a mere wish but as the summoning of all the means in our power), it would sparkle like a jewel in its own right, as something that had its full worth in itself. Usefulness or fruitfulness can neither diminish nor augment this worth.[2]

Whatever the merits of an ideal of morality based on pure reason I am interested in the extent to which external circumstances affect the will. I want to stress what Thomas Nagel describes as "the ordinary conditions of moral judgement"[3] as central to adequate understandings of moral life. Nagel in particular argues that it is widely accepted that moral ascriptions are considered inappropriate when evaluating acts that occur beyond a person's control. In other words, where there is a clear absence of control, and the examples Nagel provides include "involuntary movement, physical force, or ignorance of the circumstances"[4] then the agent in question is excused from moral judgment, whether good or bad. The problem, however, is that if these mitigating circumstances are able to be factored into a consideration of what acts are to be judged as morally significant and what are not then there is no necessarily logical or consistent reason why other circumstances (such as social or political pressures to conform) should not also be considered as potentially mitigating. Of course this is a crucial and highly contentious point in the argument and it may have been the problem concerning the demarcation of moral responsibility that led Kant to exclude potentially mitigating external circumstances in favour of assessments based on those produced exclusively by a good will. Kant's solution to this problem of separating clear absence of control from the broader range of mitigating circumstances, by excluding the latter in their entirety, is perhaps the only sure way of safeguarding the pure principles of moral assessment.

In contrast to Kant's attempt to secure the sphere of morality from contingent circumstances, Nagel writes:

> what we do depends in many more ways than these [examples where there is a clear absence of control] on what is not under our control—what is not pro-

duced by a good or a bad will, in Kant's phrase. And external influences in this broader range are not usually thought to excuse what is done from moral judgment, positive or negative.[5]

On Nagel's account, morality, far from being immune to luck, is in part dependent on it in the determination of such fundamental concerns as the ascription of praise and blame or understanding responsibilities to persons. This is to say, that luck in a person's circumstances contributes to how it is that person finds themselves in such situations in the first instance. The fact of the matter is that we are normally only likely to excuse a person's act from moral assessment if that act was performed as a result of the narrower range of excusable conditions. Yet it is also true that we continue to treat someone as an object of moral judgment even if what they do depends to a large extent on the 'broader' range of external circumstances that may also lie outside their control. Nagel treats this second situation as that which properly constitutes moral luck, be it good or bad. Nagel writes:

> Where a significant aspect of what someone does depends on factors beyond his control, yet we continue to treat him in that respect as an object of moral judgment, it can be called moral luck. Such luck can be good or bad.[6]

The difficulty here is how to take account of the presence of moral luck. Should we for example, not judge someone who was subject to a wide range of external circumstances as harshly as we would someone whose actions were not so affected? I believe that this is a question for which there is no simple answer. I do want to make the claim, however, that moral luck is a necessary factor among those factors required to reach a position that is sensitive to the complexities of situations requiring moral evaluations. In short, moral luck is relevant to moral evaluations. It is to this extent I contend that Nagel's argument is important.

Having established grounds for the existence of moral luck Nagel identifies four ways in which morality is subject to luck. These he classifies as first 'constitutive luck'; second 'luck in one's circumstances'; third 'luck in how one is determined by antecedent circumstances' and fourth 'luck in the way one's actions and projects turn out'. I argue that it is Nagel's second category, namely 'luck in one's circumstances' that most closely demonstrates, in the case of Holocaust experiences, the indebtedness of morality to luck. Browning's study *Ordinary Men*, for example shows how fate can contribute massively to ordinary people being faced with moral choices of extreme gravity. Nagel's own example further reinforces the claim that luck, as a result of one's circumstances, is a clear factor in determining the way in which the fortunes of moral agents are shaped. Nagel writes:

> The things we are called upon to do, the moral tests we face, are importantly determined by factors beyond our control. It may be true of someone that in a dangerous situation he may behave in a cowardly or heroic fashion, but if the

situation never arises, he will never have the chance to distinguish or disgrace himself in this way, and his moral record will be different. . . . Ordinary citizens of Nazi Germany had an opportunity to behave heroically by opposing the regime. They also had the opportunity to behave badly, and most of them are culpable for having failed this test. But it is a test to which citizens of other countries were not subjected, with the result that even if they, or some of them, would have behaved as badly as the Germans in like circumstances, they simply did not and therefore are not similarly culpable. Here again one is morally at the mercy of fate, and it may seem irrational upon reflection, but our ordinary moral attitudes would be unrecognizable without it. We judge people for what they actually do, not just for what they would have done if circumstances had been different.[7]

Following Nagel, my point is that citizens who were not subject to Nazi rule, force and ideology did not have to face the sorts of moral 'tests' under discussion. The 'ordinary citizens of Nazi Germany' were no different from others in terms of what might be referred to as a person's moral potentialities, it was only because of circumstances beyond their control that many of Nazi Germany's citizens had their moral sensibilities put to the test. Indeed as history records, citizens from other European countries placed within circumstances similar to those of 'ordinary citizens of Nazi Germany' were more often than not found to be as morally culpable.

If it is the case that those who were not in such unlucky circumstances are justifiably assumed to possess similar moral characters to those who were unfortunate enough to have found themselves in such difficult circumstances then what implication does this have for the wider argument concerning the apportionment of responsibility more generally? This question is of course a non-starter even if it were able to be supported empirically. My point is that, if Nagel is correct, it was only good luck that allowed such people to avoid this most difficult of 'tests'. Such knowledge should, in my view, temper any arrogance that 'we' might be tempted to display as regards our perception of what moral responsibility consists of. Ultimately, Nagel's argument demonstrates an aspect of moral life for which there may be no satisfactory resolution. The examples of Browning and Nagel show that moral judgments are conditional upon a number of factors but that in spite of this such judgments remain critical to our understanding of what it means to be moral. The fact of the matter is that we attribute moral praise or blame for acts committed, not potential acts. Luck, whilst it is an integral part of moral life, does not have the effect of making moral life itself any less demanding. If, however, it is accepted that luck is a factor in moral evaluations then such evaluations are going to be less self-righteous and more cognizant of the vulnerability that is at the core of the beliefs that we hold to be important.

In his essay 'Luck and Moral Responsibility'[8] Michael Zimmerman considers the role of luck in parallel with the question of free will. Zimmerman is committed to maintaining a conception of morality as immune to luck because as he says, there is a very strong need for it to "be possible for someone to be morally responsible for an event's occurring."[9] To this end, and acknowledging the influence of Kant, Zimmerman argues for the need to neutralise luck in determining moral responsibility. The problem that Zimmerman encounters though is that what he calls 'differential judgments' seem to be, in a sense, unjustifiable. Following an example that he uses, it is unfair to blame the collaborator more than the non-collaborator because of the difference in circumstances. In Zimmerman's example all that separates the non-collaborator from the collaborator is the idea that the non-collaborator did not have the opportunity to collaborate. If the collaborator deserves blame then it appears as if the non-collaborator also deserves blame.

The way in which Zimmerman attempts to extricate himself from this problem is by introducing the notion of free will. Acknowledging the difficulties of such a presupposition, Zimmerman nevertheless holds to the view that actions are in large part freely decided upon. For Zimmerman this is crucial as it allows attention to be focussed on the agent in question and his or her decision. In his conclusion Zimmerman writes:

> In sum, I accept that freedom of decision is crucial to the ascription of moral responsibility and thus to the ascription of praise and blame. Even if . . . it is unfair to engage in differential judgement...still there is room for praise and blame. Insofar as what happens after one has made a free decision is, in a sense, up to nature, then these events, while perhaps serving as indirect indicators of praise and blame, are strictly dispensable in the assessment of moral responsibility. . . . But the decision itself is not at all irrelevant; on the contrary, it is, one might say, the fulcrum of such ascription. And this is true even in those cases where no decision was made (as with the non-collaborator) but where one would have been made but for some stroke of fate or fortune.[10]

Zimmerman's stress on free will and the need to focus on intentions in the assessment of moral responsibility is important not least because it allows for a ready understanding of the strengths as well as the weaknesses of acknowledging luck in moral life. By foregrounding the proposition that morally assessable actions are freely willed Zimmerman is able to keep a rein on the force of responsibility. Rather than everyone being held responsible not only for what they do but also for what they would have done had circumstances been different, with the result that blame loses its force, Zimmerman argues that the actual decision is still the critical factor in the ascription of blame and praise. Luck, however may still be regarded as a factor of some significance in the sense of a particular agent being in a particular place at a particular time thereby enabling that agent to display, for example, the sort of courage necessary to win a medal. This is not to say that the element of luck present diminishes the quality of the courage or suggests that medals should be given to everyone who might have acted in the same way. What I want to emphasize is that whilst it may be true that such characteristics as courage are of importance, the point is that the circumstances in question are a key to assessing courage. An individual may be intrinsically courageous but if the appropriate circumstances never arise then this component of his/her character may never be recognised.

Nagel also argues that in certain situations moral luck can entail a moral dilemma. The important point here is that dilemma-type situations may represent stronger cases of the influence of circumstantial luck than so-called standard accounts. In respect to the dilemma-type situations Nagel, in a footnote, writes:

> An unusual example of circumstantial luck is provided by the kind of moral dilemma with which someone can be faced through no fault of his own, but which leaves him with nothing to do which is not wrong.[11]

If Nagel is correct in his assertion then there may be a case for greater consideration to be attached to the influence of luck in moral evaluations. This brings me to my reason for highlighting Nagel's account. I seek to test the significance of moral luck within the context of the sorts of situations I'm interested in. Moreover, it is my view that whilst Nagel has raised an important aspect of the role of luck in moral life, he does not scrutinise it sufficiently. Specifically my concern is that having ascribed a certain significance to the moral dilemma as an example of moral luck, he then fails to investigate whether or not it is relevant to the context within which it arises in his discussion of the 'ordinary citizens of Nazi Germany'. Instead Nagel relegates his understanding of this particular sort of circumstantial luck to the confines of a footnote in the wider discussion thereby leaving it under-examined.

The significance of this failure to test the force of this particular type of circumstantial luck in respect of the 'ordinary citizens of Germany' has also been noted by Daniel Statman in the introduction to his anthology titled *Moral Luck* [12] Statman argues that Nagel's account of a moral dilemma is flawed insofar as such a situation, where one is faced, through no fault of one's own, with a choice where one cannot avoid doing wrong, is itself implausible. In other words, Statman denies the possibility of genuine moral dilemmas. Statman writes that "if one chooses the best course of action available to one, one is acting perfectly well from a moral point of view and is not to be blamed for anything."[13] Statman seems unwilling to admit circumstances in which there is no best course of action. On a narrower view of morality, where the stress is on being able to ascribe praise or blame rationally, Statman might be right. On a more encompassing understanding of responsibility, like the understanding I am developing and the one Gowans articulates in *Innocence Lost*[14] Statman is sidestepping the possibility that acts can be understood as immoral without blaming the agent. This is especially evident in Statman's use of the Nazi example. In his attempt to make morality immune from luck he claims that genuine moral dilemmas even if possible, are always going to be different from those faced by the Nazi. The Nazi, according to Statman could have chosen otherwise thereby reducing the role of luck to merely finding oneself in a difficult situation. This seems to me to be mistaken. The presence of luck within moral life necessitates down-grading our capacity to make moral decisions with anything like the sort of self-righteousness we would wish.

Moreover, I think it is important to recognise that even if the situation of the Nazi is not in the strict sense an example in which the circumstances force the person to behave wrongly, it may still be an instance of the way luck influences morality. In this respect Statman's account of the situation that people are likely to have found themselves in, falls short of allowing for the complexity of situations people actually found themselves in. It is not necessarily the case that someone has to be faced with circumstances where there is no escape from wrongdoing in order for luck to have been a significant and perhaps telling influence on the behaviour of a moral agent. Moreover, in the case of the sort of situations to which Nagel is referring, a focus on the circumstances will often provide a significant contribution toward an understanding of the nature of moral responsibility. The 'choice less choice' scenario is problematic precisely because the extreme nature of the circumstances have reduced the very concept of moral agency to the point where it may no longer make sense to speak of a freely willed will.[15]

With respect to the accounts of Nagel and Zimmerman I have argued that circumstance is an important, if problematic factor in achieving a more satisfactory understanding of moral responsibility. On my understanding it is Nagel's account of the force of circumstance that comes closest to recognizing its role in how we might come to view our responsibilities to ourselves and to others. Both Zimmerman and Nagel recognise the significance of luck yet pursue a line of thought that ultimately underrates its significance in moral life. Both writers make an important contribution to the discussion of the complexities of moral life.

Another potentially interesting aspect of responsibility is the possibility that in situations where moral sensibility is sorely tested, the result may be some form of *akratic* behaviour. In other words, given the role of circumstance in the way in which actions come to be manifest, it might be argued that *akrasia* could be one factor contributing to an explanation of the reasons for particular actions. Returning to Browning's account I argue that the situations he details could well entail the sort of puzzle attributable, at least in part, to akratic behaviour. The puzzle is this: The profile of the average policeman from Battalion 101 contained nothing to distinguish him from an average profile from the wider populace of the time. The average policeman of the study was not in any sense inherently evil. Additionally, on Browning's own carefully supported account, the average policeman from his sample was not in any overt sense an anti-Semite nor did he have any express sympathies for Nazi ideology. Yet most of the policemen in question voluntarily acted contrary to certain primary, and for the most part commonly held beliefs, beliefs derived in large part from general social conventions about the sanctity of human life. By what further means then can the behaviour of the policemen be explained? One possibility is that the behavioural puzzle as described here may constitute a form of akrasia.

Donald Davidson in his essay 'Paradoxes of Irrationality'[16] proposes an open-ended definition of akrasia as including those situations "where the agent acts intentionally while aware that everything considered a better course of action is open to him."[17] If the feelings of revulsion were as powerful as Browning reports yet most of the policemen nevertheless acted contrary to these feelings, contrary to what they would likely have held to be their better judgment, then it could be argued, following Davidson's working definition, that the behaviour of those who participated in the killing was akratic.

If we were to pursue this line of inquiry further it would make sense to try to identify the stages of the process that can lead to akratic behaviour. This task has been much assisted by Amélie Rorty's analysis of akrasia in her book *Mind in Action*. [18] Rorty writes:

> [The] . . . stages on thought's way to action can be regarded as supplementing Aristotle's schema of the practical syllogism: the person's most general evaluations represent the major premise; his interpretation of his particular situation represents the minor premise; his intentions and decisions represent his forming the conclusion of the argument and his action is the consequence of his having drawn the conclusion. These distinctions allow us to locate the junctures where psychological akrasia can occur, in ways that explain the occurrence of behavioural akrasia.[19]

In the light of Rorty's 'stages' in the processes that lead to action it becomes possible to elaborate further in response to the question: what is happening in purported cases of akrasia? In the mind of the akrate the major premise, being his or her more general evaluation, is usurped by the minor or situation specific premise. In Rorty's terms the akratic alternative overtakes the preferred judgment. If this is so then the real puzzle is to be able to explain why and how this occurs.

One important consideration for Rorty is that the so called akratic alternative need not be irrational. On this account the agent may follow what Rorty refers to as 'a preferred course' for non-rational reasons and then modify their belief according to what they think is the rational though 'akratic alternative'. By way of substantiation, Rorty proposes that the agent may be committed to a preferred course as a result of long held beliefs. Such preferences Rorty argues may be acquired without having been thought through and the agent themself may well believe that it is non-rational to arrive at judgments in this way. In the case of the policemen of Reserve Battalion 101, I want to pose the question whether or not it is conceivable that the preferred judgment, (for example, not to participate in the killings), might have been overtaken by what the policemen believed was a rational, though akratic alternative. For example, Browning, quoting from the testimony of a thirty-five year old metal worker from Bremerhaven writes:

> I made the effort, and it was possible for me, to shoot only children. It so hap-

pened that the mothers led the children by the hand. My neighbour then shot the mother and I shot the child that belonged to her, because I reasoned with myself that after all without its mother the child could not live any longer. It was supposed to be, so to speak, soothing to my conscience to release children unable to live without their mothers.[20]

However shocking this process of rationalisation may seem it nevertheless must be conceded that the situation described by this policeman might constitute, in his eyes, a 'reasonable' akratic alternative. In other words, at some point in the mental chain of thought between the agent's general evaluations and their interpretation of the particular situation it is possible that the akratic alternative overtook the preferred judgment. Altogether then, we have a situation where the agent in question was acting voluntarily, was in full possession of his beliefs yet, in the majority of cases, the course he took, over and above what Rorty calls 'the preferred judgment', was 'the akratic alternative'. I argue that Rorty's argument is broadly consistent with the more conventional views concerning akrasia whilst at the same time allowing for a potentially greater range of scenarios where akratic action may be demonstrated to have occurred. In short, Rorty's assessment of the conceptual dimensions of akrasia serves to significantly enrich the way such behaviour might be understood.

This said it is also the case that the behaviour of the policemen in question was significantly influenced by other factors. It can be demonstrated that a number of elements germane to the situation the policemen were in crucially affected their behaviour. Such elements included peer pressure, conformity to authority and a generalisable climate of the dehumanisation of the victims in question. These factors are all known to have contributed to the behaviour of the policemen.[21]

I also find in Rorty's account of *akrasia* a certain resonance with what Nussbaum describes as the 'fragility of goodness'.[22] The policemen in the example may well have had a conception of 'the good' but it may have been, if clearly defined in the first instance, only poorly reflected upon and it is certain to have been severely tested by the circumstances the policemen found themselves in. Broadly consistent with a Nussbaumian type position, Rorty argues that the 'modern age', following in the wake of the likes of Dostoevsky, Nietzsche and Freud has "cast doubt on the doctrine that agents are essentially motivated by a conception of what is good or desirable."[23] At the very least the accounts of Nussbaum and Rorty indicate the need to question interpretations that assume that agents are inherently motivated by reason or notions of the good more than they are motivated by plain desires and emotions or even whims. In support of this latter point I am reminded of the evidence of my earlier examples of the policemen who succumbed to circumstances inherent to the situation they found themselves in. I think that the concept of *akrasia* goes some of the way to explaining the behaviour of the policemen in question. Some clarification is warranted here. Firstly, and like Rorty, I would not hold that for an action to be able to be described as akratic, it needs to be motivated by unconflicted judgments of what is best. Moreover, I would think that it would be possible for the akrate to be internally conflicted though in ways that does not reflect on their capacity to reason per se. I think that understandings of akrasia that restrict it to irrational thought processes fail to capture that which is really interesting in such cases as those of the policemen of Reserve Battalion 101. And what is potentially interesting in such accounts is the idea that akratic actions may derive from thinking, though conflicted individuals.

A fundamental condition of akrasia and perhaps even the key to the puzzle of akrasia is that the behaviour in question needs to have been undertaken willingly. In the case of the policemen this means that it has to be able to be demonstrated that the policemen were acting voluntarily. It needs to be demonstrated that the policemen acted without coercion and that other genuine options existed in order that they could have acted otherwise. I argue that on the basis of Browning's research there is some evidence indicating that the decisions of the policemen can be classed as voluntary. However, I would also say that the evidence is inconclusive. In qualified support of the view that the policemen's decisions were voluntarily made Browning writes that in advance of the commencement of the action the commanding officer gave explicit notice that:

> any of the older men who did not feel up to the task that lay before them could step out. . . . After he had taken Schimke under his protection, some ten or twelve other men stepped forward as well.

In another testimony an un-named policeman stated that:

> It was in no way the case that those who did not want to or could not carry out the shooting of human beings with their own hands could not keep themselves out of this task. No strict control was being carried out here. I therefore remained by the arriving trucks and kept myself busy at the arrival point. In any case I gave my activity such an appearance. . . . I suffered no consequences for my actions. I just mention here that I was not the only one who kept himself out of participating in the executions.[24]

The question of voluntary agency, however, is more complex than merely demonstrating that the circumstances allowed for alternative choices of action. What I'm talking about here is an ability to make decisions consciously about actions. The discussion thus far has operated under the assumption of a conceptual benchmark for what constitutes the norm with respect to moral agency and the processes that lead to morally justifiable actions. When we come to explain the actions of the akrate, however, these sorts of assumptions are unable to be relied upon. This is because the character of the akrate differs from that of the normal agent. The mental processes operating in the mind of the akrate, such that these persons can be led to a conclusion other than the preferred judgment means that something is acting on the substance of their agency that in turn leads them to deviate in this way. This at the very least suggests a sense of agency that is less rationally capable in some way than that of the 'normal' agent.

Rorty argues that the akrate is typically a conflicted person, although in ways that are more subtle than those that would disqualify the agent from being able to exercise voluntary agency. It is with regard to the possible ways that this conflict within the akrate manifests itself that is of particular interest. It would seem that the conflict that occurs within the mind of the akrate leads to a debilitated capacity for judgment. Sometimes, however, it is the specific situation within which the agent is framed that engenders the conflict in the first instance. On this, perhaps the most important point, Rorty argues that the situation an agent finds themself in can engender akratic behaviour due to, for example, an inability on the part of the agent to be able to exercise careful judgment within the parameters of the particular situation. In other words, the circumstances of the situation in question can have the effect of restricting the scope for sound judgment. Such a situation, on Rorty's account, can lead to akratic behaviour.

Alternatively, and more relevant to the example of the policemen, Rorty writes that:

> One of the ways in which power corrupts is that it allows unusual scope for the akratic release of the powerful but stressed person. The normal checks and constraints that might add weight to the preferred course are absent. The powerless are often lightning conductors for the akratic actions of the powerful. The conflicted akrate is often canny about the directions of his akrasia, acting against his better judgment primarily only against those too weak to restrain him.[25]

This added dimension of akrasia parallels very closely the situation of the policemen of Reserve Battalion 101. In Browning's study the boundaries between the powerful (those who committed the killings) and the powerless (the Jews who were killed) are expressly demarcated.

Following a line that is not dissimilar to the reasoning of Rorty's account, Alison McIntyre has argued [26] that akrasia may be profitably understood as a kind of 'renegade reason' to be explained in part by way of the circumstances that impinge upon the agent's motivations to act one way over another. In her concluding remarks McIntyre writes:

> Agents work with limited information about themselves and their situation, and they must decide how to act upon this information in a limited amount of time by exercising limited cognitive capacities. . . . We are also constantly forced to acknowledge the loose texture of our plans and the fact that the conditions for abandoning them often remain unspecified when our plans are formulated. . . . Other sorts of plans may depend on there arising no defeating external circumstances, where the list of such defeating considerations is not specified in adopting the plan, through no deliberative fault or shortcoming on the part of the agent.[27]

As with Rorty's approach, one of the key elements to McIntyre's understanding of akrasia is the need to factor in circumstance. Thus the actual reasons for action may rely more on situational factors, such as the availability of time to evaluate and even when there is time to consider, the opportunity to reconsider, than such factors as changes in an agent's evaluative judgments. Again Browning's research offers some excellent insights into how circumstances impact upon an agent's plans of action. In his description of the way duties were assigned by one of the platoon commanders in the course of the killings at the village of Jozefow, Browning writes that:

> When dividing his men into small groups of shooters, Drucker had kept about one third of them in reserve. Ultimately, everyone was to shoot . . . [however] . . . With the constant coming and going from the trucks, the wild terrain, and the frequent rotation, the men did not remain in fixed groups. The confusion created the opportunity for work slowdown and evasion. . . . After two rounds one policeman simply "slipped off" and stayed among the trucks at the edge of the forest.[28]

As mentioned in the earlier account the policeman just mentioned recalled that he remained with the arriving trucks and kept himself busy so as to avoid becoming involved in the shootings.

In some instances, however, circumstances conspired against those wanting to evade the shootings. Browning reports that some of the policemen were able to be re-assigned and some were not depending on who they approached and during what were vicarious situations. In Browning's words:

> Two policemen made the mistake of approaching Captain (and SS-Hauptscharfuhrer) Wohlauf instead of Kammer. They pleaded that they too were fathers with children and could not continue. Wohlauf curtly refused them, indicating that they could lie down alongside the victims.[29]

Given the sorts of situations that some agents find themselves in, and even where they are going to be able to exercise differing options, it may be the case that an 'all things considered judgment' will not be an option. In other words, in some situations, maybe where the person's character is stressed, they may still be considered a rational agent yet be faced with a 'situation' where the chosen course of action is inconsistent with what the agent holds to be the best course of action. Ultimately, and in the light of Browning's description of the situation, it may make more sense to interpret the actions of some of the policemen involved in the massacres in Jozefow in Poland as resulting from the most 'reasonable' though akratic course of action.

Whether or not in the final analysis there is sufficient evidence to demonstrate the existence of akratic behaviour is of secondary importance for my purposes here. It is my contention that the discussion of akrasia pointedly demonstrates the significance of circumstance, and hence of luck in regard to such circumstances, on the actions of agents. On the basis of the aforementioned discussion it can be deduced that the moral, if not the criminal, culpability of those involved must depend to a significant degree on the particular set of circumstances involved. Most of the men of Reserve Police Battalion 101, for example, faced their particular test and failed. The question of how their behaviour might best be understood however is not so straightforward. It can be argued that they, largely as a result of bad luck in their circumstances, found themselves in difficult situations faced with massively distressing choices. This is not to say that they should not be judged morally culpable but that that process of judging be tempered by the knowledge that, faced with similar circumstances, 'we' ourselves may not have behaved any differently. The choices faced by the policemen entailed factoring in a range of influences particular to the situation. Luck, as it relates to morality further complicates how we might best understand the behaviour of not only the policemen of Browning's study but moral agents more generally. That a person should find themself faced with a situation where they have to make the sorts of choices that the policemen in question had to make is tragic. My point is that luck, in the circumstantial sense, played a significant part in the policemen finding themselves in such a situation in the first instance. The mere fact of finding themselves in such a situation not only ensured the most severe test of their character but as studies have shown, also greatly enhanced the chances of those involved developing psychological disorders later in their lives. The bad luck experienced by the policemen contributed not only to the enormity of the crimes that followed but also to the conceptual complexity incurred in understanding both the crimes and the behaviour that produced them.

Given that the perpetrators were morally culpable we may also want to argue that most of those who witnessed but who remained silent share, in some measure, some degree of culpability. The magnitude of the failure is surely different but what makes it different is, in part, the difference in circumstances of those involved, not that the people involved were somehow intrinsically morally different. It is true that there are those, like the Righteous Gentiles, who stand worthy of special merit and admiration, but it is equally true that they represent an exceptional category among the many others who inhabit the moral landscape of the Holocaust. Here I would like to endorse the words of Plato:

> For experience should have taught him that few are the good and few are the evil and that the great majority of men are in the interval between them.[30]

The people who witnessed but who remained silent are not as morally culpable as those more directly implicated because they were not faced with the same sort of circumstances. Or to put it another way, they encountered differing luck in their circumstances. This being the case, it can be said of luck that it ought to be factored into the increasingly complex array of explanatory factors contributing to a more comprehensive understanding of the moral dimensions of Holocaust experiences. What remains true however, and what this chapter has demonstrated, is that there are no easy ways of taking account of luck. If it is the case, as I believe I have shown, that luck is part of the human condition itself, then it has a role to play, among the other aspects of responsibility, that ensure the complexity of moral life.

Notes

1. See Bernard Williams, *Moral Luck*, (Cambridge: Cambridge University Press, 1981) and Thomas Nagel, *Mortal Questions*, (Cambridge: Cambridge University Press, 1979).

2. Immanuel Kant, *Groundwork of the Metaphysic of Morals*, (New York: Harper & Row, 1964), 62.

3. Nagel, 25.

4. Nagel, 25.

5. Nagel, 25.

6. Nagel, 26.

7. Nagel, 33-34.

8. Michael Zimmerman, 'Luck and Responsibility' in Daniel Statman (ed.), *Moral Luck*, (New York: State University of New York Press, 1993).

9. Zimmerman, 230.

10. Zimmerman, 230.

11. Nagel, 34.

12. Daniel Statman, *Moral Luck*, (New York: State University of New York Press, 1993).

13. Statman, 21.

14. See my discussion of Gowans' account in Chapter Three.

15. See my mention of the choiceless choice scenario in Chapter Three.

16. Donald Davison, 'Paradoxes of Irrationality', in R. Wollheim and J. Hopkins (eds.), *Philosophical Essays on Freud*, (Cambridge: Cambridge University Press, 1982).

17. Davison, 295.

18. Amelie Rorty, *Mind in Action*, (Boston: Beacon Press, 1988).

19. Rorty, 230.

20. Browning, 73.

21. See the discussion of the policemens' behaviour in Chapter Two.

22. See Martha Nussbaum, *The Fragility of Goodness*, (Cambridge: Cambridge University Press, 1986). In her account Nussbaum sets up the problem of 'goodness' as a dilemma in which she explores the implications of the Greek poet Pindar's poetic image that what we must hold dear, in human excellence, is also its greatest weakness, its vulnerability. See especially 1-21.

23. Rorty, 249.

24. Browning, 65-66.

25. Rorty, 260.

26. Alison McIntyre, 'Is Akratic Action Always Irrational', O. Flannigan & A. Rorty (eds.), *Identity, Character and Morality*, (Cambridge: MIT Press, 1990).

27. McIntyre, 397-398.

28. Browning, .65.

29. Browning, 62.

30. Plato, *Phaedo*, 89e-90a, (Oxford University Press: Oxford, 1999).

BORDERLINES OF RESPONSIBILITY

In the preceding chapters my aim has been to establish the grounds for a discussion of moral responsibility at the interface of both enormity and complexity analyses of Holocaust experiences. The primary means of configuring this discussion has been to envisage a conceptual framework within which a more comprehensive understanding of such experiences might be possible. A key idea in this framework is the idea of a weave of responsibility, informed through an integration of the work of various commentators to produce an understanding of responsibility that includes the practices that mark our moral engagement with the world, a particular interpretation of responsibility as integrity, a consideration of our differing responsibilities to specific persons and the role of individual dispositions. Throughout these discussions I have maintained that individuals' various interpretations of responsibility are pivotal to understanding how we chart our moral byways. Thus my intention has been to elaborate on ways in which we might come to understand moral responsibility whilst at the same time placing an emphasis on individual agency and the factors that affect agency within the more general context of Holocaust experiences.

As the discussions have proceeded it has become increasingly evident that understanding our responsibilities within the context of Holocaust experiences is a daunting project. Distilling a working account of our responsibilities within both enormity and complexity evaluations severely tests the possibilities for such an account. In this chapter I seek to further explore the discussion by elaborating on the idea that the Holocaust was not something that someone else or some others were responsible for. I will develop another aspect of responsibility that extends much farther than the geo-political borders of National Socialist Germany. Conceived in this way, the Holocaust also implicates, in a moral sense, European civilization, European culture and European people more generally. In other words, the whole process of reinvigorating questions of responsibility, guilt and innocence contains within it powerful assertions about the nature of 'the West'. As stated in chapter one, whilst it is true that the Holocaust fits 'our' strongest intuitions of evil it is also true that it did not occur in another world and its perpetrators were not devils. The Holocaust occurred in Europe at the hands of Europeans. Whilst this is, on the one hand, an obvious statement, it is also a very provocative one. Though a statement of historical fact it also serves to blur understandings of responsibility. By interpreting responsibility in this way, I in no way intend to suggest that my account is entirely original. In fact, in support of my argument I employ aspects of the work of Peter Haas, Berel Lang, Philippe Burrin and Zygmunt Bauman in an attempt to understand what I consider to be a new articulation of this aspect of responsibility in the context of the Holocaust. I also make the wider point that whilst my argument concerning the importance of a complexity analysis depends, in part, on a focus that highlights individual differences as well as my theoretical understanding of the nature of morality, it additionally includes the idea to be explored in this chapter of a broad Western cultural constitution. I do not consider these different aspects of a complexity analysis to be in opposition but rather to be complementary.

First, however, I want to return to Jacques Derrida's comments in *Of Spirit, Heidegger and the Question,* already quoted in the first chapter.[1] I want to stress Derrida's reference to the geographical, thematic and ethical proximity of Nazism (and thus by default the Holocaust) to 'the West'. Using a forest metaphor Derrida makes the point that Nazism evolved not only in the silence and indifference of European political, social and economic life but also out of a European intellectual tradition.

Pursuant on Derrida's line of thought, my argument for this chapter takes the following form. First I will attempt to show that the Holocaust has European roots and that it is not exclusively a German phenomenon. I will then argue that, in terms of the idea of a weave of aspects of responsibility this fact implies that both a wider frame of reference for understanding the historical, social and cultural antecedents of the Holocaust and also a more nuanced understanding of the moral dimensions of this complex of events is required. If it is the case, however, that the Holocaust was a European phenomenon it is always going to be problematic to make such a phenomenon explicable within the same kind of Enlightenment-derived philosophical discourse that was used to justify the genocide of the Jews by the Nazis. For instance, if it was outrageous or perhaps even absurd that Eichmann could invoke the philosophical principles of Kant in his defence,[2] there is also a certain irony in his attempt to do so. Eichmann was able to employ Kant because the language of Kant is the language of modernity, and in particular the language of modern European moral philosophy. In another context, it has been argued by Hugo Ott[3] that it was Martin Heidegger, perhaps the most important thinker in twentieth century Germany, who perceived the German nation as the cradle, and thus the saviour, of European civilisation. Ott contends that it was in part Heidegger's ideas about the role of Germany as the saviour of 'the West' that contributed to his temporary though problematic descent into the orbit of the National Socialist propaganda machinery. Viewed from this perspective Eichmann's appeals to Kantian philosophy contain a certain bizarre logic. My immediate point is that Eichmann, irrespective of the validity of his defence, was able to draw on the same discursive tradition as Kant and the later Heidegger. Eichmann was able to utilise the language of modernity in a way that suggests that many of the basic tenets of National Socialism were derived in turn from ingredients basic to modernity itself. However, and although the tradition of modernity may give rise to Eichmanns, this is not to say that interpretations of modernity per se are linked causally with Eichmann's interpretation of modernity. Rather my wider point is that although modernity was able to give rise to differing and sometimes conflicting interpretative possibilities, there is still a certain measure of discomfort to be had from the knowledge that Eichmann himself chose to appeal to elements from within the Western philosophical tradition as a defence for what he seemingly believed to be defensible.

The idea that moral responsibility for the Holocaust is located within the historical, political, cultural and intellectual fabric of Europe more generally, resonates strongly, though not straightforwardly, with the notion of responsibility understood as comprising various aspects or what I have referred to earlier as part of a conceptual weave of responsibility. So whilst I have been primarily arguing the case for understanding responsibility in terms of individual acts and individual events I also believe that there is an aspect of the concept that relates it to a composite of events located within the historical fabric of Europe. This chapter seeks to understand this broader sense of responsibility in the context of the phenomenon of the Holocaust.

I will continue with a discussion of one commentator's understanding of where, in the broader sense, responsibility for the events of the Holocaust lay. Berel Lang's book, *Act and Idea in the Nazi Genocide,*[4] is a significant contribution to understanding the moral/philosophical dimensions of the Holocaust. In his carefully elaborated conceptual study of genocide in its Nazi configuration Lang writes that:

> genocide *is* distinctive, not, as has often been claimed, in the "uniqueness" of
> its occurrence—since we know that there may have been, and even more surely
> can be, more than one of these—but *as an idea and act of wrongdoing* [my ital-
> ics].[5]

An indication of the difficulties involved in successfully substantiating the thesis, that as an act and idea of wrongdoing the Holocaust is unique, is acknowledged by Lang himself on at least two occasions with his recognition of the mitigating effect of cultural/historical context on the way ideas, including moral understanding, are formed and acted upon. In his introduction for example, Lang writes,

> The sense of individual agency or identity that is a condition of moral con-
> sciousness cannot be imposed from the outside; still more pertinently, no one

acts or speaks in moral terms as a universal consciousness. If the history of ethics has any single lesson to teach, it is that the status of moral agents is determined by their own places in space and time: they act always, if not only, as individuals and always and only in a context.[6]

And elsewhere, although less willing to attribute the same degree of significance to the idea of historical specificity, Lang notes,

> There is nothing surprising or problematic in the claim that we come to know what a moral principle is—or, on its side, evil principle—by encountering it first in history, by seeing there, close up, its transformations and its consequences. . . . This is not to imply that the act of genocide or the judgement of it is *determined* by cultural norms, but only that such norms influence moral judgement.[7]

The substance of the difficulties of Lang's position can be traced to the content of these passages. On the one hand Lang says that individuals act *only* within a context. That is to say the moral life of individuals derives from the intentions, choices and actions of individuals within concrete situations. An agent's moral consciousness or the ability to comprehend situations with an ethical content is based on the amalgamation of deliberations and judgments accumulated over time and are the direct result of our interactions and experiences with others in the world.

On the other hand in the first passage Lang seems to imply a certain knowledge of the act and idea of genocide, as entailing wrongdoing. My concern here is admittedly subtle and requires careful unpacking. On Lang's account the Nazi genocide against the Jews entailed both 'idea and act of wrongdoing'. In other words, the extermination of the Jews expressed wrongdoing that was inherently wrong. If this is the case then the question that should follow is: What prompts individuals to act in one way rather than another if not the culturally and historically specific contexts within which these acts occur? If the answer is that individuals obtain the moral criteria for their actions from a source that transcends the singularity of the situation then judging the events of the Holocaust could be argued to be no more difficult than imposing straightforward moral 'laws'. If, however, an individual's deliberations, choices and actions derive from the way in which they understand and comprehend their particular situation then understanding the moral dimensions of such actions will also need to attend closely to the particularities of those historical situations. I would suggest that there is much to be gained from combining both answers as it were. In fact, the two answers may be complementary. I believe, however, that the difficulty lies in adequately expressing what that complementarity entails. How context is interpreted here is important. As I have argued throughout this book our moral perspectives emerge, in large part, from our cultural history which in turn provides us with the wherewithal to set a moral course to action.

The point of my elaboration of these distinctions between how we are led to moral actions relates to the importance Lang places on the idea that the Nazi genocide against the Jews represents, in his words, the "'paradigm' of moral enormity".[8] Such an emphasis, though important, can have the effect of obscuring the fact that understanding the moral dimensions of the Holocaust amounts to more than understanding its moral enormity. The moral enormity of the Holocaust, and the events that comprise it, is one facet of the phenomenon. I contend, however, that the Holocaust was also a series of events of staggering moral complexity. This fact ought not be allowed to be bypassed in favour of generalisable judgments that focus on the events of the Holocaust as conforming to some idea of pure evil. In his perceptive work, *Morality After Auschwitz* [9] Peter Haas has also argued against accounts of the Holocaust that classify it as an idealized type of evil. Concerning the claim that the modern world has placed into contention classical cosmological standards of right and wrong, Haas writes:

> To continue to describe the Holocaust and its actors in terms of pure guilt or innocence, then, eliminates the possibility of taking these modern insights into account. Rather, the Holocaust becomes a sort of medieval morality play in which angels and devils do battle. Although emotionally satisfying, such characterizations of the Holocaust seem to me to oversimplify the nature of evil and so block any deeper understanding of what occurred in Europe.[10]

Although this point is not lost on Lang, he, in my view, nevertheless pursues a line of argument that foregrounds enormity at the expense of complexity. This also seems to entail pursuing morally determinate conclusions. For example Lang argues that in the case of the Nazi genocide against the Jews "the agent of the act is voluntarily choosing to do wrong as a matter of principle—what is wrong even by his lights."[11] The difficulty here is that Lang appears not to pay sufficient attention to the possibility that a series of events as morally complex as the Holocaust resists generalisations of this sort. In my view, a claim of this level of generality is extremely difficult to sustain. More importantly, this level of generalisation precludes what at the very least warrants further investigation: namely, that those engaged in, and those who witnessed, the perpetration of the Holocaust, in Haas's words, "knew what was going on, found it to be at least ethically tolerable and consciously acted accordingly."[12] Haas's line of argument seems to be that a more subtle approach to how we understand moral responsibility in the context of the events of the Holocaust is required. Or that the way that we arrive at our sense of what it is to act in an ethically sustainable manner is considerably more complex than straightforward accounts can allow for.

Lang on the other hand, seems to be seeking an account that can be understood in a more morally austere context. To this end, he writes:

> The levels of awareness required to move through the conceptual "moments" of genocide, the kinds of evidence and rationalization required, are such that if, after acknowledging them, we still conclude the Nazis were only doing what they *thought* to be right—with the implication that ignorance may not itself be cul-

pable—we give up all hope of distinguishing morally significant judgement or action from whatever it is that anybody, at any particular moment, *does*.[13]

I believe that Lang's conclusion that we give up our ability to distinguish morally significant judgments, does not necessarily follow from the possibility that perpetrators of the Holocaust believed that what they were doing was morally sanctioned. The possibility that many Europeans, from those at the centre to those on the periphery, involved in the implementation of the Holocaust believed that what they were doing was sustainable within the framework of their moral lives indicates, at the very least the need to probe below straightforward judgments about what occurred during this time. The relationship between culpability and knowledge of right and wrong is rarely going to be as clear cut as supposed by Lang. In some cases ascriptions of guilt with respect to ignorance or an agent's moral beliefs will be more obviously appropriate. However, there will also be cases where it will be less obvious. To illustrate this point we need only consider the instance of allied leaders who, armed with knowledge of the fate of the Jews failed to act to curtail the efforts of those directly involved in the implementation of the genocide of European Jewry. Whilst this example is clearly different from the sort of situation posed by Lang I believe that it conveys the inappropriateness of simplistic delineations on these issues.

Moreover, and as I have argued at length in chapter two, with regard Browning's research of the policemen of Reserve Battalion 101, there really seems to be the need to allow for such exigencies as what J. L. Mackie refers to as the 'circumstances of injustice'. Typically, these involve "situations in which people are led to the extremes of inhumanity by steps each of which seems reasonable or unavoidable."[14]

My more general point here concerns the possibility that many Europeans, at various levels of involvement, believed that the events and actions comprising the Holocaust, were broadly supportable within the prevailing value system and that this suggests a moral topography of exceeding complexity. For example, when I argue that many individuals believed that the policies of denigration, exclusion and deportation introduced over a period of time and which eventually led to the attempted extermination of the Jews were broadly supportable, I use the word 'believed' advisedly, to incorporate a whole range of ways that knowledge of such events as those that constituted the Holocaust might be acquired, internalised and generally made sense of according to the then prevailing social orthodoxy of anti-Semitism.

Aside from the questions surrounding those people explicitly implicated in the mass murder of European Jewry (and even within this category the issues are far from simple) there are many other dimensions entailed in a more nuanced understanding of what happened that Lang's account leaves unexamined. For example there are the individuals of various governments of Europe, other than Germany, who implemented on their own initiative, their own 'solutions' to the 'Jewish problem'. If we accept that some form of intervention was possible, there were arguably also individuals from within Allied nations who, while aware of what was occurring inside the extermination camps, chose not to attempt to stem the program of mass murder. There are individuals within governments who at best remained indifferent to and at worst collaborated with the Nazis' programme of making Europe *judenfrei*. There were large numbers of individuals from every country in Europe who watched with approval the events as they unfolded. And finally there were the millions of people who witnessed or were aware of the deportations, and even the killings of Jews from villages and towns and cities across Europe, but who remained silent out of fear. Individuals in all of these categories chose a particular course of action that implicates them in some sense within the myriad of events culminating in the attempted genocide of European Jewry.

Important to Lang's thesis is the stress he places both on what he construes as a constitutive link between the intentional character of genocide, in terms of both idea and act, and the knowledge on the part of the perpetrators that this intention is endowed with evil. As Lang concludes toward the end of chapter one:

> There is thus substantial evidence, as inferred from the character of genocide in general, and visible in the course of the Nazi genocide against the Jews in particular, of the genocide's intentional character—intentional in respect both to the act of genocide and to the knowledge of its moral enormity.[15]

And elsewhere in a more specific context Lang writes:

> The process of systematic dehumanization requires a conscious affirmation of the wrong involved in it—that is, that someone who is human should be made to seem, to become, and in any event to be treated as less than that . . . here the agent of the act is voluntarily choosing to do wrong as a matter of principle— what is wrong even by *his* lights. This is a large claim to make . . . [but] . . . in the immediate context of what has been said about the occurrence of genocide, the basis for the claim can be seen in stages of deliberation which the act of genocide presupposes and without which neither the idea nor the act embodying the idea is possible. One stage of deliberation is required in order to identify apparent individuals in terms of a generic and collective essence—that is, to "see" individuals not as individuals but as exclusively defined by their membership in a group. A second stage is presupposed in the claim that this generic essence represents an imminent danger, and that it has this character not as it happens, but necessarily: a judgement is made that the essence is intrinsically a menace. A third stage of deliberation is required for the decision that only extermination of the danger, now fixed intrinsically in the *genos,* can be an adequate response to it.[16]

At issue here are Lang's connected claims that firstly, the Nazi extermination of the Jews contained within it various 'stages of deliberation' thereby according it an intrinsically intentional characteristic; and secondly, that the idea and act of genocide also necessarily included knowledge of wrong-doing. Lang also seems to be arguing that the basis for the second claim lies in being able to establish the first claim. My first point is that claims of this order of magnitude are difficult to substantiate. In the context of wider historiographical issues claims of this sort form part of the debate between what has become known within the literature as 'the intentionalists' and 'the functionalists'.[17] Lang's thesis would seem to lean toward the intentionalist interpretation that is that the extermination of the Jews represented the fulfilment of an identifiable and pre-formulated plan. So called functionalists on the other hand, argue that the Holocaust was the result of a process of persecution characterised more by incrementalism, improvisation and changing circumstances. Importantly, in terms of the veracity of Lang's thesis, much of the dispute turns on the ability to demonstrate clear intention or conversely, the absence of a definitive moment in the actualisation of the Final Solution.

My concern with Lang's claim is that he writes, in the first instance, in terms of the intention to exterminate the Jews as deriving from individual acts. This claim is then conflated with an attempt to show intention in the form of an overall plan for the extermination of the Jews. I suspect that it is not legitimate to slide between the two claims in the way that Lang does. There seems to be a difference between attempts to move from demonstrating intention with regard to a particular group of Jews and the claim that there was intention to exterminate Jews as an entire population. In any event Lang sets himself a very difficult task with the more general claim based on the idea of intention in respect to the motives of particular individuals.

Some commentators argue that the primary material required to base 'strong' intentionalist claims, such as represented by Lang's thesis, has not been found. On the question of a premeditated map of the 'Final Solution' Raul Hilberg, in an interview with Claude Lanzmann says:

> Yes, it [the idea of a 'Final Solution'] was new, and I think for this reason one cannot find a specific document, a specific planned outline or blueprint which stated: "Now the Jews will be killed." Everything is left to inference from general words. General words—the very wording "final solution" or "total solution" or "territorial solution" leaves something to the bureaucrat that he must infer. He cannot read that document. One cannot even read Göring's famous letter to Heydrich at the end of July 1941 charging him in two paragraphs to proceed with the "final solution", and examine that document, and consider that everything is clarified. Far from it. It was an authorization to invent. It was an authorization to begin something that was not yet capable of being put into words. I think of it that way.[18]

Although in agreement with Hilberg's claim that there is an element of invention in every step of the 'Final Solution', I argue that serious questions remain as regards both the intentionalist and functionalist interpretations. Nowhere are such issues more evident than in Philippe Burrin's text *Hitler and the Jews: The Genesis of the Holocaust*. In this book, one of the most careful interpretations of the evidence to date, Burrin writes:

Retracing the path to the Final Solution, I would support another explanation in which the two existing approaches are combined. Like the intentionalists, I believe that Hitler harboured the intention of exterminating the Jews; this intention, however, was not absolute, but conditional: it would be carried out only in the event of a well-defined situation, such as the failure of his planned conquests, leaving the way clear to pursue meanwhile another policy. Like the functionalists, on the other hand, I maintain that a combination of circumstances was essential to the fulfilment of his intention, for its translation into action: here the perception of the failure of the Russian campaign and of its strategic consequences played a decisive part.[19]

In this passage Burrin treads a wary path between the intentionalist and functionalist perspectives. A key aspect of Burrin's thesis is the claim that Hitler's 'plan' had been, in the absence of all out war, to divest Europe of its Jewish population. Burrin argues that inasmuch as there was an articulated plan, it was to relocate rather than exterminate European Jewry; and that the shift in policy came only after it became apparent that the war more generally would not run ultimately in Germany's favour. What Burrin presumably means is that were Germany to suffer military/territory losses then relocation of the Jews of Europe would no longer be an option. According to Burrin even after the attack on Russia in June 1941 there is evidence that the 'territorial solution' alluded to in the January 30, 1939 speech to the Reichstag was still under consideration.

The most controversial, though well substantiated element of Burrin's thesis concerns the claim that the exterminations perpetrated by the *Einsatzgruppen* were not in fact part of a general order for the total extermination of the Jews of Europe. Instead Burrin argues that the murders committed by the *Einsatzgruppen* developed in a somewhat ad hoc way and it was only by the autumn of 1941 when the Russian campaign began to slow that the idea for the total extermination of European Jewry became formalised. A fundamental problem for both intentionalist and functionalist accounts of events is the absence of clear, unequivocal and conclusive documentation to support the enshrining of the Final Solution. Burrin's evidence is based on the following: the two known documents to contain references to the 'general' instructions as to the fate of the Jews,[20] testimonial accounts of *Einsatzgruppen* and *Einsatzkommando* leaders and most importantly detailed reports from *Einsatzgruppen* leaders in the period July-September 1941.

It is Burrin's assessment of the *Einsatzgruppen* reports (*Ereignismeldungen UdSSR*) that provides the greatest insights into the problems faced by intentionalist accounts of events. Burrin argues that the reports indicate that after the initial invasion of the Soviet Union there was a step-by-step increase in killings and that the killings were selective in that the victims were mostly men. However, from early to mid-August killings of women and children increase dramatically. Burrin interprets this change as a definitive change in policy. Burrin argues that the period in question represents a change from a policy that is quite selective in its targets to a policy of the general extermination of Jews. Other accounts tend to reinforce this interpretation of events. For example, Browning's study *Ordinary Men,* provides support for Burrin's assessment inasmuch as Browning's research points to orders of the same period given to German Order Police that detail explicitly only the killing of Jewish men.

Other studies however, including Itzhak Arad's account of the extermination of Lithuanian Jews[21] and Richard Breitman's book *The Architect of Genocide,* [22] suggest that notwithstanding the uncertainty that surrounds an exact date, interpretation of the evidence points to a general order for the extermination of Jews having been given prior to the Russian campaign. Saul Friedländer in the introduction to the English translation of Burrin's text *Hitler and the Jews* sums up his reservations concerning Burrin's interpretation when he writes that:

> whatever the overall picture given by the reports about the Einsatzgruppen activities, there is no necessary correlation between this picture and the initial orders given to the killing units. There may have been an initial order for the overall extermination of the Jews on Soviet territory, although for several weeks the killings were directed mostly at men.[23]

While Friedländer's summation shows that the evidence is inconclusive as regards either group of interpretations, it does seem as though Burrin's assessment of the course of events is as plausible as it is cogently argued. The evidence of undisguised and unambiguous 'public' recognition of the fact of the total extermination of the Jews does little to aid the arguments of either intentionalist or functionalist interpretations given that such recorded evidence comes, in a chronological sense, well after the programme of mass murder is implemented. For example on 9 June 1942, on the occasion of Heydrich's state funeral, Himmler makes explicit mention of his intention to his senior staff. Cited in Peter Padfield's book *Himmler Reichsführer-SS,* Himmler is reported to have said:

> the first great task is to overhaul the whole SS and police and to fuse them together. The second task is to fetch in and fuse the Germanic peoples with us. The third task is the settlement and migration of peoples in Europe which we are carrying out. The migration of the Jews will be dealt with for certain within a year: then none will wander again. Because now the slate must be made quite clean.[24]

This passage contains evidence by inference, more than a year prior to the famous Posen speech, of Himmler's intention as regards the extermination of the Jews. There is also evidence of Himmler's 'General Plan East', no copies of which are known to have survived, in which Himmler's intentions were elaborated upon. This evidence, though, comes well after the evolution of the mass shootings of 1941-42 and the introduction of extermination by gassing, and whilst important in its own right, must be placed in the context of the course of events.

At the very least the research of Burrin and others puts the onus on intentionalist accounts such as that of Lang, to provide conclusive documentation to support the claim that the total extermination of the Jews was a part of the policy of the Nazis prior to such a policy being activated by the specific circumstances that eventuated. Though, this may prove to be possible, for example after such time as previously unexamined Soviet archival documentation is adequately assessed, the issue will remain unresolved.

Another concern lies with the second of Lang's inter-related claims that is the connection between the idea/act of genocide and voluntary wrongdoing. The way Lang develops this claim warrants closer consideration. He considers but rejects the idea of a so-called 'utilitarian' justification for the policy of genocide on the basis of the inconsistency with which such a principle might be said to have applied. Lang argues that claims by the Nazis that the Jews represented a threat to the wider body of the community as a whole, insofar as they had any coherency, were unable to be adhered to with any degree of consistency. The utilisation of medical and biological metaphors by Nazi ideologues is cited by Lang as an example of the inapplicability of principles of utilitarianism by the Nazis.[25] Lang correctly, in my view, argues that the Nazis' policy of genocide conflicted on a number of significant occasions with the requirements of self-preservation, with the implication that the value of self-preservation contained within the metaphors, and the basis of the utilitarian rationale, was not the dominant motivating factor. Lang is then led to the more general conclusion that "the Nazis were willing to increase the risk that they would lose the wider war with whatever consequences this would have for their survival individually or as a nation—in order to wage their war against the Jews."[26]

According to Lang nowhere are the contradictions between the programme to exterminate the Jews and the value of self-preservation more evident than between the war against the allies and the war against the Jews. Lang's aim is to use this contradiction as an example of the problem of utilitarian justifications as an explanation for the genocide. What should be borne in mind though, is that the two so-called wars were in some significant ways quite distinct from one another and therefore, not surprisingly, likely to come into conflict in respect to the problem of the increasingly scarce resources cited by Lang. Indeed it is hardly surprising that such conflicts over resources (the example Lang cites concerns the use of railroad transport) occurred not infrequently even within competing sections of the military, especially as these resources became increasingly scarce. It is therefore the case that the significance of Lang's argument on this question conveys more of a sense of the overall importance that was attached to the "Jewish Question" as a fundamental component of Nazi ideology than it does about the moral dimensions of the Holocaust itself. It could even be argued that Lang's account of the connection between the conflicts that arose between the war against the Jews and the wider war against the Allied forces reveals more about the logistics of distributing scarce resources (In this case railroad transport) in wartime than it does about the moral enormity of the Holocaust.

An even more important problem however, is the appropriateness of the primary evidence Lang provides in support of his thesis concerning voluntary wrong-doing. On the basis of the primary documentation provided by Lang, the conclusions that are able to be drawn are at best ambiguous. A case in point is Lang's citation of part of Heinrich Himmler's June 10, 1943 address to SS officers and high party officials at Poznan in Poland in which Himmler stated that:

> The hard decision had to be made that this people should be caused to disappear from the earth. . . . Perhaps, at a much later time, we can consider whether we can say something more about this to the German people. I myself believe that it is better for us—us together—to have borne this for our people, that we have taken the responsibility for it on ourselves (the responsibility for an act, not just an idea), and that we should now take this secret with us into the grave.[27]

Although Lang only refers briefly to this quotation in the context of the issue of secrecy his primary intention is to draw attention to Himmler's alleged sense of moral responsibility. Though secrecy is an important issue here I want to argue that it is not obvious, even in this explicit statement from Himmler, that an understanding of wrong-doing is present. In order to illustrate this point I would like to quote, at length, another address by Himmler to senior SS officers in Poznan on October 4, 1943. This passage is of interest because of its explicit elaboration of a claim of moral correctness regarding the Final Solution. Himmler stated:

> I also want to speak to you here, in complete frankness, of a really grave chapter. Amongst ourselves, for once, it shall be said quite openly, but all the same we shall never speak about it in public. . . . I am referring here to the evacuation of the Jews, the extermination of the Jewish people. This is one of the things that are easily said: "The Jewish people are going to be exterminated," that's what every Party member says, "sure, it's in our program, elimination of the Jews, extermination—it'll be done." And then they all come along, the 80 million worthy Germans, and each one has his one decent Jew. Of course, the others are swine, but this one, he is a first—rate Jew. Of all those who talk like that, not one has seen it happen, not one has had to go through with it. Most of you men know what it is like to see 100 corpses side by side, or 500 or 1,000. To have stood fast through this and—except for cases of human weakness—to have stayed decent that has made us hard. This is an unwritten and never-to-be-written page of glory in our history, for we know how difficult it would be to-day—under bombing raids and the hardships and deprivations of war—if we were still to have the Jews in every city as secret saboteurs, agitators, and inciters. If the Jews were still lodged in the body of the German nation, we would probably by now have reached the stage of 1916-17. The wealth they possessed we took from them. I gave a strict order, which has been carried out by SS *Obergruppenführer* Pohl that this wealth will of course be turned over to the Reich in its entirety. We have taken none of it for ourselves. Individuals who have erred will be punished in accordance with the order given by me at the start, threatening that anyone who takes as much as a single Mark of this money

is a dead man. A number of SS men—there are not very many—committed this offence, and they shall die. There will be no mercy.

We had the moral right, we had the duty towards our people, to destroy this people that wanted to destroy us. But we do not have the right to enrich ourselves by so much as a fur, as a watch, by one Mark or a cigarette or anything else. We do not want, in the end, because we destroyed a bacillus, to be infected by this bacillus and to die. I will never stand by and watch while even a small rotten spot develops or takes hold. Wherever it may form we will together burn it away. All in all, however, we can say that we have carried out this most difficult of tasks in a spirit of love for our people. And we have suffered no harm to our inner being, our soul, our character.[28]

In this passage, as in the previous example, there is a sense of moral responsibility but here it seems to be spelled out along the lines of a sort of moral fortitude. Central to Himmler's speech is his use of the terminology of 'right' and 'duty'. In fact Himmler goes to some lengths to point out that the moral universe as perceived by Nazi ideology would be adhered to and in strict accordance with the letter of the law as he perceives it. At the very least the matter of Himmler's alleged knowledge of wrong-doing needs to be questioned. Whether or not Himmler's claim of 'frankness' may be taken at face value, in the context of when and where this speech was delivered it must be a very real possibility that the words that were spoken were believed by both Himmler and the members of his audience.

In another section of the same speech cited by Lang, Himmler goes so far as to present the extermination of the Jews as a moral dilemma of sorts. Also cited in Roger Griffin's book *Fascism*, [29] Himmler writes:

Thus the difficult decision had to be taken to make this people disappear from the earth. For the organisation that had to carry out this task it was the most difficult one we had ever had. It has been carried out—I believe I can say this—danger that it might was a real one. The path between the two possibilities of either being too cruel and heartless and losing respect for human life, or too soft and so suffering distress to the point of a nervous breakdown—the strait between this Scilla and Charybdis is narrow indeed.[30]

In this passage Himmler's reference to the most difficult task of his organisation, delusory as it may now seem, seems to suggest a reference to what he understands as a genuine moral problem. Yet according to the way Himmler has internalised the situation he implies that the task was carried out admirably, without loss of humanity on the part those who perpetrated the crimes in question.

The claim that Himmler believed that he personally was charged, with the express sanction of the Führer (and thus by default of the German people), with the morally justifiable 'mission' to exterminate the Jews also needs to be considered in the context of when it was current. Moreover, and as a necessary adjunct to this first claim, Himmler also believed that this crusade required a moral framework able to accommodate the sorts of agendas intended by those involved in the proposed mass murder of the Jews. These matters and the important question of secrecy are addressed in a speech Himmler gave to a gathering of generals and Führer headquarters staff in early May 1944. Cited in Padfield's book *Himmler Reichsführer-SS*, Himmler is reported as having said:

> The Jewish question in Germany and the occupied countries has been solved. It has been solved in accordance with the struggle for survival of our *Volk* , in which the survival of our blood was at stake, without compromise. I tell you that as comrades. We are all soldiers, whatever uniform we wear. You might like to sympathise with me and imagine how hard it was to fulfil this soldierly order that was given me which I followed and carried through out of obedience and the most complete conviction. If you say, 'The men—that we understand—but not the children,' then may I draw your attention to my earlier remarks. In this showdown with Asia we must accustom ourselves to the ground rules and consign to oblivion the morals of past Europeans' wars which are dear and much closer to us. We are, in my opinion, even as Germans with all our deep heartfelt good-natured feeling, not justified in allowing the hate-filled avengers so that our children and grandchildren have to settle with them because we, the fathers or grandfathers, were too weak and too cowardly and left the children for them.[31]

There are a number of differing interpretations that can be put on this passage. I argue that in the midst of a wider audience Himmler makes the claim that, what he refers to as the moral 'ground rules', as regards the question of the extermination of the Jews, are different from those that pertained in previous times. Himmler seems to be arguing for a new moral understanding of the treatment of the Jews as a means of rationalising this treatment in the eyes of an audience that extends beyond the immediate circle of party faithful. This is important because it implies that Himmler himself believes in what he is saying and is attempting to convince his audience of his 'duty' as he sees it. I make this claim somewhat tentatively in view of the fact that, on the available evidence, it is difficult to interpret with any clarity what Himmler believed.

There is also the matter of secrecy to be raised here. Padfield makes the point that in this speech and others later the same month and in the months following, Himmler continues to spell out what has been achieved by way of a 'Final Solution' to audiences that fall outside the Party circles. Padfield suggests that Himmler's revelations to the wider audience may well have been due to a number of reasons including the aim of drawing this audience into complicity, a booster for morale or a genuine expression of the pride at having accomplished the extermination of a greater part of European Jewry in the face of considerable moral and practical difficulties. The point here though is that less than a year earlier Himmler had warned the Posen audience that the fact of the extermination was a secret that needed to be taken with them to the grave. Yet this series of revelations through 1944 diminished the seriousness with which Himmler regarded the need for secrecy. This is also the case as regards the need to maintain a distance between the fact of the extermination and the order for the extermination as having originated from the Führer. In the passage above the phrase 'this soldierly order that was given me' strongly implicates Hitler as the source of the order to exterminate the Jews.

In his book *Memory, History, and the Extermination of the Jews of Europe* [32] Saul Friedlander examines aspects of Himmler's notorious 1943 Posen speech. Looking to explain in his words, "the 'why' and not the 'how' of the 'Final Solution'", Friedlander refers to the extreme 'dissonance' evident between the concept of the genocide of the Jews and the idea that this could be achieved in a morally satisfactorily way. Of importance here, however, is the fact that Himmler's own understanding of the moral enormity of his words have not escaped him. Hence the key sentence: "This is an unwritten and never to be written page of glory in our history."[33] As Friedlander points out, this sentence indicates Himmler's awareness that future generations would never be able to understand. Friedlander argues that this sentence together with Himmler's vow of secrecy point to doubts Himmler himself might have had. Friedlander's position does seem to lend support to the idea that as moral enormity escalates so, too, does the requirement for censorship of that which has been morally transgressed.

There is further evidence problematising Lang's arguments concerning the idea that act and idea in the perpetration of the Holocaust were inherently bound up with a knowledge of voluntary wrong-doing and the issue of secrecy. I justify the need for more detailed attention to these problems here because of the importance they hold for my thesis. Due to the need to demonstrate the controversial and conflicted nature of the above problems I will consider the evidence of some lengthy textual excerpts. Examples of such evidence can be found in a volume comprising entirely of primary research titled *"The Good Old Days": The Holocaust as Seen by Its Perpetrators and Bystanders.* [34] In the editorial preface Klee, Dressen and Riess write that among the powerful documents are:

> contemporary texts (diaries, letters and reports) and the minutes of interrogations in which the murderers, accomplices and onlookers give an unembellished account to their interrogators of how the mass murder of the Jews was organised and carried out to the bitter end.[35]

The book also contains a large number of photographs conveying interesting images. These pictures do not portray fanatics foaming at the mouth as they commit murder but rather perpetrators (spurred on by spectators) performing their 'work' and who afterwards, exhausted but satisfied, enjoyed a few beers in their spare time[36]. The pictures show people whose appearance does not betray a knowledge of active participation in the mechanics of unjustified murder, but rather as ready and willing operators of the machinery of the Holocaust. The frankness of the material seems to also indicate with some clarity the extent to which the National Socialist 'Weltanschauung' (world-view) was rooted in the German popular consciousness, part of the thinking of the time, and regarded as quite natural by large sections of the population.

In other words, the editors of this collection of primary material are claiming that their evidence supports what seems to be true of any social system and not just the Nazi regime: that is, that the system of values that drove the Holocaust influenced behaviour in such a way that the behaviour could be judged appropriate for those for whom it was intended. The Nazi ethic was considered by its adherents as a distinct and ethically sustainable system for judging right and wrong behaviour. Put another way, communities that function with any degree of social cohesion must possess some form of an ethic as a function of that cohesion. In conjunction with this it is reasonable to suggest that ethical systems, as a component of their role, channel behaviour. To recapitulate it seems implausible to suppose that those who perpetrated and those who silently witnessed the Holocaust were suddenly unable to distinguish between what they believed to be right and wrong. This is not to suggest that there were not those who thought that what they were doing was wrong. What I am claiming, though, is that it was at least a possibility that the effect of the policies of the Nazi regime was to reinforce the degree to which entire systems for discriminating between ethical and unethical behaviour were able to be absolutely impoverished for the express purpose of the extermination of European Jewry. And, if what I argue is plausible then it is also possible that the Holocaust represents a shocking example of how a particular way of viewing the world (that of the Nazis) was able to modify the attitudes and behaviour of large segments of populations in the systematic dehumanization and murder of large sections of their own populations as a matter of ethical routine. In short, what was achieved was the degradation, through propagandisation, of moral life.

Whilst I believe that there is some merit to the above argument I also think that it ought not stand without qualification. The evidence of Klee, Dressen and Riess presents a day to day routine of the perpetrators that seems bereft of moral anxiety. Appearances, of course, can be deceptive. It seems counter-intuitive to believe that the actions of those directly involved in the implementation of the 'Final Solution' did not generate moral conflict of one sort or another. And even more difficult to sustain is the claim that National Socialist ideology was readily accepted by 'all sections of the population'. Regarding the more modest claim that the perpetrators of the Holocaust regarded their 'work' as at least ethical sustainable, the evidence is far from conclusive. Klee, Dressen and Riess themselves cite many instances in the diaries, reports and testimonies of those charged with the implementation of the 'Final Solution', of the severe psychological effects of mass murder. And in the now infamous October 4, 1943 speech in Posen, Himmler himself acknowledges the moral/psychological costs that inhere in such situations. Himmler is also reported to have been physically revolted by the sights he witnessed on one of his inspections of SS operations in Minsk. As recalled by SS General Karl Wolff, Himmler's liaison officer at Hitler's headquarters:

An open grave had been dug and they had to jump into this and lie face downwards. . . . And Himmler had never seen dead people before and in his curiosity he stood right up at the edge of this open grave. . . . While he was looking in, Himmler had the deserved bad luck that from one or other of the people who had been shot in the head he got a splash of brains on his coat, and I think it also splashed into his face, and he went very green and pale; he wasn't actually sick, but he was heaving and turned round and swayed and then I had to jump forward and hold him steady and then I led him away from the grave.[37]

The effects upon the moral character of those who had to carry out and/or witness such 'work' would likely have been profound. What is even more certain is that such trauma was far from isolated. As for Klee, Dressen and Riess's claim that the German population at large endorsed the Nazis' eventual intention to murder all the Jews of Europe it is unlikely such a proposition would be able to be substantiated even if true. Further it does not follow that the beliefs of the population in general can be adduced from the beliefs of one section of the population, however representative that sample of the population may be. Finally, and to reiterate the point of this extended discussion of aspects of Lang's thesis, the evidence of Klee, Dressen and Riess does, in my view, dilute the validity of Lang's overly generalised claim that the events of the Holocaust were necessarily bound up with a knowledge of wrong-doing.

Perhaps the single most significant question raised by Lang is the question of the secrecy cloaking the 'Final Solution'. In this matter Lang makes the claim that secrecy, in regard to the "Final Solution", was structurally linked "to an intention to do evil."[38] The problem here, though, is the difficulty of explaining conflicting evidence. As Lang himself is prepared to recognise, "There is no means, it seems clear, of proving conclusively that the phenomenon of concealment on the scale that it was practiced by the Nazis is a reflection of guilt rather than a calculation of prudence."[39] Nevertheless it is true that the question of secrecy remains an important issue, and alongside such attendant questions as the evidence of the psychiatric care required by SS and other personnel involved directly in the mass murder of the Jews, it represents the single most persuasive component in Lang's argument that the Holocaust represents the paradigm case of evil intention.

Opinion on the issue of secrecy remains divided. Reinforcing Lang's thesis Yitzhak Arad has argued that:

> The orders for the total destruction of the Jews were delivered verbally and were regarded as top secret. Evidence to this effect was given by leaders of *Einsatzgruupen* (A. Ohlendorf and others) at their trials after the war.[40]

Some surviving documentation clearly supports this claim. In Heydrich's instructions on policy and the operations concerning the Jews in the occupied territories, dated 21/9/1939 he writes:

> I refer to the conference held in Berlin today, and again point out that the *planned total measures* (i.e., the final aim-*Endziel*) are to be kept *strictly se-*

cret.[41]

There is much primary evidence, however, showing that the issue of secrecy in regard to the 'Final Solution' remains a contentious one. In many instances, mass murder was carried out in full public view, over long periods and in a manner that Klee, Dressen and Riess argue "can only be described as 'execution tourism'."[42] This last claim is well supported by numerous eye witness extracts. These extracts also attest to the moral enormity of the events in question and as such warrant extended and detailed inclusion. I want to emphasise that these extracts do not completely discredit the claim to secrecy but they do, in my view, lessen the significance of the issue of secrecy as it relates to Lang's claim that the genocide of the Jews entailed generalisable and intentional wrong-doing.

In the first extract reported in 1941 in the town of Kovno, Lithuania an Adjutant of the rank of Colonel reported:

> Before the start of the Russian campaign, between 21 June and 1 July 1941, the staff of Army Group North under the command of Field Marshal Ritter von Leeb was based at 'Waldfrieden', a health resort some 10 km from Insterburg. As Adjutant (11a) to this staff I received orders to travel to 16th Army HQ, which was stationed in Kovno, and arrange quarters for the staff of the army group liaising with them. I arrived on the morning of 27 June. While I was travelling through the town I went past a petrol station that was surrounded by a dense group of people. There was a large number of women in the crowd and they had lifted up their children or stood them on chairs or boxes so that they could see better. At first I thought this must be a victory celebration or some type of sporting event because of the cheering, clapping and laughter that kept breaking out. However, when I inquired what was happening I was told that the 'Death-dealer of Kovno' was at work and that this was where collaborators and traitors were finally meted out their rightful punishment! When I stepped closer, however, I became witness to probably the most frightful event that I had seen during the course of two world wars. On the concrete forecourt of the petrol station a blond man of medium height, aged about twenty five, stood leaning on a wooden club, resting. The club was as thick as his arm and came up to his chest. At his feet lay about fifteen to twenty dead or dying people. Water flowed continuously from a hose washing blood away into the drainage gully. Just a few steps behind this man some twenty men, guarded by armed civilians, stood waiting for their cruel execution in silent submission. In response to a cursory wave the next man stepped forward silently and was then beaten to death with the wooden club in the most bestial manner, each blow accompanied by enthusiastic shouts from the audience.[43]

On 7 August 1941 in Zhitomir, Ukraine a truck-driver from Technical Battalion 6 reported:

> One day a Wehrmacht vehicle (police vehicle?) drove through Zhitomir with a megaphone. We had been lodged in the electrical plant where we had been working. Over the loudspeaker we were informed in German and Russian

(Ukrainian) that at a certain time that day Jews would be shot in the market-place or something to that effect. As I had that particular day off I went at that appointed time to the market-place. I was alone. Upon arriving there I saw fifty to sixty Jews (men, women and children) had assembled there and were being held under SS guard. There were about eight guards. Round and about stood about 150 civilians watching. There were also, of course, members of the Wehrmacht among the onlookers. The Jews sat on the ground. I had made my way through the spectators and had stopped about two meters from the Jews. I can therefore say with certainty that they were all wearing civilian dress and could therefore not have been prisoners of war. The guards asked the people standing around if they had any scores to settle. Thereupon more and more Ukrainians spoke up and accused one or other of the Jews of some misdemeanour. These Jews were then beaten and kicked and ill-treated where they were, mostly be Ukrainians. This went on for about forty-five minutes. Then three [two-Ed.] from this group were taken out and executed on a gallows. The wooden structure was ready and waiting. There were three nooses hanging from it. The three delinquents had to climb on a truck. After the nooses had been put around the necks of these males the truck drove away. That is how the execution was carried out. This part was also carried out by SS people. Finally all of the Jews assembled there had to get onto the truck. They stood herded tightly together. Then an announcement came over the loudspeaker that we should all follow the lorry to the shooting. This announcement was directed toward the spectators. [44]

On 3 January 1942 Major Rösler reported:

At the end of July 1941 Infantry Regiment 528 was on its way to Zhitomir from the West, where it was to move to resting quarters. At that time I was regimental commander. On the afternoon of the day we arrived I was taking up my staff quarters with my staff when we heard rifle salvoes at regular intervals, followed after some time by pistol fire. The shots were not coming from far away. I decided to go and look into this matter and so together with the Adjutant and the Ordonnanoffizier . . . set off in the direction of the rifle fire to find out what was happening. We soon realized that a cruel spectacle was taking place out there for after a while we saw numerous soldiers and civilians pouring onto an embankment in front of us, behind which, as we were informed, executions were being carried out at regular intervals. . . . When we finally climbed onto the embankment we were completely unprepared for what we saw. . . . In the earth was a pit about seven to eight meters long and perhaps four meters wide. . . . The pit itself was filled with innumerable human bodies of all types, both female and male. . . . Behind the piles of dug earth from it stood a squad of police under the command of a police officer. There were traces of blood on their uniforms. In a wide circle around the pit stood scores of soldiers from the troop detachments stationed there, some of them in bathing trunks, watching the proceedings. There were also an equal number of civilians, including women and children.[45]

These examples indicate that during this phase of the 'Final Solution' at least, (the occurrence of mass shootings in the immediate aftermath of the invasion of the Soviet Union) secrecy was clearly not an issue, or indeed possible in the eyes of the perpetrators.

Elsewhere, and as regards knowledge of the purpose of such camps as Auschwitz, Belzec, Sobibor and Treblinka, the evidence shows that people who lived in the immediate vicinity were well aware of what was happening. In the interview with the Pole named Borowi cited earlier in chapter four, the interpreter reports that:

> He was born here in 1923, and has been here ever since.
> *He lived at this very spot?*
> Right here.
> *Then he had a front row seat for what happened?*
> Naturally. You could go up close or watch from a distance. They had land on the far side of the station. To work it, he had to cross the track, so he could see everything.
> *Does he remember the first convoy of Jews from Warsaw on July 22, 1942?*
> He recalls the first convoy very well, and when all those Jews were brought here, people wondered, "What's to be done with them?" Clearly, they'd be killed, but no one yet knew how. When people began to understand what was happening, they were appalled, and they commented privately that since the world began, no one had ever murdered so many people that way.
> *While all this was happening before their eyes, normal life went on? They worked their fields?*
> Certainly they worked, but not as willingly as usual. They had to work, but when they saw all this, they thought: "Our house may be surrounded. We may be arrested too!".
> *Were they afraid for the Jews too?*
> Well, he says, it's this way: if I cut my finger, it doesn't hurt him. They knew about the Jews: the convoys came in here, and then went to the camp, and the people vanished.[46]

Another unidentified man from present-day Treblinka aided by an interpreter reported that:

> He had a field under a hundred yards from the camp. He also worked during the German occupation.
> *He worked his field?*
> Yes. He saw how they were asphyxiated; he heard them scream; he saw that. There's a small hill; he could see quite a bit.[47]

These two examples show that the overall question of secrecy was more complicated than a generalised connection between an alleged knowledge of voluntary wrong-doing and the requirement to keep this knowledge secret. Rather the evidence indicates that many chapters of the Holocaust were in fact offered up for those present to bear witness and in some instances to participate as willing spectators.

Sereny, in *Albert Speer: His Battle With Truth,*[48] demonstrates the need to distinguish carefully between differing categories of knowing. She argues that knowledge of the gassings was not, at the time of its occurrence, widespread. Sereny does, however, distinguish knowledge of the gassings with the knowledge of the mass shootings that had followed the early advances into the Soviet territories. The mass shootings, she claims, were hardly a secret, especially since many thousands of ordinary German soldiers and officers had participated in the murders and many more civilians had witnessed them. As for Sereny's more specific account of Albert Speer's knowledge of events she writes:

> The obsession of Speer's life after Nuremberg . . . was Hitler's murder of the Jews. The ambivalence, however, was that while he sincerely grasped every opportunity to reiterate his sorrow and his pain at having been—the automatic formula he used—"a part of a government that committed such crimes", he was totally incapable of saying that he had known about them at the time.[49]

On Sereny's account, and on the basis of the evidence she introduces, it is almost certain that Speer had at the time been aware of the mass shootings but possibly not of the gassings. On the question of Speer's knowledge of an intention to exterminate the Jews as a matter of Nazi policy, it has been substantiated that Speer was present at the infamous conference at Posen on October 4, 1943. And whether or not Speer was actually present at Himmler's evening speech of the same day in which official intentions were spelt out, several of Speer's close colleagues were present. Speer himself maintained in private conversations with Sereny that he could not recall the exact occasion of Himmler's speech. What seems more certain, though, is that given the established extent of knowledge of the genocide of the Jews of a number of Speer's friends and colleagues it is highly improbable that Speer was not aware, at the very least in a generalizable sense, of what was happening to the Jews.

Sereny also demonstrates that secrecy regarding the extermination of the Jews continued, through to the end of the war, to be a matter of importance in official references to the subject. Citing correspondence between top SS officials Sereny makes it clear that for official purposes the need for secrecy was paramount. Thus in a letter to Ernst Kaltenbrunner, Heydrich's successor as chief of Security Police and SD, and written on 9 April 1943, Sereny cites Himmler who writes:

> I have received the Inspector of Statistics' report on the Final Solution of the Jewish Question. I consider this report well executed for purposes of camouflage and potentially useful for later times. For the moment, it can neither be published nor can anyone [outside the restricted circle] be allowed sight of it.[50]

As Sereny correctly points out, Himmler's reference to "for purposes of camouflage" can only indicate the need to maintain an official secrecy. The question of the use and proliferation of euphemistic terminology by the Nazis is also clear evidence of the importance of secrecy on these matters. Abraham J. Edelheit and

Hershel Edelheit in their book *History of the Holocaust* [51] describe how Nazi terms such as *Sonderzüge* (Special trains), *Übersiedlung* (Resettlement) and *Umgelegt* (Liquidated) were primarily used to describe nothing other than the mass murder of Europe's Jewry. Evidence such as the employment of euphemisms is unequivocal proof of the desire on the part of the Nazis to shroud their true intentions in secrecy. I want to argue that this evidence and Sereny's claims of secrecy need to be tempered by Himmler's dissemination of information of the fact of extermination to audiences other than those within the core of the Nazi Party hierarchy. The point is that the evidence is ambiguous regarding the matter of secrecy.

As significant as all of these questions of secrecy undoubtedly are it is also important to note that issues that test knowledge of Holocaust events are not restricted to matters surrounding the mass shootings or gassings of Jews. Whilst these questions remain crucial to being able to distinguish between criminal and lesser forms of responsibility, as is the case in respect to individuals such as Albert Speer, they do not constitute anywhere near the full spectrum of possibilities of knowledge of 'events' within a broader understanding of the moral dimensions of the Holocaust. For example, a strong case exists to extend moral responsibility to include the more widely known, and in many instances condoned, day by day, year by year alienation, brutalisation and ghettoisation of European Jewry. With regard to this more generalisable sense of moral responsibility encompassing a whole range of anti-semitic measures employed by governments throughout Europe, including the dissemination of racist propaganda, restrictions on the ownership of property, economic and legal segregation and eventual deportation and ghettoisation, there is and could never be any real question of maintaining secrecy.

Some commentators argue that a generalisable and tacit consensus existed with respect to not only less extreme manifestations of anti-Semitism but also toward the eventual implementation of the policy of mass murder. Commensurate with this line of argument Padfield writes:

> The Himmler-Heydrich solutions to the 'population problem' in the occupied areas and the 'biological' problem of Jews and gypsies were undoubtedly radical, but they were agreed by virtually everyone who counted in the top leadership of the Party and the doctors, lawyers, academics and industrialists and managers who served the Party and the SS. They [also] received assent in a significant proportion of those who did not belong to either. [52]

Admittedly, Padfield only cites examples of 'consensus' from the military leadership as evidence of a wider audience acceptance of the Nazi 'logic' that led to the 'Final Solution'. The point is, however, that commitment to the idea of the liquidation of every Jew within the reach of an expanding Reich was tolerable to many more than an inner circle of fanatics.

A detailed insight into more formal concerns internal to the organisation of the SS over the issue of secrecy and their understanding of the distinction between morally acceptable and morally unacceptable behaviour is contained in the volume of documents edited by Klee, Dressen and Riess. On 24 May 1943 a secret verdict of the SS and Police Supreme Court in Munich concerning the case of SS Untersturmführer, Max Taubner, in which the said person was accused of executing Jews without authority and in a manner unbecoming of an SS officer, photographing the executions, having the film developed without discretion in photographic shops in Germany and distributing them among his wife and friends, included the following deliberations:

> The accused shall not be punished because of the actions against the Jews as such. The Jews have to be exterminated and none of the Jews that were killed is any great loss. Although the accused should have recognized that the extermination of the Jews was the duty of Kommandos which have been set up especially for this purpose, he should be excused for considering himself to have the authority to take part in the extermination of Jewry himself. Real hatred of the Jews was the driving motivation for the accused. In the process he let himself be drawn into committing cruel actions in Alexandriya which are unworthy of a German man and an SS officer. These excesses cannot be justified, either, as the accused would like to, as retaliation for the pain that the Jews have caused the German people. It is not the German way to apply Bolshevik methods during the necessary extermination of the worst enemy of our people. In so doing the conduct of the accused gives rise to considerable concern. The accused allowed his men to act with such vicious brutality that they conducted themselves under his command like a savage horde. The accused jeopardized the discipline of his men. It is hard to conceive of anything worse than this. Although the accused may have otherwise have taken care of his men, by his conduct however he neglected his supervisory duty which, in the eyes of the SS, also means not allowing his men to become psychologically depraved. The accused is therefore to be punished under section 147 of the MStGB [Militärstrafgesetzbuch: Military Penal Code]. Since however the provisions of this punishment only provide for imprisonment or detention of up to fifteen years, it is recommended that section 5a of the Special War Punishment Statutory Order be applied, since such a deterioration of discipline requires a severe sentence. . . . By taking photographs of the incidents or having photographs taken, by having these developed in photographic shops and showing them to his wife and friends, the accused is guilty of disobedience. Such pictures could pose the gravest risks to the security of the Reich if they fell into the wrong hands. It would be extremely easy for them to be leaked out of Southern Germany to Switzerland and used for enemy propaganda. The accused was also aware of this considerable danger. His disobedience is therefore to be viewed as a particularly serious case. By contrast the SS and Police Supreme Court does not consider that this conduct constitutes a deliberate undermining of Germany's military power. It is convinced that the accused never even entertained the thought that the showing of such pictures to people of weak dispositions could undermine the fighting spirit of the German people, and thus he did not take such a possibility into consideration. For this crime the accused is to be punished under section 92 of the MStGB. . . . The SS and Police Supreme Court has sentenced the accused to a total of ten years imprisonment. The accused has been expelled from the SS and

declared unfit for service. The conduct of the accused is unworthy of an hon-
ourable and decent German man. For this he has been given under section 32 of
the RStGB the additional sentence of ten years' deprivation of his civil rights.[53]

There are number of questions at issue in this passage. First, in the eyes of the
SS court, anti-Semitism as a system of belief is viewed, in this case, as a justifiable reason to murder Jews without prior military authority. In other words, although the accused acted without authority in the murder of Jews it was judged
by the court that he had acted with sufficient reason. If it had been the case that
the accused had acted on the basis of reasons not recognised by the state the outcome on this point of law may have been different. That is to say, the outcome
of this court's deliberations is tantamount to an official recognition of state sanctioned anti-Semitism. The real problem it seems was not the killing of Jews
without authority but the apparently debased manner in which these people were
murdered. The SS court had found it morally unacceptable that an SS officer had
killed in this depraved way. It appears that what was ethically abhorrent was not
the killing of innocent people for no other reason than the fact that they were
Jewish but rather that the way in which the killing was undertaken placed into
risk the overall discipline of the men under his command. In the eyes of the SS
court the accused had not behaved in accordance with the code of conduct of an
SS officer. Paramount in this regard was the concern over the perceived deterioration of military discipline and the inappropriateness of the behaviour of the accused in his role as an SS officer. The murder of Jews is deemed by the court as
ethically acceptable and even in the right circumstances, correct behaviour.

Second there is the question of secrecy in the judgment of the SS court. The
court is obviously concerned with the possibility of photographic evidence
reaching the 'outside' world. One possible reading of this is that the 'outside'
would find these images morally unacceptable. It is difficult, however, to conclude this with any real certainty from the evidence of the court's deliberations.
It is just as likely for example that the court was concerned about this potential
leak for reasons similar to those they cite concerning the possible effect the photographs would have on the wider German population. In other words, the court
might have been concerned that the leaking of such images to a wider audience
'of weak disposition', not just a German audience but any audience possessing a
'weak disposition', would weaken the general resolve necessary for the 'work'
of the extermination of the Jews. In other words, one possibility is that the SS
court believed its own ethic sanctioning and thereby legitimating the 'Final Solution'. A noteworthy postscript to this example is the fact that Himmler personally interceded in this case to exonerate the actions of the accused and have the
case dismissed and the accused pardoned.

To recapitulate, I claim that whilst the question of secrecy as regards various aspects of the Holocaust is of central importance, the evidence is anything
but straightforward. There is some evidence indicating that secrecy was linked to
a knowledge of wrong-doing. The efforts of those responsible for the operations

of the camps to conceal their existence is testimony enough to the attempt to maintain secrecy. As to the question of the knowledge of wrong-doing itself, Browning's research has demonstrated with some certainty that at the level of individual moral consciousness there was an awareness that the actions being performed conflicted violently with what individual moral agents believed to be ethically sustainable. The wider point here, though, is that the evidence is variable at best and quite ambiguous at worst. The result of this variation and ambiguity is an overall picture of exceeding complexity. The sheer numbers of those involved victims, perpetrators and bystanders, coupled with the vast organisation and machinery required, mitigated against the possibility of such large numbers of people being murdered in an environment of secrecy. In addition to this there is also significant evidence testifying not only to the lack of any pretence to secrecy but also to the wide knowledge of the occurrence of the Holocaust as it happened.

Finally, the Holocaust was, as Lang recognises, a complex of events of overwhelming moral enormity. However, this aspect of the Holocaust must not be allowed to outweigh the evidence demonstrating a moral terrain of exceeding complexity. The questions that surround issues of individual intentional wrongdoing, generalised intentions to exterminate the Jews as a people and questions of secrecy as they relate to a wide variety of people involved all point to a complex moral analysis.

Midgley, in her book *Wickedness,* discusses the view that wrongdoers possess an alternative morality of their own. Midgley goes on to suggest that the possibility of alternate moral universes has led:

> people to suppose that (for instance) the Nazis must have been original reasoners, with an independent, consistent and well-thought-out ethical theory—a view that their careers and writings do not support at all.[54]

Midgley goes on to claim, with regard to the absence of an ethical defence at the Nuremburg trials, that "it was also because there was not really much coherent ideology that could be defended."[55] I think that Midgley commits an error in dismissing too readily important components of the thesis that the Nazis possessed a coherent yet different ethical worldview. It needs to be pointed out that this thesis, that the Nazis possessed an alternative ethic, is not the same as arguing that the possession of an alternative morality was or could be consistently adhered to, although even this might be able to be successfully argued in respect to the Nazis' policy on anti-Semitism. Moreover, Midgley's example of the behaviour of the chief defendants at the Nuremburg trials is problematic inasmuch as it is hardly surprising that in this situation the individuals in question would have been unlikely to defend an ideology in the event that such a defence would be tantamount to an admission of guilt. The thesis that the Nazis believed that what they were doing constituted an ethic, in any substantive sense of the word, may well be problematic but it is all the same a thesis of sufficient complexity as to be unable to be dismissed out of hand. One commentator to take seriously the idea that the Nazis possessed what could be considered an ethic is Haas. In his challenging book *Morality After Auschwitz: The Radical Challenge of the Nazi Ethic*. Haas advances the thesis that:

> any formal system that enables evaluations . . . is an ethic, no matter what its particular judgments or contents might be. That is why I am able to call the Nazi standard of right or wrong an ethic—without thereby claiming that it was proper or moral.[56]

Haas develops the claim that a Nazi ethic existed in the sense that National Socialism was able to establish and sustain a scheme of behaviour deemed by a large social group to constitute tolerable or even correct behaviour. Haas writes:

> The assumption made in this study is that the Holocaust as a sustained way of acting in Europe was possible because a new ethic was in place that did not define the arrest and deportation of Jews as wrong.[57]

These are substantial claims and it is arguable to what extent the evidence extends in their favour. It would seem that at the very least a distinction needs to be made between tolerating such measures as the curtailment of certain rights or deportation and the extension of this component of an ethic into the idea of the absolute genocide of European Jewry. One important aspect of Haas's argument is the idea that the Holocaust was the product of a 'Nazi ethic' but that this ethic in turn was well entrenched by the fifteenth century. Haas writes:

> the content of Nazi ideology carried forward a number of political, religious and social themes that had been a part of European thinking for centuries. The Holocaust was possible because so much of its intellectual, and therefore ethical form was already familiar.[58]

More specifically this aspect of Haas's thesis is based on the proposition that the National Socialist (re)construction of the Jew-as-other was so successfully acted upon because of already entrenched, centuries old ideas of race and anti-Semitism and an ability to utilise 'legitimately' the well developed legal/moral/bureaucratic/technological frameworks of modern society. This is an important idea as it points to an understanding of the moral dimensions of the Holocaust that moves beyond conceptualising responsibility as something to be confined within the boundaries of the German nation.

In the elaboration of his argument Haas cogently shows how the Nazi ethic appropriated and utilised the entrenched moral concept of the just war with the difference being a shift in the definition of that which legitimately constituted the 'enemy'. Haas also argues that this process was made immeasurably easier by the fact that the category of 'the Jew' already comfortably fitted the historical European paradigm of the quintessential 'enemy'. This is of course a view already well supported in the literature by such authors as Richard Rubenstein,

Martin Gilbert and Raul Hilberg.[59] All of these authors have shown that the construction of the Jew as mythical 'other' was well entrenched by the sixteenth century. By the nineteenth and twentieth centuries theological discourse equating Jewry with evil was strengthened by newly emerging quasi-scientific theories of race. All of these forces of the past millennia and more, combined in the social manufacture of European Jewry as a pariah people. Having established a historical backdrop of the category of the Jew as the enemy of the Christian West, Haas then proceeds to interpret the success of National Socialism as stemming, in the main, from a combination of the socialist critique of European economic development, endemic post-First World war nationalist sentiment and racism. Piecing these historical elements together Haas argues that when amalgamated they formed a powerful world view to explain Germany's problems.

Another account that adopts a wider frame of reference as regards the origins of Nazism and the Holocaust is Zygmunt Bauman's text *Modernity and the Holocaust* . Expressing a sentiment not dissimilar to that of Haas, Bauman writes that:

> It is not the Holocaust that we find difficult to grasp in all its monstrosity. *It is our Western Civilization which the occurrence of the Holocaust has made all but incomprehensible.*[60]

Bauman argues that the Holocaust is not solely about National Socialist ideology, Germany and 'Germanness'. The Holocaust is proximally much more discomforting to those who would seek to maintain that it was no more than a temporary aberration on the moral/historical/social/political landscape of twentieth century Europe. Instead, argues Bauman, the Holocaust is really all about 'our' modern world. On Bauman's account the Holocaust needs to be viewed as a "characteristically modern phenomenon that cannot be understood out of the context of cultural tendencies and technical achievements of modernity."[61] Bauman's point is different from Haas's but the two accounts also converge in respect to how we might profitably understand the origins of the Holocaust.

In his careful explanation of the Holocaust as a "legitimate product"[62] of our modern civilization, Bauman pinpoints the link between the Holocaust and ingredients germane to modernity. Specifically, he identifies the way in which links can be sustained between first, the Holocaust and modern industry; second, the Holocaust and modern forms of rationality; third, the Holocaust and the powerful methods and apparatuses of modern government, especially bureaucracy; fourthly, and perhaps most significantly, the Holocaust and the concomitant diminution of what had previously counted as accepted moral behaviour. In the comparison between the Holocaust and modern industry Bauman cites Feingold's description of Auschwitz as 'merely' the ultimate expression of organised industry translated into the organised machinery of destruction. What has come to be symbolised by the very word 'Auschwitz', is a previously unavailable technological capacity for reducing human beings to dust to be dumped into the Sola river. Technologically, Auschwitz was perhaps epitomised by the small pellets of 'Zyklon B', the specific chemical used in the process of gassing the Jews. Together with such essential 'industrial' expertise, the system designed to exterminate the Jews relied upon an extensive network of machinery for the mass movement of millions of people, all of which was orchestrated by a modern bureaucratic command and control system. Underpinning this 'system', this technological and bureaucratic regime, were the central principles of rationality, efficiency and optimal goal implementation. Indeed it is asserted by Bauman that such principles were essential to the successful management and implementation of the goal of the 'Final Solution'.

Perhaps the most engaging aspect of Bauman's analysis is his identification of the connection between the Holocaust and the impoverishment of the then existing value structures. Bauman views the Holocaust as the most terrifying example in modern history of the "Social production of moral indifference."[63] A little further on Bauman writes:

> I propose that the major lesson of the Holocaust is . . . to expand the theoretical model of the civilizing process, so as to include the latter's tendency to demote, exprobate and delegitimize the ethical motivations of social action. We need to take stock of the evidence that *the civilizing process is, among other things, a process of divesting the use and deployment of violence from moral calculus, and of emancipating the desiderata of rationality from interference of ethical norms or moral inhibitions.*[64]

I would concur with Bauman that what is required is to heed the evidence of the Holocaust, especially the way in which the principles and imperatives of rationality have submerged ethical considerations. But whilst I am prepared to accept that there is evidence to support Bauman's claim that the 'civilizing process' has separated out and prioritized the rational over the ethical, I am also of the view that this same evidence demonstrates with as much force the heart of what I hold to be at issue in this book. That is the tension between enormity and complexity. It is this very tension that makes the 'lesson' that Bauman speaks of, though essential, so difficult.

Returning to Bauman, he claims that amongst those elements that are of primary significance to understanding how the Holocaust became a reality, there are two important signifiers: uniqueness and normalcy. He surmises that:

> Two among those factors [anti-Semitism as it evolved with the advent of Nazism and the application of that anti-Semitism into the practical policy of a powerful centralised state] ... could be seen as coincidental—not necessary attributes of a modern society, though always a possibility. The remaining factors [state control of huge, efficient bureaucracy, wartime conditions, and a largely passive population], however, are fully normal.[65]

On Bauman's account the factors he lists substantiate the 'normal' side of the equation. If such factors as he identifies are present then the precondition of normal conditions to enable the Holocaust to occur is satisfied. For Bauman the added presence of the other side of the Holocaust, its uniqueness, serves to contribute further to a point where a certain inevitability almost seems to take over. In other words, if the uniquely endemic elements of anti-Semitic attitudes are present then the road to Auschwitz would indeed appear to contain a certain banal logic. Bauman writes, "When the modernist dream is embraced by an absolute power able to monopolize modern vehicles of rational action, and when that power attains freedom from effective social control, genocide follows."[66]

As I see it, however, one of the problems Bauman has is in shifting from a situation of 'unique normalcy' to being able to explain the society-wide suspension of moral mechanisms "that make people refrain from resistance against evil."[67] His explanation of how it is that "the typically modern, technological-bureaucratic patterns of action and the mentality they institutionalize, generate, sustain and reproduce,"[68] constitute the crucial factors in overcoming and silencing ethical concerns, is an important component in the development of an understanding of the preconditions that made the Holocaust possible. Bauman's argument that the ideology of technology was an important factor in the implementation of the Holocaust and that this ideology was tied to modernity is a strong one. Interestingly enough it is apparent that whilst the ideology was of significance there is evidence indicating that the actual technology itself was sometimes found to be less than efficient.[69]

Returning to Haas and his argument concerning the idea of a Nazi ethic, he claims that the Nazi Party ideologues did in fact possess an ethic in the sense of a clear and coherent set of values and ideas that were a basis for actions and behaviour. Haas suggests that it is in the relatively brief period between Hitler's accession to power and the construction and management of the death factories that the realisation of the Nazi ethic occurs. Haas writes:

> These years . . . are a study of how people fitted reality into the grid of meaning created by a formal ethical discourse. In the crematoriums of Auschwitz we see clearly how completely ethical discourse does in fact create worlds.[70]

One of the strengths of Haas's analysis lies in his recognition of the Nazi ethic as having evolved only gradually and cautiously. It was never, according to Haas, a matter of the immediate application of an idea but rather a stage by stage process of *Gleichschaltung* within which the Jewish Question came to assume increased prominence in the overall evolution of the ethic itself. His claim would seem to accord with the idea that an ethic, as a set of practices is something that becomes habituated over time as opposed to something that is imposed. Haas builds a convincing argument on the grounds that those propagating the Nazi ethic were able to tie together the perception, in the minds of a significant number of people, that the ethical system being advanced was closely related to the values already held to be important along with the idea that the Jews represented a threat to these core values. In other words, it was not so much a matter of failing to behave ethically in their own eyes but rather as Haas puts it "certain activities"[71] were judged according to a different understanding of what it meant to be ethical in one's own behaviour. Haas contends that if this were not the case or had the Nazi "ethic been counterintuitive in this sense, it could not have established the hold that it did."[72]

The real difficulty that Haas faces, however, once having explained the successful germination and establishment of a Nazi ethic within Germany, is further explaining exactly how that same ethic was able to be exported so rapidly over the German border and into Europe more generally. As it turns out Haas is well aware of the complexities that inhere in any adequate explanation of this question. He explores such factors as the effect of wartime conditions themselves and the way that such conditions are able to sanction behaviour that would not otherwise be tolerated; the degree to which the Nazi ethic was able to be imposed by whatever means necessary in those satellite countries where Germany imposed its own puppet regimes, and perhaps most significantly the fact that many European countries already possessed distinct if different histories of anti-Semitism that lay dormant awaiting the appropriate trigger to set in motion what for the most part found expression only occasionally and in more restrained ways.

Haas possesses a sharp awareness of the difficulties that derived from the efforts of the Nazis to export their self-styled ethic and his account has a special focus on the German qualities pertinent to the Holocaust. It is true that the ethic that brought into being and sustained the Holocaust evolved in Germany. This truth should not however be allowed to cloud the fact that in other national/cultural contexts the Nazi ethic was not dominant or in some instances even relevant. It is also well documented that in some of these other contexts mass murder of the Jews was effected in some instances with a tenacity and fervour that surprised even the Nazis.

Haas gives a clear account of the success of the Nazi ethic outside of Germany. The implementation of the Holocaust in Hungary is a case in point. On the liquidation of Hungary's Jews he writes:

> Despite a clear knowledge of what was being done, despite the full survival of the Jewish communal structure, and despite the imminent defeat of Germany, the entire community was arrested, deported, and gassed. . . . The fact that this could be done so thoroughly, openly, and quickly in a country not committed to an alliance with Germany, and to a community that was aware of what was about to happen, and while the world watched in full awareness shows how overpowering and persuasive the ethic had become.[73]

Haas's analysis is continuous with other knowledge that Hungary had remained within the orbit of German military partnership. In fact Admiral Horthy was the last head of state to have the dubious honour of an audience with Hitler as the latter desperately sought to shore up the rapidly disintegrating Reich.

Randolph Braham in *The Politics of Genocide in Hungary*,[74] deepens and elaborates on Haas's insightful account with his evidence that Hungary, whilst it had, prior to the spring of 1944, refrained from wholesale genocide, possessed both a clear history of anti-Semitism and a not insignificant political faction of extreme anti-Semites. It is entirely likely that it is primarily on the basis of the deadly combination of these two factors that the disaster that befell the Jewish community in Hungary was made possible. In other words, had it not been for a pre-existing 'culture' of anti-Semitism augmented by sporadic pogroms and the later involvement[75] of the well organised para-military machinery of the Arrow Cross fascist party, Eichmann and his team would not have been able to implement, with the ease with which they did, such a terrible train of events ending in the mass deportation of Hungarian Jews to Auschwitz. This is not to say that the presence of Eichmann, as the key representative of the Nazi ethic, in Hungary was not of importance in understanding the fate of Hungarian Jewry. On the contrary Eichmann was a crucial element. However, Eichmann and the ethic he embodied were one element among others.

In the light of these accounts Haas's thesis throws up a number of other important insights. Perhaps the most important of these is firstly, his identification of where the parameters of responsibility for the Holocaust lay. The Holocaust was a European phenomenon in its origins and in its execution. And second, that it is not at all obvious that the moral universe within which the crimes of the Holocaust were committed, was dedicated to evil. On these two fundamental points Haas writes:

> Europeans committed what we judge to be heinous crimes under Nazi rule not because they were deficient in moral sensibility, and not because they were quintessentially evil and brutal people, but because in fact they were ethically sensitive people. They were fully aware of what they were doing and displayed principled acquiescence. The difference is that for them such deeds were simply no longer understood to be evil.[76]

Haas's argument, whilst contentious, nevertheless resonates strongly with the evidence. It needs to be noted that Haas is not saying that we are not justified in asserting that the Nazis were mistaken. On the contrary Haas's analysis extends our understanding not only of such questions as why people do what we might think they presumably know to be wrong but also questions that focus on how Nazi ideology itself may be more fruitfully understood, and how some people came to comprehend the nature of the ethical more generally. To summarise this chapter then, I want to return to my idea of a weave of responsibility. My immediate aim has been to pull back from the fibres of the weave to allow a view of the wider pattern of how we might be able to understand the moral fabric of the Holocaust. Whilst they widen the horizon of our conceptual vision, the themes of secrecy, possibilities of knowledge of wrong-doing, the existence of a Nazi ethic and the role of modernity also re-affirm my argument that the events of the Holocaust are characterised by morally complex issues. My claim has been that when viewed from the broader perspectives employed by Lang, Burrin, Bauman and Haas our understanding of the Holocaust, as a phenomenon of moral significance, remains complex. So whilst I continue to hold to the view that it is in terms of individual responsibilities that we reveal our moral engagement with the world I believe that wider angle investigations of the sort undertaken by these commentators lend context to individual behaviour as the source of complexity analyses.

Notes

1. Derrida, 109.

2. Hannah Arendt in *Eichmann in Jerusalem* (135-136) notes that during his trial Eichmann, under questioning from Judge Raveh, made mention that he had read Kant's *Critique of Pure Reason* and, after further questioning, even produced an approximate definition of the 'Categorical Imperative'.

3. Hugo Ott, *Martin Heidegger, A Political Life*, (London: Harper Collins, 1993).

4. Berel Lang, *Act and Idea in the Nazi Genocide*, (Chicago: The University of Chicago Press, 1991).

5. Lang, 4.

6. Lang, xiv.

7. Lang, 29.

8. Lang, 8.

9. Peter Haas, *Morality After Auschwitz: The Radical Challenge of the Nazi Ethic*, (Philadelphia: Fortress Press, 1988).

10. Haas, 2.

11. Lang, 22.

12. Haas, 2.

13. Lang, 28.

14. J.L. Mackie, *The Miracle of Theism: Arguments for and against the Existence of God*, (Oxford: Clarendon Press, 1982), 162.

15. Lang, 28.

16. Lang, 22.

17. See Philippe Burrin's characterisation of this debate in his book *Hitler and the Jews, the Genesis of the Holocaust*, (London: Edward Arnold, 1994).

18. Lanzmann, 72-73.

19. Burrin, 23-24.

20. The documents refered to here are first, the letter from Heydrich of 2nd July 1941 to higher SS and police chiefs summing up instructions to the heads of *Einsatzgruppen* and second, a 17th July order from Heydrich that 'all Jews' amongst Russian prisoners of war should be executed.

21. Itzhak Arad, *Vilna Hayehudit Bemaavak Uvechilayon*, (Tel Aviv: Sifriat Poalim,

1976).

22. Richard Breitman, *The Architect of Genocide: Himmler and the Final Solution,* (New York: Knopf, 1991).

23. Saul Friedlander, 'Introduction' in Philippe Burrin, *Hitler and the Jews,* 6.

24. Peter Padfield, *Himmler,* (London: Macmillan, 1990), 385.

25. Examples of the sort of metaphors cited by Lang (see p.16 in *Act and Idea in the Nazi Genocide*) include analogies such as 'various types of bacilli or cancer' and incorporate such terms as 'cancers', 'plague' and 'tuberculosis'.

26. Lang, 16.

27. Lang, 3.

28. Heinrich Himmler, 'From a speech by Himmler before senior SS officers in Poznan, October 4, 1943', in Yitzak Arad, Yitzak Gutman and Andre Margaliot, (eds.), *Documents on the Holocaust,* (Oxford: Yad Vashem & Pergamon Press, 1987), 344-345.

29. Roger Griffin, *Fascism,* (Oxford: Oxford University Press, 1995).

30. Griffin, *Fascism,* 162.

31. Padfield, 484.

32. Saul Friedlander, *Memory, History and the Extermination of the Jews in Europe,* (Bloomington: Indiana University Press, 1993).

33. Arad, Gutman & Margaliot (eds.), 344-345.

34. Ernst Klee, Willi Dressen & Volker Riess, *"The Good Old Days": The Holocaust as seen by Its Perpetrators and Bystanders,* (New York: The Free Press, 1991).

35. Klee, Dressen & Riess, xvii.

36. This would be a view corroborated by the donation in 2007 to the United States Holocaust Memorial Museum of the photo album attributed to SS Obersturmfuhrer Karl Hocker.

37. Based on the recollections of former SS General Karl Wolff, The World at War, Thames Television Documentary, London, 27 March, 1974 and cited in Martin Gilbert, *The Holocaust: The Jewish Tragedy,* (London: Fontana Press, 1987), 191.

38. Lang, 24.

39. Lang, 26.

40. Arad, Gutman & Margaliot (eds.), 368.

41. Arad, Gutman & Margaliot (eds.), 173.

42. Klee, Dressen & Riess, xx.

43. Klee, Dressen & Riess, 28.

44. Klee, Dressen & Riess, 109-110.

45. Klee, Dressen & Riess, 117-118.

46. Lanzmann, 24-25.

47. Lanzmann, 25-26.

48. Gitta Sereny, *Albert Speer: His Battle with the Truth,* (London: Macmillan, 1995).

49. Sereny, 340.

50. Sereny, 347.

51. Abraham J. Edelheit & Hershel Edelheit, *History of the Holocaust*, (Boulder: Westview Press, 1994).

52. Padfield, 348.

53. Klee, Dressen & Riess, 201-202 and 205-206.

54. Midgley, 61.

55. Midgley, 61.

56. Haas, 4.

57. Haas, 7.

58. Haas, 13.

59. See Richard Rubenstein & John K. Roth, *Approaches To Auschwitz: The Holocaust and its Legacy*, (New York: John Knox Press, 1987), Martin Gilbert, *The Holocaust: The Jewish Tragedy*, (London: Fontana Press, 1987) and Raul Hilberg, *Destruction of the European Jews*, (New York: Holmes & Meier Publishers, 1985).

60. Zygmunt Bauman, *Modernity and the Holocaust*, (Cambridge: Polity Press, 1989), 89.

61. Bauman, xiii.

62. Bauman, xii.

63. Bauman, 18.

64. Bauman, 28.

65. Bauman, 94-95.

66. Bauman, 93-94.

67. Bauman, 95.

68. Bauman, 95.

69. For examples of ineffeciencies see Raul Hilberg, *The Destruction of European Jews*, 338 and Ernst Klee, Willi Dressen & Volker Riess (eds.), *The Good Old Days*, 242 and 235.

70. Haas, 59.

71. Haas, 7.

72. Haas, 5.

73. Haas, 108.

74. Randolph Braham, *The Politics of Genocide in Hungary*, (New York: Colombia University Press, 1981), 1-38.

75. On most accounts Arrow Cross involvement in the deportation of Jews really began in September, 1944.

76. Haas, 2.

LISTENING TO THE HOLOCAUST

The aim of this final chapter is to incorporate the individual voices contained in testimonies of survivors within an understanding of the tension between complexity and enormity analyses of the Holocaust. An important theme of this book has been the idea that the Holocaust, as a compilation of experiences and events, is fundamentally about lived experiences. The universal death which the Nazis tried to inflict upon the entire Jewish people, individually and as a whole identity, is a common point of reference for interpretations of the Holocaust. For many commentators the attempt to universally exterminate Jewish identity remains one of the most morally significant markers of the Holocaust. But as important as it is to underline the moral enormity of Nazi plan for the 'universal death' of European Jewry there is also the equally valuable task of understanding the significance of the individual voices of survivor testimonies. This is not to suggest that the voices of individual Jews are in some way intellectually more significant than other voices from this disaster. My point, however, is that the voices of individual Jewish survivors represent the most tangible, concrete examples of the refusal of the universal death that the Nazis attempted to impose upon the Jewish people. Thus one of my claims here is that this aspect of the Holocaust, the testimonies of individual survivors, is at least as much about the meaning of survival as it is about the attempted genocide of European Jewry.

I aim to stress not only the importance placed on the moral enormity contained in the attempt at 'universal death' but more especially on the complexity that is contained in our understanding of our responsibilities as the mark of our moral engagement with the world. I have argued throughout this book that our understanding of moral life, from the standpoint of the Holocaust, will be most satisfactorily enhanced by recognising the importance of moral complexity as a factor integral to our lives. Support for my position concerning the significance of moral complexity as a component of moral life is present in the work of the historian Richard J. Evans when he writes that:

> Nazism and its effects cannot be made real to people who were born long after
> the event, if they are presented in crude terms of heroes and villains. . . . The
> nature of the moral choices people had to make can only be accurately judged
> by taking into account the full complexities of the situations in which they
> found themselves.[1]

Given the context of his discussion on moral choices I understand Evans to mean
that there is a need to take account of the complex interplay of factors that make
it possible for us to understand the moral dimensions of the situations we find
ourselves in. That is to say, in order to understand the choices people make we
need to weigh the influence of such factors as circumstance, individual disposition, the importance people attach to their values and beliefs, people's responsibilities to themselves and others and the role of luck. I have also argued that
complexity analyses are best articulated in terms of a weave of responsibility
and that this weave is in turn most usefully thought of as a way of understanding
the different senses of responsibilities that I am seeking to convey. Responsibility, understood as concrete and specific responsibilities to persons, as practices
that hold together moral life, as including a consideration of the situations we
find ourselves in, as entailing provision for our personal dispositions and as the
very framework of our moral life serves to give a sense of our moral engagement
with the world.

Signposts demarcating experiential rupture and narratives of disaster abound
in accounts of the Holocaust. Such accounts lend themselves well to enormity
analyses. As I have argued throughout, however, Holocaust stories are also often
morally complex. An adjunct to this latter claim is the idea that there may be no
moral comfort to be derived from the individual experiences of survivors of the
Holocaust. This idea is based, in part, upon a particular and mediated understanding of experience as a source of evidence and explanation. In an article titled 'The Evidence of Experience'[2] Joan W. Scott charts the play between identity, experience and historical explanation. On Scott's account, experience
should not be viewed as an unquestioned ground for explanation. She argues that
experience is meaning producing. However, it also needs to be understood that
experience and the meanings that derive from experience differ in accord with
the way the experience is interpreted. Thus Scott writes that:

> Experience can both confirm what is already known (we see what we have
> learned to see) and upset what has been taken for granted (when different mean-
> ings are in conflict we re-adjust our vision to take account of the conflict or to
> resolve it—that is what is meant by "learning from experience," though not
> everyone learns the same lesson or learns it at the same time or in the same
> way).[3]

Importantly for Scott, what counts as experience is never self evident or straightforward and as I understand the matter cannot be used to ground arguments seeking, for example, to determine identity. Approaching Holocaust testimonials as linguistic expressions of experience, with a similar qualification, I argue that the testimonies are, nevertheless, meaningful historical narratives. By meaningful historical narratives I mean that such testimonies are context bound and temporal but for all of this no less valid as sources of meaning. To this extent I aim to hold onto the idea that they can yield an understanding of the moral landscape of the Holocaust. In other words, I proceed on the basis that it is possible to maintain a measure of critical distance with regard to the material and in so doing, acknowledge one's own interpretive role in the process of attempting an understanding of the events.

I do not consider Holocaust testimonies to be true or authentic in the sense that they represent indisputable truths. The necessary activity of locating such experiences in the temporal context of past, present and future means that the testimonies are more like 'situated truths' inasmuch as they are always the subject of interpretation. When I refer to the testimonies as 'subject to interpretation' I mean that they are subject to the usual intellectual activities that test their consistency within and among connecting historical narratives and are, therefore, always open to contestation.

My other claim here is that, as accounts of specific instances of individual survival, such testimonies represent individual efforts *in extremis*, to sustain the human values by which these same individuals had lived before the Holocaust. I believe that the examples that I make use of in this chapter will bear this point out. For this reason alone testimonial material is a key element not only toward understanding the moral dimensions of the Holocaust but also as a means of extending understanding of the nature of the 'moral' itself. My justification for this claim stems from the idea that individual survivor testimonies depict the endurance of a certain sense of human value and moral agency albeit within a very localised and individual frame of reference. In other words, I am not arguing that survivor testimonies represent some sort of singular moral truth out of which we can derive moral comfort. I am saying that survivor experiences can be consistently interpreted as revealing evidence of the existence and survival of individuals who are morally engaged with the world in which they live. This also means that interpretations of such experiences can and should be contested if intellectual life is to breathe the air of fresh ideas.

I will show that, as diverse and varied as the experiences spoken of in the testimonies are, their evidence depicts the existence and survival of both moral agency and individual human values. To re-iterate here, this is not to say that individual testimonies convey anything like the triumph of good over evil. This would be to erode the whole idea of moral complexity that I am seeking to convey. However, individual testimonies do demonstrate contingent and specific moral facts about the Holocaust. The metaphor of the weave is important here, as these moral facts depend upon and derive meaning from the different senses of responsibility I have examined in previous chapters. Moral facts however, like facts more generally, are not like pebbles lying around waiting to be picked up. Moral facts are always a question of interpretation.

I need to carefully explain what it is I am seeking to establish here. By moral facts I mean aspects of moral life that are able to be recognised consistently enough as to be declared true. What I'm seeking to convey here is something like what Margaret Walker expresses as the existence of a 'moral floor'[4] comprising a raft of understanding built up out of the basic human goods of trust and responsibility. Walker argues that sometimes the moral floor that we possess is so weak that we are liable to despair but it is precisely these fluctuations in our understandings of what morality is that provide us with the raw materials for criticism. Thus moral facts may be factual but not in the sense that they consist of a declaration of a moral reality that is beyond contestation. The factual aspects of moral life are always subject to interpretation and thus might be recognised, in some instances, as more akin to understandings than certainties. Indeed, and as Walker also contends,[5] it is just such aspects of moral inquiry, our understandings of what morality is, that are not only the basis of our most fruitful moral insights but also serve as the ground for practical moral deliberations and moral judgments. I construe this aspect of Walker's assessment of moral life as consistent with my argument that moral life is complex and often fraught with complications, ambiguities and uncertainties.

In *Admitting the Holocaust*[6] Lawrence Langer considers the significance of survivor testimonies for our understanding of the Holocaust. Borrowing from Kierkegaard, Langer writes:

> life is lived forward and understood backward, and I suspect that for most of us this continues to be an attractive premise. But just the opposite is true for the Holocaust experience: we live it backward in time, and once we arrive there, we find ourselves mired in its atrocities, a kind of historical quicksand that hinders our bid to bring it forward again into a meaningful future.[7]

However, if Kierkegaard is correct, then Langer is claiming a privileged position for Holocaust experience. My concerns with this account stem from two important issues. First, Langer approaches Holocaust testimonies as if the 'experience' they are able to render contains inherent truths. Dominick LaCapra in his book *History, Theory, Trauma: Representing the Holocaust* summarises this concern as deriving from what he calls Langer's 'idealization of experience'. On LaCapra's account this problem also contains the extra dimension of Langer's own unexamined position as transparent mediator of the 'reality' of the original experience. LaCapra argues that Langer leaves largely unexamined the relation between testimonial material and the way that that material is understood historically from a moral perspective. LaCapra's point is a difficult one to flesh out but I believe that it is an important one. My view is that Langer himself is unclear as to what value, ultimately, can be attributed to testimonial material. This lack of clarity is conveyed in *Holocaust Testimonies: the Ruins of Memory*[8] in a footnote when he writes that:

Beyond dispute in oral testimony is that every word spoken falls directly from the lips of the witness. Not as much can be said for written survivor testimony that is openly or silently edited. Whether this seriously limits the value of some written memoirs is a question that still needs to be investigated.[9]

Whilst I recognise the importance of oral testimonies, my point is that Langer's account sidesteps the compromises entailed in interpreting oral testimonies. In other words, the testimonies do not speak for themselves. They acquire meaning in accordance with the sorts of processes Langer himself undertakes. The act of listening itself implies interpretation as testimonies become transmitted to other parties.

Admittedly Langer's position in respect to the relation between testimonial material and the interpretation of that material is a good deal more nuanced than I have allowed thus far. Recognising the concerns of Langer, regarding the uses of testimonial material, I nevertheless want to stress the value of testimonial material as evidence of the moral complexity of Holocaust experiences. However this brings me to my other concern regarding Langer's approach to Holocaust testimonies. In his assessment of the possible responses to the 'trauma' that for Langer necessarily follows in the wake of Holocaust experiences, he opts for a theoretical position that never really escapes from the strictures incurred by the idea of trauma itself. Thus, he presents a case whereby all possibilities for understanding Holocaust testimonies are tempered by the fragmentary and repressive effects of the trauma associated with the original experience.

What seems to be important for Langer is what he refers to as 'durational time'. Langer writes:

In the realm of durational time, no one recovers because nothing is recovered, only uncovered then re-covered buried again beneath the fruitless struggle to expose "the way it was". Holocaust memory cannot be used to certify belief, establish closure, or achieve certainty. Hence chronological time is needed to intrude on this memory by those who insist on rescuing belief, closure and certainty from testimonies about the disaster. Durational time resists and undermines this effort.[10]

Langer sets up a distinction between 'durational' and 'chronological' time in a way that seems to be something like the psychological distinction between the unconscious and the conscious. Thus Holocaust survivor experience, because of the moral trauma that it entails, necessitates a process of forgetting in which the experience survives though in a shape that is not readily accessible to memory. For Langer, Holocaust memory is always problematic because, although, 'always-present', it becomes for both the witness, and in narrative forms, a problematic representation of the past.

Langer's account also seems to resonate with the debates surrounding the problem of interpreting historical material more generally. That is to say, if it is the case that historical interpretations are just that, interpretations, then there may be no unmediated access to the original experience. The facts, if they do not speak for themselves, always entail interpretation. The twist here, however, is that Langer argues that in the case of Holocaust experiences, because of the nature of the experience itself, representation of the material, as in the case of testimonials, involves a certain sort of loss. In the transition from that which is always-present but 'forgotten' to the presented past Langer argues that we get led astray by the disjuncture that persists between chronological and durational time. Holocaust experiences, according to Langer, remain imprisoned within the unrepresentable past of those who experienced but cannot convey the content of the experience.

I claim that there are dangers associated with an unquestioned acceptance of any account that might place insurmountable barriers in the way of projects seeking to understand the voices of the testimonies. Aside from tendencies of ahistoricism that pervade such accounts there seems to me to be a real possibility that they run the risk of de-legitimising testimonial voices altogether. Langer relies heavily on Lyotard's account of the effects of trauma upon the memory. I argue that whilst moral trauma may induce disruption, shock and discontinuity in terms of the way memory functions, I don't think it renders memory completely untrustworthy. My evidence is the testimonies that follow. I want to suggest that the evidence of the testimonies can be interpreted as constituting concrete and meaningful lived experiences. As long as we are alive and in possession of our usual faculties we are moral agents with stories to tell.

The fact that any voices at all have come back to us from Auschwitz is important and it is in this context that I find Langer's attempts to mediate between that which may or may not constitute a legitimate voice problematic. On the one hand Langer writes that whilst "Auschwitz is often described . . . as an "anti-world", a separate planet . . . in fact the camp was in Poland in Europe on planet earth, run by men and women like the rest of us."[11] Elsewhere however, in connection with the testimonies that tell the stories of a more familiar world, Langer writes:

> The tales they [survivors] tell paralyse the will as well as the word. Unintentionally, they ridicule our naïve notions of choice, heroism, and resistance, those verbal creatures of the imagination that shrivel and disappear in their other world of the Holocaust, where the inhuman imagination holds sway.[12]

Langer claims that the testimonies challenge our naive understanding of the notions of choice, heroism and resistance. In this sense Langer seems to align himself with the task "not to acknowledge heroic lives, but to mourn melancholy deaths."[13] An example of such an alignment is Langer's treatment of the diaries of Etty Hillesum, a Dutch Jew who perished at Auschwitz after an extended internment at the Dutch deportation camp at Westerbork. The trouble for Langer, it seems, is that the diaries of Hillesum portray a meaningful, emotionally and intellectually enriched life in the face of the abyss that awaited her. Langer writes as if seeking to reduce the record of Hillesum's experience to a form of evasion in the face of 'how it really was'. He says that:

> Our hindsight, however, darkens her efforts to reconcile hope with annihilation, making her buoyancy seem pathetic and exasperating rather than praiseworthy. . . . It may be unfair to call Etty Hillesum's vocabulary like "fate", "suffering", and "destiny" specious—"inappropriate" would be a juster term—but at least we should pursue the direction in which it leads (and misleads) us, in order to perceive more accurately the scenario of her vision.[14]

Langer's more important point is that knowledge of the wider contexts gives greater perspective to these stories. While I concur with Langer my point is that there is every possibility that Hillesum's life was for her meaningful and sustainable precisely because it occurred in our world and not some 'other world'. Of greater significance, though, is the possibility that Langer, by questioning Hillesum's description of her experience, is missing the point that Holocaust experiences, on account of the differences, discontinuities and complexities that they contain, highlight the lack of conformity to a standard pattern of experiences. Jewish experiences of the Holocaust do not fit any one moral agenda, Nazi or otherwise. As I intend to demonstrate Jewish experiences of the Holocaust resist unified moral classification as they bear witness to the survival of a complex array of emotions, values and manifestations of moral life.

Langer's account of the significance of moral trauma in the context of the Holocaust is important. Nowhere is this more evident than in the way he identifies the intensity of the impact on the lives of those who were the targets of the Nazi attempt at genocide. In the tradition of Levinas,[15] those targeted were the 'other' of those events. In a sentiment that I think is sympathetic to that of Langer's account, the editors of *Different Voices: Women and the Holocaust*, Rittner and Roth, cite Gertrud Kolmar as having posed what was for them one of the most confronting of questions. Kolmar, a German Jew from Berlin was deported to Auschwitz-Birkenau in the Winter of 1943 where she was killed. Prior to her deportation Kolmar wrote, "So then, to tell my story, here I stand. . . . You hear me speak. But do you hear me feel?"[16]

In this half statement, half plea, there lies a difficulty, certainly for historical, but more especially for moral philosophical interpretations of the Holocaust. For Rittner and Roth this difficulty is invoked in the testimonies of the victims, in the "Listening for that question, hearing it, heeding it, responding to it."[17] For Rittner and Roth, Kolmar's question, in turn, raises another most pressing question: To what extent does the Holocaust represent an obstacle to meaning? Or to put it in a different way, is it possible that the nature of the events of the Holocaust themselves represent, in certain respects, obstacles to understanding the events themselves. And could it be the case that the most unmediated and most sensitive expression of this problem for understanding the Holocaust is to be located in the voices of its most primary victims?

For Langer too, there are particular barriers facing attempts to retrospectively extract meaning from what remains of the evidence. This is true for both those who experienced the Holocaust first hand and those that did not, though the barriers for each might be of a different sort. Among the difficulties to be overcome are concerns over the accuracy of survivor recollections, differing interpretations of such recollections and, with the passing of time, fewer and fewer individuals remaining alive to give their account of events. Such problems, daunting though they are, are compounded by the very nature of the experience itself. For example there are arguments in support of the view that the experiences of survivors in some sense entailed an actual disruption of the processes of their ascribing moral meaning.[18] I do not want to suggest that some Holocaust experiences are morally unfathomable but as I argued throughout, some Holocaust experiences are demonstrably morally complex. One aspect of this complexity relates to the way in which some experiences can induce moral trauma. And by moral trauma I am not only referring to the psychological shock that is experienced but also want to identify the way an individual's stock of values and beliefs can be desecrated to such an extent that it can affect their ability to maintain their moral bearings.

Something approaching the sort of experience referred to above may be present in the description of events as re-counted by the survivor Ida Fink. In a section of her account describing what she refers to as a 'scrap of time' Ida Fink recalls:

> I want to talk about a certain time not measured in months and years.... This time was measured not in months but in a word—we no longer said "in the beautiful month of May", but "after the first 'action', or the second, or right before the third." We had different measures of time. . . . We call the first action—that scrap of time that I want to talk about—a round-up. . . . Our transformation [though] was not yet complete; we were still living out of habit in that old time that was measured in months and years, and on that lovely peaceful morning, filled with dry, golden mists, we took the words "conscription of labour" literally.[19]

Elsewhere in her account and recounted later in this chapter Fink described her subsequent flight from the market place with her sister as marking a break in her experience of time "because it was then *that time measured in the ordinary way stopped* [my emphasis]." [20] It might be argued that this moment in Fink's experience, when, as she describes it, the measurement of time 'in the ordinary way' ceases, represented a shock to the processes within which we normally apportion meaning. What I'm suggesting Fink is referring to when she speaks about the cessation of time measured 'in the ordinary way' is a suspension of time according to its linear conception. That is to say, the suspension of time according to its representation on clocks, calendars and even with the rising and setting of the sun. It might be objected that experiences of the sort described here are not peculiar to the Holocaust. In fact my point is not that Fink's experience is in some way unique, although I may in other contexts want to say that her experience conveys a certain sort of unique quality. Rather I want to argue that Fink's experience is sufficiently different from other more 'common' experiences on the basis of the extreme, and in my interpretation, confounding impression that it left upon her moral imagination.[21]

For Fink, time appeared to be disrupted at a certain point in her experience, to the extent that it was no longer, after this juncture, possible for it to be registered linearly. Instead linear time was replaced by measuring the passing of time in accordance with particular 'places' and 'events'. The way in which Fink thought after this event, the way in which she would ascribe meaning to it, was altered as a direct result of the event itself. Perhaps also, Fink's account suggests that certain Holocaust experiences are sufficiently socio-psychically disruptive as to cause a re-formatting or re-arrangement of the way not only time is experienced but also the way we allocate meaning to these experiences. To reiterate, however, my reason for singling out the story of Fink is to focus upon the effect that the experience she describes had on her moral understanding of the world. Fink talks about the process in terms of a transformation. What I'm suggesting is that this transformation came about as a result of what I refer to as a certain sort of moral trauma. The sort of trauma I am arguing for concerns a connection between the dramatic affront to her values and her entire spatial/temporal bearings.

Perhaps one of the key difficulties with these speculations lies in not being able to adequately explain an experience that falls beyond the edge of moral comprehension. This might be true not only for Fink but for everyone. Some commentators, for example Lyotard,[22] go so far as to claim that certain Holocaust experiences, typically those of the most extreme kind, are so disruptive to the way individuals receive, order and generally make sense of their experiences that they can only be accommodated at the level of the unconscious. That is to say, that it is in the nature of Holocaust experiences that they may only be experientially catalogued at the level of the unconscious, thus rendering their availability subject to particular conditions and beyond the reach of what might be referred to as our readily available memory.[23]

The voices in the testimonies that follow are part of a complex tapestry of voices and stories that testify to both the near disappearance of a moral order and the survival of multiple senses of responsibility in the face of disaster. This is also to refer to the refusal of Jewish identity to go the way of the 'universal death' intended by the Nazis. The evidence of the testimonies runs counter to the simplification implied by universal death. More than this though, each strand in the tapestry of testimonial voices bears witness to a complex array of emotions, intellectual currents, ambiguities, conflicting demands and other moral responses that go to the core of the complexity that comprises moral lives. The examples presented here extend understanding of our moral engagement with the world. This is a crucial point. The testimonies themselves represent evidence of the multitude of possibilities for moral agency. I argue that such evidence emerges from the chronicling of the stories themselves. It needs to be borne in mind that what I am suggesting here is a long way from attempting to create some sort of normalised memory based around ideas of natural innocence or innate dignity. In this respect I am indebted to the arguments of Lawrence Langer and the case that he mounts against the possibility of understanding memory in this sense. As the testimonies to follow show, such possibilities as essentialised notions of the 'good' are absent from Holocaust experiences. Rather, one aspect of what is at issue is, as Michael Bernstein writes:

> the truly difficult question of decorum in its full ethical sense: the ongoing at-
> tempt to work out which modes and techniques of representation are appropri-
> ately responsive to the exigencies of so monstrous a series of events.[24]

I believe the question of decorum as Bernstein expresses it is a real challenge. In view of the testimonies that follow I also think that there is a difficulty in sustaining the idea of innocence. In the light of testimonial evidence I question the idea of innate moral innocence. In other words, the testimonies of survivors substantiate the gravity of morally tragic situations by exposing the limits and possibilities of moral life. By highlighting morally tragic situations, testimonial material thereby reveals some of the difficulties associated with the idea of moral innocence. On the substance of moral innocence, Gowans writes:

> The ideal of moral innocence . . . puts forward a standard of perfection that,
> though difficult to attain, is nonetheless thought to be within the reach of each
> of us. The standard is moral innocence, or moral purity, the ideal of living one's
> life in such a way as to fully, comprehensively, harmoniously understand and
> respond to the requirements of morality, and thereby to entirely exclude all
> forms of wrongdoing.[25]

Gowans also argues that there lies within 'our' general understanding of morality, a deep desire for an 'ideal of moral innocence'. He claims that this aspiration is present in spite of the fact that the ideal is most likely unattainable. On Gowan's account moral innocence is premised on the hope for moral purity. Following Gowans, I argue that if we accept the existence of the sorts of morally tragic choices symbolised, for example, by 'Sophie's choice', then this is tantamount to an admission that the ideal of moral innocence is problematic. Make no mistake, though. I do not seek to impugn the purity of Sophie's choice. The Sophies of this world did their best and it is plainly wrong to ask more of such people. But it seems to me that there is something tragic with a world in which negative outcomes, of the sort depicted in Sophie's choice, are sometimes unavoidable. Such situations leave the idea of moral innocence somehow tainted. Of some importance here is the contention that the stories contained in some Holocaust testimonies show that sheer effort of will to attain the ideal of moral innocence is not enough to maintain belief in such an ideal. And as Gowans demonstrates in his account of inescapable wrongdoing, the possibility of moral dilemmas remains deeply offensive to any sense of moral purity or goodness that seeks to transcend the situations we sometimes find ourselves in. In the same vein, I argue that testimonial material highlights some of the problems that accrue in attempts to preserve the ideal of moral innocence.

If some Holocaust testimonies demonstrate morally tragic situations they at the same time show the importance of what it means to live conscious of life's moral content. There are many examples in the testimonies that reinforce the absolute centrality of ideas of good and bad intentions, responsibilities, choices, judgements and consequences within a given moral life. But rather than indicating an ability to visualise some sort of ideal of moral purity, the testimonies throw into sharp relief the limits, possibilities and fragility of unflawed moral agency. The significance of stories about the Holocaust, as opposed to other stories more generally, is important here. Holocaust stories, because of the way they push moral sensibilities in every possible direction and because of their geographical spread, their diversity along ethnic, cultural and gender lines, are a compelling subject for moral scrutiny. This is not to make a claim for uniqueness on the part of the Holocaust. Holocaust testimonies do, however, demonstrate the importance of moral agency in the broader canvas of human agency more generally.

By capturing something of the idea of limits to positive moral outcomes and the variety of possibilities of moral agency, the testimonies are a harsh reminder of the human capacity for wrongdoing. Stories of moral courage do exist and many of the testimonies themselves are proof of this. But it is also the case that the overwhelming majority of accounts of Holocaust events tell other stories. It seems to me that the evidence presented in earlier chapters, is overwhelmingly weighted in favour of stories of either moral wrongdoing, moral failure, moral ambiguity, moral indifference or what might be called a kind of moral silence in the face of events. The reasons for this are, not surprisingly, a part of the complexity of moral life that this thesis seeks to convey. More often than not the complexity that I refer to comprises a subtle amalgam of factors. My intention is to use the testimonies that follow as tangible examples to further illuminate my argument connecting the moral complexity of Holocaust experiences. As I have argued throughout, it is, in most instances, as a direct result of the situations that people find themselves in that moral tragedy is invoked.

Another important claim here is that, included in the various ways of understanding responsibility as it pertains to the raft of Holocaust experiences, should be a listening to the voices of Holocaust testimonies. There is a certain stress here on the value of listening as a means of accessing the feelings, emotions and thoughts that comprise the raw material of Holocaust stories. The sense of the significance of Holocaust testimonies as powerful conductors of how we might understand moral complexity has links with Raimond Gaita's understanding of the accounts of the testimonies as evincing what he terms 'knowledge of the heart'.[26] On Gaita's account this kind of understanding derives, in part, from feeling, though a certain sort of feeling, or what he refers to as disciplined feeling. In describing this type of knowledge Gaita distinguishes between the knowledge imparted by SS reports of killings in the ghettoes and that of the chroniclers of *Oneg Shabbes*. [27] For Gaita the sort of knowledge provided by the *Oneg Shabbes* is entirely distinct from what may be an equally factual report of events documented by the SS. Gaita suggests that we read the *Oneg Shabbes* in a way that is similar to how we might read Martin Gilbert's book *The Holocaust,* that is 'with bleeding eyes'. Gaita's insight in my view derives from his understanding of such knowledge as being inscribed with a certain sort of feeling. My claim is that some testimonial material yields a similar sort of understanding thereby providing more than a mere testament to events as they occurred.

The testimonies I draw on in the following discussion include, as far as I am aware the until now, unreviewed voices of 9 Hungarian survivors of Auschwitz. As eye-witness accounts of the horror that was Auschwitz they are remarkably free of embellishment but express, in my estimation, a desire to respond meaningfully to the events as the interviewees understood them. On one level, understanding testimonial material of this sort means recognising both its intensely personal dimension and the idea that such material also represents a commentary on the parameters, limits and complexities of moral life more generally. To this extent such testimonies recount intensely individual stories whilst at the same time invoking a much wider audience in the attempt to comprehend the moral dimensions of life itself. I think testimonies are a powerful conductor of the 'flesh and bloodness' of the events as they happened.

My thoughts on the importance of getting as close as possible to the source of the experience relates also to Langer's footnote, cited earlier, that written survivor testimonies may be compromised, as a result of the processes of editing, in ways that oral testimonies might not. I take Langer's point that editing can constitute a form of mediation, especially if it additionally entails translation, but respond with the claim that the testimonies used in this chapter are different to those most often cited in work on the Holocaust. The testimonies used are among those recorded by local authorities in Budapest immediately upon the interviewees' return from Auschwitz, shortly after the camp was liberated by the Russian forces. The testimonies were recorded between 9th July and 26th November 1945. Consequently, I believe they are close to the rawness of the experience of life in Auschwitz. These testimonies represent a proximity to events as they occurred not just in the chronological sense but also in terms of the unembellished matter of fact air they impart. Unlike such collections of testimonies as the Fortunoff Video Archive at Yale University, the intention of which is to convey the moral magnitude of the experiences documented, the testimonies I present were born of another purpose. As I understand it the interviews were carried out as part of the process of providing positive identification in the chaotic aftermath of the liberation and reconstruction of Budapest. And as I shall demonstrate, they convey a special sort of integrity in their description of everyday life in Auschwitz.

It is also my contention that the examples that follow give life to the variety of philosophical issues embedded within the simultaneous combination of moral enormity and moral complexity. These voices can be interpreted as conveying a keen sense of both complexity and enormity analyses that play such an important part of the moral tragedy of Holocaust experiences. I want to emphasise this last point that the testimonies represent a vivid record of the human drama that was Auschwitz with an example that, whilst dispassionate in its style, is emotionally evocative in terms of the images it conveys. Recounting their arrival at Auschwitz, Mrs. O. P. and her daughter Q. R. write:

> We arrived in Birkenau on the evening of the 3rd of June. We had to leave our luggage in the wagons and stand in queues of five. They then selected the old and young from those who could work. . . . We stood there on the street of the lager for three or four hours. We saw two huge chimneys in the distance spitting fire and smoke. It was a peculiarly horrible sight in the night.[28]

Just as is the case with the example above, the testimonial material that follows is intended to convey particular moments within the intensely personal stories of moral tragedy. More pointedly, the stories vividly represent some of the most powerful data available for the complexity analyses elaborated in the preceding chapters.

The material is organised according to how it contributes to an understanding of Holocaust experiences as morally complex depictions of morally tragic situations. Thus I have chosen stories that show the systematic dehumanisation of moral agency, the issue of luck, both good and bad, bystander predicaments, the behaviour of SS and non-German personnel, and accounts that identify individuals by name as possessing extraordinary moral fortitude.[29]

In addition to what can only be described as base brutalisation and terrorisation a number of the testimonies contain evidence of what I would call the systematic dehumanisation of moral agency. That is to say, the testimonies contain powerful evidence of efforts that were made to strip the interviewees of their sense of what it meant to be human. One such example is recorded through the eyes of the then fifteen year old Ms A. B. Upon arriving at Auschwitz, A. B. recounts the feelings of humiliation she experienced as she and others from her transport were provided with Russian military uniforms and men's underwear infested with lice. Describing how she felt A. B. writes:

> We could not recognise each other, we did not even feel like women, but rather we looked like animals[30]

A. B.'s example very clearly demonstrates how the Nazis intended to strip these people of core aspects of their moral selves. A similar sentiment is conveyed in E. F.'s description of her arrival at Auschwitz. She recalled that:

> They herded us out of the wagons and took our remaining belongings away. . . . We walked 1 kilometre amongst electric fences to the bathhouse. When we arrived we had to undress and stand naked in front of the SS and Slovakian girls. . . . We were standing there ashamed; everything had been taken away from us.[31]

This is a poignant and telling description of how lacking in worth a person can be made to feel. Understanding the moral dimensions of such experiences, enormous though they undoubtedly are, also entails accounting for such apparently confounding, and therefore complicating aspects such as those described here. Without exception all of the testimonies describe a life in Auschwitz designed to manufacture a logic to justify the murder of people on the grounds of their racial affiliation. Human beings, solely on account of their race, were put through a planned ordeal of dehumanisation designed to strip them of their dignity and respect.

The testimonies also convey some powerful examples of behaviour that can restore faith in the idea of a residue of positive moral agency in the face of morally tragic situations. That such examples are able to exist at all in the context of life in Auschwitz is a point worth highlighting. Some of the examples that I want to consider would not perhaps be described as heroism under fire. We should not, however, let their modest appearance fool us into under-estimating their importance as evidence of the presence, in difficult circumstances, of the possibility for goodness. One example of what I describe as modest goodness in the face of moral tragedy concerns a female SS guard, Maria Reich. Auschwitz survivor, Dr. I. J. wrote:

> I would like to recount another episode as well. In August I took 9 patients to the Horst Hospital with the escort of a female SS guard. As we crossed the street there was an old woman coming from the opposite direction, carrying a tray full of baked fruit bread. When she saw us she took it off her head and gave some to each of us. The guard told her she was not allowed to do that. However, the old woman did not take any notice of this. She told her not to be so cruel; could she not see how hungry these poor women were? . . . The SS woman did not report this event in the lager; I know that for sure. . . . On another occasion I saw her kneel in front of a sick haftling and help her do up her shoes.[32]

These two acts of kindness, seemingly nondescript, would likely have been risky lapses of kindness with potentially serious consequences for the guard had the episodes been reported to superiors. Likewise the pity shown by the old woman also needs to be recognised as an act of bravery under the circumstances recounted by I. J. The same survivor, I. J. also writes about two doctors at the Horst Hospital,[33] Dr. Bertran and Dr. Eugen Gang, who:

> tried to heal and look after our haftlings with the utmost altruism, and succeeded in saving some of them from the terrible fate of the lager by keeping them in the hospital as long as they possibly could. They did not even let them go at the order of the Gestapo. The haftlings only returned when it was time to evacuate the hospital. Then they let them go with blankets, clothing and food.[34]

This example like the previous one would seem, on the face of it, to represent less than extraordinary behaviour. However, under the circumstances such behaviour is surely noteworthy. Almost certainly the SS guard and the two doctors took risks that might have had serious repercussions for them. If the accounts of I. J. are accurate then Maria Reich, Dr. Bertran and Eugene Gang all made a significant moral choice in difficult circumstances. I want to argue that their choices are all the more remarkable in the light of the overwhelming number of instances in the testimonies of other sorts of moral choices.

Perhaps the most difficult group of examples to understand among the instances of expressions of responsibility within this group of testimonies are those who might be best described, to borrow Michael Marrus' categorization, as bystanders. Although I have already examined bystander behaviour at some length in chapter four I think that this group of examples, given the sorts of behaviour evidenced, warrants further consideration.

The behaviour of those who witnessed the maltreatment of the Jews covers a broad spectrum. In the testimonies used here behaviour ranges from the sorts of moral stands made by those cited above by I. J., through to instances that can be described at best as morally suspect and at worst as behaviour that beggars description. In another testimony, Hungarian Auschwitz survivor, C. D., upon returning to her hometown in Bekescsaba prior to being forced into the town's ghetto noted that:

> After the arrival of the Germans my father was daily insulted even by the citizens. Generally they behaved very nastily; they drew different signs on the walls.[35]

This is an interesting observation on the part of C. D. It seems to depict a situation where the arrival of the Germans served as a trigger for the legitimisation of anti-semitic behaviour. And although it's not clear from the testimonial material, it seems also that this description was intended to contrast with life before the arrival of the Germans. Prior to the arrival of the Germans it would seem that life was, if not lived in harmony, at least tolerable for the Jewish population of the area. Even after surviving Auschwitz, but prior to the arrival of the Russians, C. D. wrote that masquerading as 'Aryans' she and a friend stayed in a camp for displaced 'foreigners' where:

> we got to know a Hungarian family who took us in. . . . We stayed there until the Russians arrived on May 16. Then we confessed that we were Jews. We could see that our hosts did not like it too much, so we left.[36]

Sadly, accounts depicting this sort of behaviour can be found throughout the testimonies. After being interned in the Balassagyarmat ghetto prior to her deportation to Auschwitz, Dr. I. J.'s impressions were that:

> The Christians had mixed feelings toward us, some of them disputed these rules [Here Schenk is referring to the fact that she was not allowed out of the ghetto to attend a patient without a written permit from the police, an armed escort and

a relative of the patient] but the majority were happy with the separation of the Jews. A lot of them were curious and wanted, for differing reasons, to get into the ghetto. People looked at me as if I was a curious breed of animal.[37]

On June the 5th I. J. and others were moved to a tobacco barn in the town of Nyirjespuszta. She writes that:

> The transportation proceeded in cars and on foot. On the streets there were a lot of people standing and watching us with interest. No traces of good or bad intentions could be seen on their faces, only curiosity. However, even before we left, the looting in the Jewish flats in the ghetto had started. They took food, movable objects etc. We could see these items being taken away from the derelict houses, and I personally witnessed one of the gendarmes looking after us, go into a flat, and stuff his pockets full of cigarettes, handkerchiefs and women's silk stockings.[38]

Curiosity would seem to me to be an odd choice of words, by I. J. here. Perhaps the passivity she encountered in the faces of the onlookers was that of indifference. This is of course speculation on my part but I would venture to say that curiosity and indifference might present the same 'face'. Curiosity or indifference aside, the looks that I. J. encountered were not interpreted by her as conveying any sort of concern on the part of the onlookers. This in its own right is a cause of concern. It is very difficult to ascertain the nature of the 'interest' being shown. For some of those looking on there might have been malice in their faces. For some it might have been concern for their own fate and even feelings of helplessness in the face of the plight of these people. A sign of how some of the local population viewed the situation of the deportation of the Jews is evident in I. J.'s claim that some of them began to loot the possessions of Jewish families even before they had left the scene. This would seem to represent not only a generalised lack of respect for the property of others but outright contempt for those Jews whose comprehension of what was happening was already stretched to breaking point.

Toward the end of her long ordeal but by now working in a munitions factory in Germany, I. J. recalled that:

> In Sommerda the majority of people were very hostile towards us. It was the case, for example, that doctors did not want to refer our patients to surgery, commenting: "Jews can die". I am unable to name one doctor in Sommerda Hospital who behaved humanely toward our patients. They were so hostile and unfriendly that even our SS guard found it too much and reported it to the commandant.[39]

The behaviour that I. J. observed at the hospital must have been extremely difficult for her to understand, especially as she herself was a medical doctor. I. J. makes a very interesting observation about the change in behaviour of the local population once it became clear that the arrival of the Americans was imminent.

I. J. writes:

> In April the environs of Sommerda were heavily bombarded by the Allies, es-
> pecially Erfurt, 30 kilometres from us and the airport of Koleda, 10 kilometres
> from us. . . . On the 3rd of April the order came with Himmler's signature to
> empty the lager. . . . As soon as the situation changed, the people became
> friendlier. When we left Sommerda on foot, on the 4th of April, both the work-
> ers and the civilians behaved in a friendly way.[40]

If I. J.'s testimony can be taken on face value then the behaviour displayed to the
Jews, though consistent with self-interest, would seem to be duplicitous. Later,
after the surrender of Germany when I. J. was attempting to find her way back to
Hungary she arrived in the German town of Kaden where:

> the behaviour of the German civilians changed immensely. Those who previ-
> ously did not want to give us any food or accommodation now begged us to
> stay with them. The German civilians provided us with everything from cooked
> meals to cube sugar and cakes.[41]

Describing their initial incarceration in the ghetto in the Hungarian town of Kisvárda, Mrs O. P. and Ms Q. R. write, in a joint testimony, that:

> Non-Jewish civilians generally behaved cowardly, or at best were merely pas-
> sive. There were also those who seemed happy with our sad fate.[42]

One can only speculate at how difficult it must have been for Mrs O. P. and Ms
Q. R. to comprehend the indifference and even the expressions of apparent satisfaction on the faces of people from their own community as they and other Jews
were maltreated by Hungarian authorities. As difficult as it is to understand what
it must have been like, like Lawrence Langer, I want to refrain from the claim
that the testimonies represent some sort of, "homage to "the indomitable human
spirit""[43] because in my view such tributes contribute little to further understanding of the subtle and not so subtle complexities of the moral lives of these people. Part of what I'm seeking to convey here is a sense of the difficulty of understanding how people themselves understand their responsibilities to others and to
themselves.

I believe that there is evidence for the claim that the difficulties entailed in
trying to fathom the emotions and reasoning of those whose experiences are revealed in the testimonies stems in part from a sense of moral disorientation that
such experiences would likely have visited on the individuals involved. There
are a number of instances in the testimonies of a feeling of the moral faculties
being overwhelmed by events. In fact, there are moments in most of the stories
when the interviewees convey a sense of incomprehension or incredulity of what
was happening to them and why.

For example, in her testimony E. F. describes the way she felt just after the
'selection' process at the time of her arrival at Auschwitz. E. F. writes that "I

walked on numb, not even realising what this [the selection] meant."[44] Perhaps what E. F. is describing here is a certain kind of numbness or incredulity at what she is experiencing. It is not certain whether this numbness stemmed from some sort of moral incomprehension but there is a good chance that it did. In the joint testimony of Mrs K. L. and Mrs M. N. they talk about continuous brutalisation leading up to their arrival at Auschwitz. Recounting the selection itself they write that:

> [it] happened so quickly that members of families did not even have time to say goodbye. We were somewhat numb from the trip, the excitement and the volume of traffic at the station.[45]

The extracts from the testimony of E. F., and that of K. L. and M. N., whilst perhaps inconclusive, suggest difficulty in comprehending the moral practical implications of the events that confronted them. It is as if the events prior to, and including, their arrival at Auschwitz represented a moral universe of such horrifying proportions that they were unable to align them with their previously acquired precepts for what constituted acceptable behaviour. The point I would make is that such evidence as the testimonies, is evidence of both enormity and complexity; enormous in the horror conveyed and complex in terms of the factors that come in to play in order to understand such experiences.

The degree to which luck played a part in the survival of particular individuals is striking in the testimonies. By 'luck' is meant luck in one's circumstances that carries with it a moral dimension insofar as luck impacts upon the way we conduct our lives, the sorts of choices and judgments we make and the consequences we bear responsibility for. One instance where luck was of paramount significance was during selections in Auschwitz. For example, after surviving the horrors of Auschwitz for eight months A. B. recalled the selection of December 13th [1944]. She writes:

> I will always remember this day. They woke us up at 2.30a.m. and made us stand in the meadow just as we had stood at the beginning of the first transportation. From my transport there were only six women left. We stood there all day. Eventually, at 6p.m. they let us back into the barrack. There Frau Dreschler, Aufseherin Wolkenrath, Lagerkommandant Scwartz and Oberaufseherin Frau Mandel were waiting for us. We had to jump over a one meter wide trench. Those who succeeded would be left alive; those who did not were immediately taken away. Naturally the malaria and typhus had left a lot of women weak and unable to jump. They were all sent to the gas. On that horrible day, of the 25,000-30,000 left, only 4,000 remained. All of the others were taken away by trucks. I can still hear the screams of these poor women. They were even then still 2,000 short for their 'death transport', so they randomly chose another 2,000 people and took them too. One of my girlfriends died in this random way.[46]

Clearly A. B. herself is well aware of the role of luck in surviving such moments. In another very poignant example of how life can hang on an apparently insignificant choice C. D. describes the details of the selection of herself and her mother and sister after arriving at Auschwitz. She writes that:

> After five days we arrived at Auschwitz-Birkenau at 10 a.m. We were taken off the wagons by Polish boys dressed in stripy suits and the men were immediately separated from us. . . . I was standing in front of an SS officer together with my mother and younger sister and he immediately sorted us. The aim of the selection was to separate families and it was done on the basis of similar features. This was my perception but others said so too. My sister was put in my group. My mother cried out after us, my sister went over to her and thus they found themselves on the side from which nobody ever returned.[47]

In spite of the matter of fact way that C. D. writes one can only wonder how she must have felt at being separated from her mother. And then when her sister rejoined her mother what did she feel? She would almost certainly have been very frightened and disoriented. She would also have been very anxious as to her fate and the fate of her family. In another testimony and writing also about the nature of selections that were a pivotal part of life and death in Auschwitz, K. L. and M. N. recall that:

> The most usual motif of life in Auschwitz apart from the appels [roll call] was the selections. They happened in the open air, we had to march in front of Mengele stark naked. He did not only select the sick and the very thin, but he was very unexpected in his choices and reasons.[48]

Such uncertainty, as recalled by K. L. and M. N. must have been very difficult to deal with emotionally and displayed the absolute power over life and death wielded by those in control.

The joint testimony of mother and daughter, Mrs O. P. and Q. R., recounts the role that luck played in being able to stay together during their stay in Auschwitz. They recall that:

> It was a huge thing that we could stay together all the way through. We had to think of all sorts of things to be able to stay together. . . . At the end of September Q. R. came down with Scarlet Fever. The doctor realised and put me in hospital. I was supposed to be there for two weeks and we were constantly expecting Dr. Mengele. After 5 days and constant begging from my mother I thought it better to deny my temperature in order that I could be released. So somehow still feverish I managed to get out of the hospital. I was lucky, as a week later there was a huge selection that hardly left any patients there.[49]

In the case of O. P. and Q. R. it seems that luck played an integral part in the determination of their survival. I am not saying that luck is the only factor here. Indeed, in the example above it is clear that both women possessed a good understanding of what it meant to be ill for too long. I would reiterate though that, together with the manifestly close bond between mother and daughter, their will to survive and the knowledge of life in the camp, luck needs to be considered in an explanation of their survival. The point here is that luck looms larger in the circumstances depicted than for most of us thus contributing to the moral complexity quotient of the moral dimensions of the examples.

One of the most important aspects of the testimonies examined here concerns the rare and contemporary insights that they offer on the issue of the behaviour and motivation of those Germans and Hungarians involved in the operations of the ghettoization and transportation of Jews from Hungary to Auschwitz. As contemporary sources they represent a valuable insight into how the perpetrators of these crimes acted and how they might have been thinking at the time that they committed these acts. In my attempt to understand the behaviour of those Germans and Hungarians who participated in the implementation of Nazi Jewish policy I have mostly focused on accounts of individuals who have been identified by name in the testimonies. Some of the people identified have been documented elsewhere. Others I have been unable to locate in other sources.[50] Where possible I have sought to provide secondary evidence that corroborates the identification of these individuals.

My primary aim here has been to shed additional light on the attitudes and motivations of those 'ordinary people' who committed such 'extraordinary' crimes. Following the excellent work of Browning[51] I am seeking to unpack some complex questions. For example, what were the motivations of the rank and file SS personnel? Were they driven by anti-semitic sentiments? Or were they themselves driven by a range of factors, some external, and some specific to the psychological makeup of the individuals concerned? Or was it a combination of all of these factors? I am also very interested in whether or not the Holocaust perpetrators made significant distinctions between their victims. Did they distinguish between Jews and non-Jews? And very importantly, did the perpetrators act with moral consistency? It is certainly the case that different categories of people are explicitly identified in the testimonies. The testimonies refer specifically to career SS, ordinary German army personnel, Hungarian special police and ordinary Hungarian police. It also seems to be the case that a variety of motivations for behaviour is able to be seen.

First I shall consider SS personnel mentioned by name in the testimonies. Perhaps the most infamous of these is Joseph Mengele. Mengele was a medical doctor at Auschwitz and, as has been well documented, was personally responsible for many selections and the infamous experiments on twin children. One particular testimony makes note of certain aspects of Mengele's behaviour which seems to stand at odds with the overall welfare of the inmates of Auschwitz. In spite of being personally selected for the gas chamber by Mengele, a Hungarian-Jewish survivor of Auschwitz, C. D. is able to note Mengele's apparent expressions of humanity, attention to cleanliness, a pre-occupation with personal attire and is even able to speculate on the possibility of Mengele's feelings toward one of the Jewish doctors. C. D. writes:

In August I was taken to the hospital with typhoid. Here Dr. Mengele put me in the transition camp together with the dead and dying, saying I was unable to work. There a woman doctor friend of mine from Szeged (Dr. Klara Nagy) swapped me for a corpse, after Mengele had selected me, so the numbers were matching and Mengele did not look for me. He was a wonderfully handsome man, and was always walking around nicely dressed up. We thought he was in love with Klara Nagy. He checked out the toilets very thoroughly, generally it was clean in the lager, thanks to him.[52]

This description conveys an image of a man who seemingly went about his work with a certain thoroughness and attention to detail. It is difficult to imagine how this description of the level of cleanliness can be believed given the general level of squalor that has been described in many other accounts of life in Auschwitz. Moreover Mengele was, undoubtedly, personally responsible for the deaths of countless lives by virtue of his role in the selections. As for C. D.'s remarks concerning the appearance of Mengele, her story is corroborated by some of the other testimonies. On this issue of the SS personnel's attention to personal appearance, Inga Clendinnen writes:

Inside Auschwitz, as in every SS run camp, distinctions between 'guard' and 'prisoner' were highly visible and deliberately dramatised. . . . Their elegant, emblematic uniforms and cultivated ease of bearing was in constant contrast with the physical squalor, ludicrous clothing, cropped heads, and histrionically abject demeanours imposed on their prisoners.[53]

Clendinnen's comments on this contrast form part of her wider argument that it is possible to 'read' life in Auschwitz as ritualised drama. I will consider her interpretation in more detail a little later in the chapter when I look more directly at the question of the behaviour of the SS in the camps.

Returning to Mengele, it is important to note that his active participation in the selections for the gas chambers is repeatedly mentioned in the testimonies. C. D. writes:

In September almost every day there were selections. We had to march naked in front of Dr. Mengele and the soldiers. He usually looked at the stomachs. Those with hunger flattened stomachs were not put into the work transports.[54]

In a description of an 'appell', E. F. recalled:

Around 2 a.m . . . they chased us out into the night with sticks and dog whips. It was terribly cold and the rags we were wearing did not warm us. They made us stand in rows of five, but apart, so that we could not warm each other. We had to stand there like this until 11 a.m. the next day. . . . We lived like this for four days. . . . After this we had to get undressed again and we felt ashamed. We had to march in front of Dr. Mengele (the handsome man) holding our right arms above our heads.[55]

One testimony in particular depicts Mengele as a man capable of measured brutality. In the joint testimony of Mrs O. P. and her daughter Q. R., Q. R. recalls an incident in which Mengele tried to separate mother from daughter. They write that:

> A German civilian factory owner came to ask for workers, we were already happy to get out of there. Mengele appeared and chose me but not my mother. I acted as if I had not noticed the direction he was pointing me to. My mother began to come toward me. Mengele called me and hit me so hard I fell on the floor. He called the SS women and the bitches hit me with sticks or with their boots wherever they could get me. When they tired of it Mengele told them to throw me into the corner, where there were already about 40 people.[56]

In addition to physical violence Mengele also seemed to find some sort of macabre pleasure or satisfaction in the fear that he was able to generate in the inmates. Continuing the recollection of Mengele's attempt to separate Q. R. from her mother, mother and daughter write:

> We stood there for a while. Then he shouted at us "Hinein in die Gazkammer!" They then pushed us into a small gas chamber, which they used to disinfect blankets in. I was desperate. I heard someone shout: "We are still young, we want to live!" I looked around; we were in a small room. . . . It was almost pitch dark. On one of the doors there was a small window. There were two big holes in the ceiling with taps. . . . They opened one of the taps then the SS women herded us out. We were screaming.[57]

Mengele's interest in the suffering of human beings has been well documented.[58] Further corroboration of Mengele's predilection for watching people suffer comes in the form of the joint testimony of Mrs K. L. and M. N. In their testimony on a particular aspect of life at Auschwitz they write that:

> The sick were taken to hospital, where they were treated by haftling doctors. It was a nicely furbished hospital with medication. Then Dr. Mengele appeared, had a look at the sick and sent 80% of them to the gas chamber. Initially it took 2-3 minutes to die of the gas. However, later on when the gas was running out or they put a smaller amount in, people suffered for about 10 minutes. Dr. Mengele and his escort watched the suffering from the outside. To my knowledge they did not leave anybody under the age of 12 alive, except twins.[59]

There are some concerns about this account of Mengele as it is written as though they are retelling the story of someone else. While there is no reason to doubt the veracity of what they say it is not clear as to whether or not their 'knowledge' is based on an eye-witness account or on what they had heard from someone else. Where, for example would their knowledge of the experimentation on twins have come? It even seems unlikely that they would have been able to observe Mengele as he watched the gas chamber in action. My concerns about the reliability of the testimony of K. L. and M. N. are allayed somewhat by the fact that not dis-similar recollections of Mengele occur in most of the testimonies.

Aside from Mengele a number of other career SS personnel at Auschwitz receive special mention in the testimonies as a result of their behaviour. It seems plausible that these men and women would have been hand picked for their anti-semitic attitudes and enthusiasm for brutalizing and killing Jews. Some of the examples cited in the testimonies are noteworthy for what they reveal about the antipathy of the SS personnel toward the Jewish inmates. In some of the accounts of the behaviour of the SS personnel in Auschwitz, for example, it seems clear that a sense of pleasure was derived from the suffering of others. A. B. in her testimony describes being moved to the 'Effekten kommando' (inmates who were responsible for the sorting and storing of items confiscated from Jews after their arrival at Auschwitz). Referring to the senior SS non-commissioned officer at the Effektenkommando she writes:

> There we had a nasty Schaarfuhrer. One day, for example, he chose ten men and told them he would perform 'Mittagspause' (lunchbreak) with them (This bastards name was Wiegleb). The men were taken to a warehouse full of lice-ridden clothes. There they had to dress up in furs and gasmasks and run for an hour, then lie down, run some more, then lie down. In the meantime they were flogged until they collapsed.[60]

It is difficult to ascertain with any certainty the purpose or reason for such seemingly gratuitous violence. Inga Clendinnen builds a complex and interesting argument in an effort to shed some light on this issue. She claims that there are a number of factors that would likely comprise the motivation for the sort of behaviour described. She begins by identifying the tradition of discipline that permeated not only German military culture but that of German civil culture too. She uses the example of Auschwitz commandant Rudolph Hoess as a way of illustrating this point. Citing Hoess's own emphasis, in his biography, on the significance of discipline as necessary for obedience and submission to rule, Clendinnen also makes the point that the requirement for discipline in the camp, whilst a factor, is insufficient to explain situations of the sort I have identified above. As she puts it discipline as an explanation fails, on its own "to comprehend the apparently gratuitous 'disciplines' inflicted inside camp boundaries but outside official hours of work, and inflicted with sinister enthusiasm."[61] Clendinnen's remarks here seem to come close to the heart of the issue. She pursues her line of thought with references to remarks by survivors Elie Cohen and Primo Levi who talked of the absurdity and ridiculousness of the behaviour of the SS. She proceeds to speculate that for the SS personnel the 'squalid reality' of not only the lives of the Jewish inmates, but their own lives as well, would have required the maintenance of the fiction of moral, intellectual, physical superiority in the face of the 'enemy'. Hence Clendinnen invites the hypothesis that:

> the rounds of disciplinary procedures so ardently enforced by the Auschwitz SS

not only met cultural criteria of discipline and punishment, but were also consciously theatrical, and that these pieces of SS theatre, constructed and enacted
daily, reanimated the SS sense of high purpose and invincibility, authenticated
the realism of their absurd ideology, and sustained both morale and self-image
in what was, indubitably but inadmissibly, psychologically a hardship post.[62]

Clendinnen's argument is very interesting and I concur with most of what she
has to say. Her description of the theatre of 'arrival', of 'initiation', of 'roll calls'
and of the forms of 'sport' that the SS conjured up all align convincingly with
notions of the ritualised drama of life in the camp. However, one aspect of her
interpretation of Auschwitz is less convincing. Her claim that the sort of behaviour in question would have aided morale and self-image is not uncontentious as
there are other plausible interpretations of the behaviour she describes. For example, it seems possible that such behaviour was designed to denigrate and de-
humanise inmates as a means of affirming the anti-semitic ethic that Jews were
sub-human. Whatever the reason, I also hold to the view that such behaviour is
morally complex and that interpretations are thus, by definition, also going to be
complex. Clendinnen is also aware of how complex and difficult answers are to
come by. On the one hand she says that she favours explanations of an anthropo-
logical kind.[63] Yet by the time she arrives at her concluding remarks on the behaviour of the SS she seems willing to concede that the story also needs to take
account of such factors as the moral psychology of individuals and the role of
the circumstances that individuals find themselves in.[64]

   Examples of gratuitously cruel behaviour abound in the testimonies. In
some instances there are clues as to why such cruelty might have been inflicted.
In some instances anti-Semitism is almost certainly a factor. For example, in his
testimony of events in the Hungarian city of Munkács prior to his deportation to
Auschwitz, Dr. G. H. writes that with the authority of the camp commander
Márton Zöldi:

> Women were tied up in the most impossible positions or turned upside down
> and forced to sing Hungarian folk songs until they fainted.[65]

The reference here to Hungarian folk songs is noteworthy as it serves to mark
out, albeit anecdotally and fragmentally, the historical/cultural presence of anti-
semitic attitudes within sections of the Hungarian population.

   Later in the same testimony, when recalling life in a deportation camp in
Ebensee in the final weeks of the war, G. H. writes of the differences between
the treatment meted out to Jews and non-Jews. In particular G. H. singles out the
behaviour of the two 'block' leaders. He refers to the senior man of one of the
blocks as a 'Christian Pole' who treated those unfit for work so cruelly that they
soon died as a result of his behaviour. Of the Ebensee deportation camp G. H.
writes:

> In none of the deportation camps where I had so far been was anti-Semitism as

strong as in Ebensee. The Jewish captives were meticulously separated from the
Christian ones, including those who were sick, there being an area for Christian
sick people and another special area designated for the Jewish sick.[66]

In this camp, G. H. writes that there were about 12,000 prisoners of whom about
4,000 were Jewish. The balance according to G. H. was Christian Poles,
Frenchmen and Russians. The other senior block leader to whom G. H. refers
was an Austrian named Lorenz. G. H. singles this man out as being especially
brutal. In one incident G. H. testifies that Lorenz, on the pretext of not being able
to find his pencil, accused the Jewish prisoners of having stolen it. As punishment, eighty Jews were forced to stand naked in the open where they were
flogged.

The record shows that the examples of cruelty of SS and other camp personnel were not restricted to men. For example, A. B. recorded that during a delousing routine in Auschwitz an 'Aufseherin', named Lotte Claus would beat the
women with a hot poker.[67] Elsewhere in the testimonies specific mention is
made of SS women brutalising the prisoners.

In several of the testimonies some interesting distinctions are made between
the behaviour of local Hungarian police and officials, Hungarian special police,
SS personnel and regular German army personnel. The observations made regarding the differences in the behaviour of the different personnel are interesting
in that they suggest that behaviour was not uniformly inhumane. In other words,
the differences described in the testimonies indicate differing sorts of behaviour
amongst perpetrators and between separate organisations and jurisdictions. For
example, in her testimony, Dr. I. J. describes markedly different treatment
among the different personnel responsible for the various stages of her deportation to Auschwitz. At the train station in her home town of Balassagyarmat in
Hungary, I. J. describes how in her wagon the only bucket of fresh water for the
journey was kicked out onto the ground by the station official directing deportations. This man, whom I. J. identifies as having the surname of Pongrác is
quoted by her as having remarked that "the Jews do not need that much water."[68]
In another incident at the same station I. J. made a request to the gendarme captain (whom I. J. claims had the surname of Bretány) that an elderly woman who
was dying be allowed to be taken off the train. I. J. writes that the captain
laughed and answered "Would you be so cruel as to leave one of your fellow
Jews out of this fun?"[69]

On the third day of their deportation to Auschwitz at the town of Kassa the
Hungarian police handed over escort of the train that I. J. was travelling on to SS
personnel. It is noteworthy that I. J. writes that after the SS took over control of
the train the Jews were provided with fresh water more regularly than they had
been when the escort had comprised Hungarian police. I. J. notes that after the
changeover to the SS the Jews were also given toilet buckets and were allowed
to renew their water supply if the train stopped long enough at some stations. I.
J.'s testimony concerning the differences in the behaviour between the German
SS personnel and the Hungarian authorities is corroborated by some of the other

testimonies.

The strongest corroboration of I. J.'s observations on the difference in behaviour between the German SS personnel and the Hungarian police, both standard and specially recruited, comes from the testimony of Dr. G. H.. In his testimony G. H. gives an account of the behaviour of the Hungarian special police
during the initial roundup of Jews in the town of Munkács in Hungary. It is my
opinion that G. H.'s testimony is second to none in terms of its depiction of the
level of ferociousness and sheer brutality that was meted out on the part of the
Hungarian authorities. G. H. expressly makes the point that the police in question were not local gendarmes but 'special constables' drafted from other towns
in the province. This of course raises the question as to whether or not the police
were chosen on the grounds of their anti-semitic sentiments. Whilst I have no direct evidence that this was the case it seems at least possible that the policemen
in question were selected in large part because of their prejudices. If this were
the case it would certainly help to explain the more brutal behaviour of these
special police. G. H. writes that en route from the ghetto to the place of deportation:

> They [the 'special constables'] were armed with heavy sticks and rained blows
> on the Jews, making no distinction between men, women and children. . . .
> Numerous people were killed this way during the short distance of some two
> kilometres from the ghetto to the brickyard, among them Géza Schönfeld, a
> wholesaler dealing in bicycles, gramophones and motor parts, and the account-
> ant Márton Weiss. . . . I daresay that never during the whole period of my de-
> portation in Germany did I witness scenes as terrible as those.[70]

G. H. identifies two Hungarian nationals as being especially brutal in their
treatment of the Jewish people held in a brickyard whilst awaiting deportation to
Auschwitz. G. H. claims that a special constable from the town of Sárospatak
with the surname of Németi, would daily make all the men between the ages of
eighteen and sixty do exercises whilst hitting them about the head with a club,
often so hard that they would collapse unconscious. G. H. records that in another
incident, apparently authorised by Márton Zöldi[71] the senior officer and an ex-
officer in the regular Hungarian police, fifteen rabbis were gathered and tortured
into signing a declaration that Jewish people use Christian blood in making their
Passover bread. After a savage beating the rabbis were then buried up to their
necks in sewage. According to G. H. none of these rabbis survived this ordeal.
G. H. claimed that all fifteen subsequently died en route to Auschwitz as a result
of injuries sustained at the brickyard. This last incident is solid evidence of anti-
semitic sentiment which must rate as a key motivating factor in the behaviour of
the individuals in question. In particular the individual Márton Zöldi is, on the
basis of historical record, known to have been a rabid anti-Semite.

The testimony of Dr. G. H. is also interesting for what it reveals as regards
the distinctions perpetrators made between Jews and non-Jews. Recounting one
particular incident concerning the relationship between a Jewish woman named

Anna Grünberger and a man named József Kocsis whom G. H. describes as her Christian fiancé, he writes they were:

> tied together . . . to a horse which was then made to gallop hauling the couple along for several kilometres. The young man suffered this punishment after he was accused of hiding his bride to be.[72]

It is clear from this account that non-Jews, too, could be summarily brutalised and murdered if it was thought that they were assisting Jews in some way. In her description of the behaviour of regular Wermacht soldiers an altogether different behaviour is noted by Dr. I. J.. Upon being moved from Auschwitz to an artificial fuel factory in Gelsenkirchen I. J. writes that:

> Immediately on entering the wagons we were somewhat relieved to see that the soldiers looking after us, apart from the officer, all belonged to the Wermacht. They proceeded to treat us in a more humane manner.[73]

I. J. records that during the course of a ten day journey they were given fresh water, were allowed to wash and even received food from the personal supply of their escorts. At one point in the journey I. J. claims that one of the escorts made a point of saying that "No one should tell anyone about this."[74] My point is that the testimonial evidence shows that it is problematic to generalise about the behaviour of people. The behaviour of the soldiers escorting I. J. and her fellow prisoners is a case in point. It is at least a possibility that the men in question felt it was their responsibility to behave as humanely as they believed possible under the circumstances as they understood them. The testimonies convey a measure of evidence that anti-semitic feelings or indeed any feelings of an inhumane sort toward the people they were escorting was less evident among regular army soldiers.

For the Jews of Europe choice very often only offered itself fleetingly and in situations surrounded by panic, confusion and terror. It is also true, though, as the following examples show, that amidst the horror, the stories strongly invoke some of the subtleties and nuances of moral life. A Jewish survivor Inge Deutschkron recalls:

> I remember the day when they made Berlin *Judenrein*. The people hastened in the streets; no one wanted to be in the streets; you could see the streets were absolutely empty. . . . And I remember this day very vividly because we saw police cars rushing through the streets of Berlin taking people out of the houses. They had herded Jews together, from factories, from houses, wherever they could find them. . . . They were going off not very far from here on one of the tracks at the Grünewald station, and this was the day when I felt so utterly alone, left alone, because now I knew we would be one of the very few people left. I felt very guilty that I didn't go myself and I tried to escape the fate that the others could not escape. There was no more warmth around, no more soul akin to us, you understand.[75]

Aside from her particularly poignant description of the deportation of the Jews of Berlin, what is especially noteworthy is the way Inge Deutschkron takes up her understanding of responsibility for the events as they unfolded. I take her feelings of guilt to be entirely legitimate and emblematic of the processes individuals undergo when working through the vicissitudes of moral life. Though her guilt is ironic given that guilt ought to have been the sole property of those perpetrating the crimes against the Jews, it shows that she possessed a heightened awareness of the plight of others and was able to empathise with that plight. The example of Deutschkron contrasts with that of my earlier examination of the example of Pola inasmuch as the former chose to escape the fate of the others. Both examples, however, bear witness to the anxiety that derived from the choices they had to make.

Revisiting the earlier Fink example juxtaposes even more starkly the differing consequences of crucial initial choices. Recalling the difficult choice that she and her sister had made compared with that of her cousin, and the differing consequences of those choices, Ida Fink writes:

> We called the first action—that scrap of time that I want to talk about—a round—up, although no one was rounding anyone up; on that beautiful, clear morning, each of us made our own way, not willingly, to be sure, but under orders, to the marketplace in our little town. . . . This beautiful, clear morning that I am digging out of the ruins of my memory is still fresh; its colours and aromas have not faded: a grainy golden mist with red spheres of apples hanging in it, and the shadows above the river damp with the sharp odour of burdock, and the bright blue dress that I was wearing when I left the hose and turned around at the gate. It was then, probably at that very moment, that I suddenly progressed, instinctively, from an infantile state to a still naive caution—instinctively, because I wasn't thinking about why I avoided the gate that led to the street and instead set off on a roundabout route, across the orchard, along the riverbank, down a road we called "the back way" because it wound through the outskirts of town. . . . My sister, too, was not yet afraid; it was only when we went further along the street, beyond the bridge, and the view of the marketplace leapt out at us from behind the building on the corner, that we suddenly stopped in our tracks. . . . I don't know what it was exactly. I only know that we suddenly stopped and my sister began to tremble, and then I caught the trembling, and she said, "Let's run away," and although no one was chasing us and the morning was still clear and peaceful, we ran back to the little bridge . . . we ran for a long time until we were high up the steep slope known as Castle Hill—the ruins of an old castle stood on top of it—and on this hillside, the jewel of our town, we sat down in the bushes, out of breath and still shaking. We sat there for an hour, maybe two, I don't know, because it was then that time measured in the ordinary way stopped. Then we climbed down the steep slope to the river and returned to our house, where we heard what had happened in the marketplace, and that our cousin David had been taken. . . . First we learned that the women had been told to go home, that only the men were ordered to remain standing there, and that the path chosen by our cousin had been the opposite of ours. We

had been horrified by the sight of the crowd in the marketplace, while he was drawn towards it by an enormous force, a force as strong as his nerves were weak, so that somehow or other he did violence to his own fate, he himself, himself, himself, and that was what he asked people to tell his mother, and then he wrote it down: "I myself am to blame, forgive me."[76]

I justify quoting this example at length on the grounds of the moral force that permeates the story. Ida Fink, her sister and her cousin David all made crucial choices within the context of very specific circumstances. Ida and her sister could have chosen to do as they had been instructed to do. They could have chosen to remain with their family but they chose instead, perhaps out of an impending sense of fear, to take another path. Their cousin David chose otherwise. Though we will never know for certain the reasons for their respective choices it seems to me that the story conveys a strong sense of foreboding of the impending disaster that awaited those who gathered in the marketplace. Maybe the foreboding is evidence of the hindsight that Ida brings with her recollection of events. Perhaps she could see and feel that nothing good could come from the treatment of people in this way.

Other examples in this catalogue of episodes reveal circumstances of an even bleaker sort. In terms of what has become known as 'choice less choices' what makes these sorts of situations more extreme is the way they entail a shift beyond the option of life or death to circumstances defined by the need to decide between one form of abnormal response and another. Central to these sorts of situations is the victim's impotence in the face of circumstances imposed from outside their control. Typically the agent in such an extreme situation finds her or himself restricted with regards to the parameters of time and space. That is to say, the need for a decision is often sudden and unexpected, with no way of avoiding the requirement to decide. Situations epitomising these sorts of 'choices' are sometimes found in eye witness recollections of extermination camp selection processes. For example, Olga Lengyel shortly after her arrival to Auschwitz in May, 1944 writes:

> Today when I think about our arrival at the camp, the cars of our train appear to me as so many coffins. . . . The order came, curt and demanding: Get out!" As soon as we left the cattle cars, my mother, my sons and I were separated from my father and my husband. We now stood in columns that extended for hundreds of yards. The train had discharged from four to five thousand passengers, all as dazed and bewildered as we were. More commands, and we were paraded before about thirty SS men, including the head of the camp and other officers. They began to choose, sending some of us to the right and some to the left. This was the first "selection", in the course of which, as we could not dream could be true, the initial sacrifices for the crematories were kicked. . . . The only explanation came from an SS officer who assured us that the aged would remain in charge of the children. I believed him, assuming naturally that the able bodied adults would have to work, but that the old and very young would be cared for. Our turn came. My mother, my sons, and I stepped before the "selectors".

Then I committed my . . . terrible error. The selector waved my mother and I to the adult group. He classed my younger son Thomas with the children and aged, which was to mean immediate extermination. He hesitated before Arvad, my older son. My heart thumped violently. This officer, a large dark man who wore glasses, seemed to be trying to act fairly. Later I learned that he was Dr. Fritz Klein, the "Chief Selector". This boy must be more than twelve he remarked to me. "No," I protested. The truth was that Arvad was not quite twelve, and I could have said so. He was big for his age, but I wanted to spare him from labours that might prove too arduous for him. "Very well," Klein agreed amiably. "To the left!" I had persuaded my mother that she should follow the children and take care of them. At her age she had a right to the treatment accorded to the elderly and there should be someone to look after Arvad and Thomas. "Very well," he again acquiesced. "You'll all be in the same camp. How should I have known. I had spared them from hard work, but I had condemned Arvad and my mother to death in the gas chambers.[77]

Again I include a lengthy passage because of the intensity of the moral story it contains. On the basis of Olga Lengyel's description it is quite apparent that she made what she thought was the best decision in the circumstances. But what is more significant with regard to the matter of choice is the extreme poverty of the circumstances in question and within which the options, such as they were, were confined. I argue that Olga Lengyel's situation is a situation within which concern over whether or not her judgment was an 'all things considered' best judgment or not are secondary to the poverty of the available options. Even if Olga Lengyel had known more about the mechanics of the selection process her capacity to make a more meaningful choice than the one she did in fact make may not have been enhanced by this extra knowledge. Ultimately, she was in a no win situation and more importantly, a situation within which it may in fact not make much sense to speak about 'best judgments'. Some situations may be such that they offer no possibility for what may be meaningfully called 'good' judgments. It is important to note, though, that Lengyel took responsibility for the situation at hand within the extreme confines of the knowledge she had to hand. Moreover, in spite of the limits of the situation, she was able to maintain her moral integrity. Another survivor Abraham Bomba recalls, in an interview, a situation during a time in the camp when he was responsible for cutting off the hair of women prior to their being gassed. The situation Abraham Bomba describes portrays a situation similar to that in which Olga Lengyel was 'placed' by virtue of the circumstances she had found herself in. In response to the interviewers questions Abraham Bomba recalls:

You said there were about sixteen barbers? You cut the hair of how many women in one batch?
In one day there was about, I would say, going into that place between sixty and seventy women in the same room at one time. After we were finished with this party, another party came in...
But I asked you and you didn't answer: What was your impression the first time

you saw these naked women arriving with children? What did you feel?
I tell you something. To have a feeling about that . . . it was very hard to feel anything, because working there day and night between dead people, between bodies, your feeling disappeared, you were dead. You had no feeling at all. As a matter of fact, I want to tell you something that happened. At the gas chamber, when I was chosen to work there as a barber, some of the women that came in on a transport from my town of Czestochowa, I knew a lot of them. I knew them; I lived with them in my town. I lived with them in my street, and some of them were my close friends. And when they saw me, they started asking me, Abe this and Abe that—"What's going to happen to us?" What could you tell them? What could you tell? A friend of mine worked as a barber—he was a good barber from my home town—when his wife and his sister came into the gas chamber . . . I can't. It's too horrible. Please.
We have to do it. You know it.
I won't be able to do it.
You have to do it. I know it's very hard. I know and I apologize.
Don't make me go on please.
Please. We must go on.
I told you today it's going to be very hard. They were taking that in bags and transporting it to Germany.
Okay, go ahead. What was his answer when his wife and sister came?
They tried to talk to him and the husband of his sister. They could not tell them this was the last time they stay alive, because behind them was the German Nazis, SS men, and they knew that if they said a word, not only the wife and the woman, who were dead already, but also they would share the same thing with them. In a way, they tried to do the best for them, with a second longer, a minute longer, just to hug them and kiss them, because they knew they would never see them again.[78]

The barber described by Abraham Bomba was confronted with a 'choice less choice'. For the barber there was no 'all things considered' 'best judgment'. In terms of its moral dimensions the circumstances that the barber found himself in offered no unconscionable option. The example pointedly foregrounds the role of circumstance as an important part of the process by which people come to moral decisions. The example also highlights once again how circumstance is pivotal in influencing how we, as moral agents, take up responsibility for the situations we find ourselves in.

Other variations on the idea of the 'choice less choice' include the sorts of decisions forced on some of the 'Judenrat' leadership (the term used to describe the councils of Jewish leadership under the control of the Germans and responsible for the day to day operation of the ghettoes) to assist the Germans in the removal of 'non-essential' Jews. Justification for such decisions on the part of the leadership of the Judenrat centred on the argument that their involvement would not only reduce the worst excesses of the 'actions' as they took place but also actually enhance the bargaining position of the Judenrat and thereby increase the possibility of saving remaining Jews in the ghettoes. In the words of the Jewish leader Gens to other Jewish leadership in Vilna on the 'action' in the

Oszmiana ghetto in October 1942 he reports:

> Gentlemen, I asked you to come here today in order to relate to you one of the
> most terrible tragedies in the life of the Jews—when Jews led Jews to their
> death. . . . A week ago Weiss of the SD came to us in the name of the SD with
> an order that we were to travel to Oszmiana. There were about 4,000 Jews in
> the Oszmiana ghetto and it was not possible to keep so many people there. For
> that reason the ghetto would have to be made smaller—by picking out the peo-
> ple who did not suit the Germans, to take them away and shoot them. The first
> to go should be children and women whose husbands were taken away last year
> by the "snatchers." The next to be taken would be women and families with a
> large number of children. When we received this order we replied: "At your
> command." Mr. Dessler and Jewish Police went to Oszmiana. After two or
> three days the Jewish Police observed and reported to the *Gebeitskommissar* (in
> Vilna) that, first of all, the women whose men had been taken away last year
> were now working and could not be taken away, and, secondly, that there were
> no families with 4 or 5 children. The largest were families with two children.
> There were only a few [families] with three children. So that would also not
> work. (I forgot to say that no fewer than 1,500 persons had to be taken away.)
> We said that we could not provide such a number. We started to bargain. When
> Mr. Dessler arrived with the report from Oszmiana, the number dropped to 800.
> When I got to Oszmiana with Weiss, the number dropped again to 600. In real-
> ity the situation was different. We argued about the 600 and during this time the
> question of the removal of women and children was dropped. There remained
> the question of old people. In reality, 406 old people were   collected   in Osz-
> miana. These old people were handed over. . . . The Jewish Police saved those
> who must live. Those who had little time left to live were taken away, and may
> the aged among the Jews forgive us. They were a sacrifice for our Jews and for
> our future.[79]

In this example, Gens' rationalisation of the actions of the leadership of the
Vilna ghetto invokes a number of difficult questions. Among these is the question of the ever present danger and serious problem concerning the use of the
principles of utilitarianism to justify a course of action. The question needs to be
asked: Whose interests are really being served in this process of rationalisation,
reasonable though it may seem? Or is it a question of the situation generating a
terrible desperation which sees the Vilna leadership, as a means to stall for time,
bargain with the Nazis with the lives of their own people? These are vexed questions that are in my view devoid of straightforward answers.

If the nature of intention, choice and moral responsibility is complex and
quite subtle in respect to those who were the targets of the policies of mass murder of the Nazis, the sense of moral responsibility conveyed by those who were
quite literally targeting the Jews is no less problematic. On the one hand, some
evidence shows a level of detachment and mundaneness that seems to efface all
signs of the enormity of the moment of decision. On the other hand the same
evidence sometimes seems to convey a clear awareness of a sense of moral responsibility. The survivor E. F. recalls her moment of 'selection' in a testimony

recorded shortly after her return from Auschwitz to Budapest in 1945. E. F. writes:

> we arrived in Auschwitz at 3p.m. on July the tenth. At that time I was still with my brother, sister-in-law and a cousin. On the station I saw men dressed in striped outfits. As it was forbidden to speak they remained silent. They herded us out of the wagons and removed our remaining belongings. We were left with nothing except the clothes we were wearing. The men were separated from us, and I held onto my sister-in-law tightly, so that at least she would remain with me. In the meantime we reached the gate of the lager. I saw a very nice looking SS man [Dr. Joseph Mengele] approaching from the opposite direction. When he saw me holding on tight to my sister-in-law he motioned for me to go to the right and for her to go to the left. He did not even take his hand out of his pocket. I walked on numb, not even realising what this meant.[80]

On E. F.'s account, the selector, Dr. Joseph Mengele seeks to betray the moral enormity of the 'work' of selecting those who were, on the one hand, to be sent to their immediate death and those, on the other hand, who were to be afforded some sort of reprieve. It is now well documented that the desire for calm upon the arrival of transports was due to reasons of a more practical sort. In order to maintain acquiescence even in such close proximity to the moment of death, playing down the significance of the choices made by Mengele, allowed the process to proceed with less panic than would otherwise have ensued. This explanation for the attitude of Mengele can be evidenced in many of the accounts of the arrivals of Jews at the extermination camps. As for Mengele himself it is almost certainly the case that, in spite of his calm disposition, he would have been well aware of the moral profundity of his actions. I would also argue, though, that such an awareness, if it existed, fails to capture all that is pertinent to the story. It is possible that Mengele's officiousness and workman like attitude was indicative of a belief in the moral authority and maybe also the moral correctness of his actions, albeit within the confines of a Nazi ethic. If this is the case then it is a further indictment of a social system that produced such a flawed sense of moral responsibility in the face of such absolute abuse of human life.

Thus I conclude that the evidence of the testimonies shows that the behaviour of the perpetrators, like that of others who were involved in one way or another, was not uniform. Tragically, however, the diversity and complexity of the behaviour evidenced was unable to produce any sort of wholesale difference to the outcome. The testimonies depict enough individuals eager to brutalize and kill Jews, in the process dehumanizing themselves. The testimonies are also a powerful record of, to borrow Browning's term, how a large number of 'ordinary' people can be conscripted to perform the often mundane 'bureaucratic' work of the Holocaust. It needs to be noted that without such work the Holocaust itself wouldn't have been possible on anything like the scale it occurred. The testimonies also portray how a smaller group of similarly 'ordinary' individuals are able to, largely as a result of their compliance with the circumstances they find themselves in, commit heinous crimes. Finally the testimonies are also testament to the possibility of goodness in the face of morally tragic situations. There are enough vital examples of what Zvetlan Todorov refers to as individuals exhibiting 'ordinary virtues' to be able to lend substance to the claim of the presence of goodness in such difficult circumstances. Together these fragments combine to provide some understanding of the complexities of the moral behaviour of those who were killed or suffered, witnessed or participated in the Holocaust.

The testimonies are valuable because they make it possible to chart the nature of the complexity that comprises the moral lives of individuals. I want to recapitulate here on the idea of a 'weave of responsibility'. In the moral life of an individual there will be many and varied relationships that establish, over time, patterns of behaviour for a given situation. The structure of our relationships to others depends on our ability to, as moral agents, sustain and nurture those relationships. It is on the basis of relationships in which commitment and expectations are high that we develop what, Margaret Walker calls, a "responsibility ethic."[81] The problem, though, is that such an ethic can only ever be a rough guide to chart our responsibilities to others. Problems readily arise when situations are sufficiently morally different as to generate differing, and sometimes conflicting, responsibilities and demands to differing persons in such a way that we may be required to make morally vexed decisions. Moreover there may also be the need for an awareness that we are unable to guarantee the consequences of behaviour and/or actions. All the same, I propose that understanding responsibilities as akin to a weave is a useful way of understanding how moral lives relate to one another. As I have attempted to show in this thesis understanding the differing senses of responsibility is testimony to the complexity of moral life. This should not be a deterrent, though, to the task of seeking to understand the conceptual elements of this complexity. Indeed, in the case of the historical period I have undertaken to examine I believe that the task of understanding what it is that makes our lives morally complex, is all the more important.

Whilst I have said that moral lives can be morally complex and that our responsibilities can conflict, I am not suggesting, for a moment, that any sort of relationship or value that might derive from our relationships or history of relationships can license avoidable indecency to anyone. With regard to the testimonies I have examined it is clear that, among perpetrator behaviour, some, though not all, was sadistic. I believe that this observation is crucial. There is an aspect of the evidence of Holocaust experiences that has seldom been given due consideration. The evidence has demonstrated that most perpetrators of evils are not 'other' people. On the contrary, they are like us and they are capable of heinous crimes. They are, for the most part, ordinary people, caught up in circumstances out of their personal control. This observation should, in my view, be cause for careful contemplation.

In her reflections on our capacity for good and bad Claudia Card asked "What can sustain us in the realization that implication in the infliction of evil appears to be a continuing aspect of the human condition?"[82] It is the case that of the accounts that I have considered, the idea of a moral commitment to others based around a certain understanding of responsibility to others was so impoverished and depleted, over a short space of time, as to result in a moral tragedy of undeniably overwhelming proportions. Morally tragic though the testimonies may be, I also believe that they significantly enrich our understanding of the complexity of moral life in the context of this historical period. In response to Card's question I propose that it is precisely the capacity to enrich our understanding of the complexities of moral lives of the sort examined in this thesis that can and ought to sustain us. Such a response may appear in the eyes of some as inadequate. Be that as it may my response provides, at the very least, a justifiable standpoint from which to understand some of the possibilities of the levels of responsibilities that comprise our lives. I believe I have demonstrated that 'implication in the infliction of evil' may well be something that we have to permanently contend with. However, the book has also sought to show that understanding the tension between analyses of complexity and enormity can have a positive effect on the struggle to contend with the presence of evil. Understanding can reduce our arrogance and our self-righteousness. Reiterating an earlier statement, how we ought to live depends very much on how we understand how we do live.

This book has sought to meet my interpretation of what David Carroll has referred to as an "obligation to thought."[83] That is to say, to understand the tension between the moral complexity and moral enormity of Holocaust experiences. The presence of the tension, although it makes understanding of the Holocaust more difficult, is fruitful. It is productive because it demonstrates the need to take account of both of these aspects of the Holocaust. To this end I have tried to show that the need to understand this tension is as compelling as it is difficult. It has been a major aim to show that understanding the tension can serve as a basis to reconfigure our moral understandings of the Holocaust. Such a reconfiguration, though inconclusive in its articulation would, as I have attempted to show, place our sense of our responsibilities, to ourselves and to others at the centre of the discussion. At the forefront too, would be the notion of the 'ordinary virtue' of dignity, as a kind of self-respect and caring for others, along with understandings of the role of internal dispositions, lived experiences, circumstances and luck in moral life.

Moral life is morally complex. The weave of differing understandings of responsibility, expressed in my analysis of individual testimonies, adds veracity at this point. As I have sought to show, the Holocaust and the experiences that comprise it are also morally complex. In the final analysis, the tension between enormity and complexity, evident in the discussions of Holocaust experiences, confounding though it may seem, brings to light subtle and illuminating ways of understanding these very experiences.

Notes

1. R. J. Evans, *In Hitler's Shadow: West German Historians and the Attempt to Escape from the Nazi Past*, (New York: Pantheon, 1989), 12.

2. Joan W. Scott, 'The Evidence of Experience', in James Chandler, Arnold I. Davidson and Harry Harootunian, *Questions of Evidence: Proof, Practice and Persuasion across the Disciplines*, (Chicago: The University of Chicago Press, 1994).

3. Scott, 383.

4. Walker, 211-212.

5. Walker, 211-212.

6. Lawrence Langer, *Admitting the Holocaust*, (New York: Oxford University Press, 1995).

7. Langer, *Admitting the Holocaust*, 6.

8. Lawrence Langer, *Holocaust Testimonies: the Ruins of Memory*, (New Haven: Yale University Press, 1991).

9. Langer, *Holocaust Testimonies*, 21.

10. Langer, *Admitting the Holocaust*, 15.

11. Langer, *Holocaust Testimonies*, 5.

12. Langer, *Holocaust Testimonies*, 28.

13. Langer, *Holocaust Testimonies*, 55.

14. Langer, *Holocaust Testimonies*, 70-71.

15. See Emmanuel Levinas, 'As if Consenting to Horror', *Critical Inquiry*, Winter 1989.

16. Gertrud Kolmar, *Dark Soliloquy: The Selected Poems of Gertrud Kolmar*, Henry Smith (trans.), (New York: The Seabury Press, 1975) and cited in Carol Rittner & John Roth, Different Voices: Women and the Holocaust, (New York: Paragon House, 1993), 1.

17. Rittner & Roth, 16.

18. I refer in particular to the account of Jean-Francois Lyotard, *Heidegger and "the jews"*, Andreas Michel & Mark Roberts (trans.), (Minneapolis: Univeristy of Minneapolis Press, 1990).

19. Ida Fink, *A Scrap of Time and Other Stories*, M. Levine & F. Prose (trans.), (New York: Schocken Books, 1989), and cited in Rittner & Roth, 41-43.

20. Fink, 43.

21. This discussion of Fink's experience of shock and the change in the way she measured time may also have some connection to Langer's distinction between time as 'duration' and 'chronology' in *Admitting the Holocaust*, 14-20.

22. See Jean-Francois Lyotard, *Heidegger and "the jews"*.

23. I do not subscribe to this view though my reservations as regards Lyotard's account are outside of the scope of this thesis.

24. Michael Bernstein, 'Against Comfort', in *The Times Literary Supplement*, May 5, 1995, 10.

25. Gowans, *Innocence Lost*, 219.

26. Raimond Gaita, 'Remembering the Holocaust: Absolute Value and the Nature of Evil', *Quadrant*, December 1995, 15.

27. *Oneg Shabbes* can be translated as 'enjoyment of the Sabbath'. Its founder was Emmanuel Ringelbaum and it is an account of events of the Warsaw ghetto as recorded by Jewish writers in the ghetto.

28. From the testimony of Mrs. Gyulá Weinstock and Vera Weinstock, recorded on 10 October, 1945, M. Fellman and K.Dobos(trans.), unpublished. Appendix, 430.

29. The full translated transcripts are provided in the appendix and were orginally sourced from the archive of the Jewish Synagogue in Budapest, Hungary in 1991.

30. From the testimony of A. B., recorded on 10 October, 1945, M. Fellman and K.Dobos(trans.), unpublished. Appendix, 375.

31. From the testimony of E. F., recorded on 4 October, 1945, M. Fellman and K.Dobos(trans.), unpublished. Appendix, 391.

32. From the testimony of I. J., recorded on 18 November, 1945, M. Fellman and K.Dobos(trans.), unpublished. Appendix, 418-419.

33. The "Horst" hospital cited by I. J. was located somewhere near where Schenk was working after being moved from Auschwitz. Its exact location is not identified.

34. From the testimony of I. J., recorded on 18 November, 1945, M. Fellman and K.Dobos(trans.), unpublished. Appendix, 419.

35. From the testimony of C. D., recorded on 14 September, 1945, M. Fellman and K. Dobos (trans.), unpublished. Appendix, 383.

36. From the testimony of C. D., recorded on 14 September, 1945, M. Fellman and K. Dobos (trans.), unpublished. Appendix, 388.

37. From the testimony of Dr. I. J., recorded on 18 November, 1945, M. Fellman and K. Dobos(trans.), unpublished. Appendix, 407.

38. From the testimony of Dr. I. J., recorded on 18 November, 1945, M. Fellman and K. Dobos (trans.), unpublished. Appendix, 408.

39. From the testimony of Dr. I. J., recorded on 18 November, 1945, M.Fellman and K.Dobos(trans.), unpublished. Appendix, 420.

40. From the testimony of Dr. I. J., recorded on 18 November, 1945, M.Fellman and K.Dobos(trans.), unpublished. Appendix, 421.

41. From the testimony of Dr. I. J., recorded on 18 November, 1945, M.Fellman and K.Dobos(trans.), unpublished. Appendix, 424.

42. From the testimony of Mrs O. P. and Q. R., recorded on 10 October, 1945, M.Fellman and K.Dobos(trans.), unpublished. Appendix, 430.

43. Langer, *Holocaust Testimonies*, 2.

44. From the testimony of E. F., recorded on 4 October, 1945, M. Fellman and K.Dobos(trans.), unpublished. Appendix, 391-392.

45. From the testimony of Mrs K. L. and M. N., no record of the date of the testimony, M.Fellman and K.Dobos(trans.), unpublished. Appendix, 426.

46. From the testimony of A. B., recorded on 10 October, 1945, M. Fellman and K.Dobos(trans.), unpublished. Appendix, 379.

47. From the testimony of C. D., recorded on 14 September, 1945, M. Fellman and K.Dobos(trans.), unpublished. Appendix, 384.

48. From the testimony of Mrs K. L. and M. N., no record of the date of the testimony, M. Fellman and K.Dobos (trans.), unpublished. Appendix, 426.

49. From the testimony of Mrs O. P. and Q. R., recorded on 10 October, 1945, M.Fellman and K.Dobos(trans.), unpublished. Appendix, 432.

50. Such sources include Yitzak Arad, Yishmail Gutman and Abraham Margaliot, *Documents on the Holocaust*, (Jerusalem: "Ahva" Cooperative Press, 1988), Abraham Edelheit & Hershel Edelheit, *History of the Holocaust*, (Boulder: Westview Press, 1994) and the Simon Wiesenthal website.

51. I refer specifically here to Browning's books *Ordinary Men: Reserve Police Battalion 101 and the Final Solution in Poland*, (Harper Perenial: New York, 1993) and *Nazi Policy, Jewish Workers, German Killers*, (Cambridge: Cambridge University Press, 2000).

52. From the testimony of C. D., recorded on 14 September, 1945, M. Fellman and K. Dobos (trans.), unpublished. Appendix, 386.

53. Inga Clendinnen, *Reading the Holocaust*, (Melbourne: Text Publishing, 1998), 159.

54. From the testimony of C. D., recorded on 14 September, 1945, M.Fellman and K.Dobos(trans.), unpublished. Appendix, 387.

55. From the testimony of E. F., recorded on 4 October 1945, M.Fellman and K.Dobos(trans.), unpublished. Appendix, 392.

56. From the testimony of Mrs O. P. and Q. R., recorded on 10 October, 1945, M.Fellman and K.Dobos(trans.), unpublished. Appendix, 432.

57. From the testimony of Mrs O. P. and Q. R., recorded on 10 October, 1945, M.Fellman and K.Dobos(trans.), unpublished. Appendix, 432.

58. See Robert Lifton, *The Nazi Doctors: Medical Killing and the Psychology of Genocide*, (New York: Basic Books, 2000).

59. From the testimony of Mrs K. L. and M. N., no record of the date of the testimony, M.Fellman and K.Dobos(trans.), unpublished. Appendix, 426.

60. From the testimony of A. B., recorded on the 10th of October, 1945, M.Fellman and K.Dobos(trans.), unpublished. Appendix, 380.

61. Clendinnen, 161.

62. Clendinnen, 166.

63. Clendinnen, 166.

64. Clendinnen, 180.

65. From the testimony of Dr. G. H., recorded on the 6th of August, 1945, M.Fellman and K.Dobos (trans.), unpublished. Appendix, 400.

66. From the testimony of Dr. G. H., recorded on the 6th of August 1945, M. Fellman and K.Dobos(trans.), unpublished. Appendix, 403.

67. From the testimony of A. B., recorded on the 10th of October, 1945, M.Fellman and K.Dobos (trans.), unpublished. Appendix, 380.

68. From the testimony of Dr. I. J., recorded on the 18th of November 1945, M. Fellman and K. Dobos (trans.), unpublished. Appendix, 409.

69. From the testimony of Dr. I. J., recorded on the 18th of November 1945, M.Fellman and K.Dobos (trans.), unpublished. Appendix, 409-410.

70. From the testimony of Dr. G. H., recorded on the 6th og August 1945, M.Fellman and K.Dobos (trans.), unpublished. Appendix, 399.

71. In his testimony G. H. claims that Márton Zöldi had been a prominent figure in the pogroms against the Jews and Serbs in Novisad in January 1942 and that he had been sentenced to death for his actions by a Hungarian military court but that he had escaped custody and fled to Germany. G. H. further claims that Zöldi had returned to Budapest after the forced occupation of Hungary in 1944 as an Oberschaarführer (Non-commissioned officer) in the SS. I have been unable to corroborate this aspect of the testimony of G. H. elsewhere.

72. From the testimony of Dr. G. H., recorded on the 6th of August 1945, M.Fellman and K.Dobos (trans.), unpublished. Appendix, 400.

73. From the testimony of Dr. I. J., recorded on the 18th November 1945, M.Fellman and K.Dobos (trans.), unpublished. Appendix, 415.

74. From the testimony of Dr. I. J., recorded on the 18th of November 1945, M.Fellman and K.Dobos (trans.), unpublished. Appendix, 415.

75. Lanzmann, 50-51.

76. Rittner & Roth (eds.), 41-43.

77. Rittner & Roth (eds.), 70-72.

78. Lanzmann, 115-117.

79. Arad, Gutman & Margaliot (eds.), 440-442.

80. From the testimony of E. F., recorded on the fourth of October 1945, M. Fellman & K. Dobos (trans.), unpublished, Appendix, 391.

81. Walker, 107.

82. Claudia Card, 'Living with Evils', in J. G. Haber and M. S. Halfon (eds.), *Norms and Values: Essays on the Work of Virginia Held*, (Lanham: Rowman and Littlefield, 1998), 125.

83. David Carroll in the 'Foreward' in Jean-Francois Lyotard, *Heidegger and "the jews"*, xxv.

APPENDIX

This appendix consists of the testimonies of nine Hungarian-Jewish survivors of Auschwitz-Birkenau. The source of this testimonial material is the archive of the Jewish Museum, Budapest. Under the auspices of The Jewish Agency for Palestine, Department of Documentation these testimonies were originally transcribed in Hungarian (with one exception having been transcribed into German) between July 9 and November 26, 1945. These testimonies are reproduced here in their entirety for the first time to my knowledge in an English translation.

The authors of the following testimonies have been de-identified out of respect for the people concerned.

Testimony of:
1. Ms A. B.
2. Ms C. D.
3. Ms E. F.
4. Dr. G. H.
5. Dr. I. J.
6. Mrs. K. L. & Mrs. M. N.
7. Mrs. O. P. & Ms Q. R.

GLOSSARY
(G) German
(P) Polish
(H) Hungarian
Alternberg: Might refer to the town in Saxony in Germany.
Appell: (G) Twice daily roll call in the concentration camps where the inmates were forced to stand at attention.
Augsberg: City in Southern Germany.
Auschwitz/Birkenau: (G) The Auschwitz/Birkenau complex, near Cracow, Poland, covered approximately forty square kilometers and was made up of three camps: Auschwitz I, the base camp; Auschwitz II (Birkenau), the killing centre; and Auschwitz III (Monowice/Buna), I.G. Farben's synthetic rubber plant. Auschwitz/Birkenau was the largest death camp and has come to symbolize all camps. At least four million people died there.
Balassagyarmat: Town in Northern Hungary.
Belzec: (P) Death camp in Poland where approximately 550,000 people died.
Bereg: County in the former Kingdom of Hungary.
Bergen-Belsen: (G) Detention camp in Germany, which functioned as the official reception and interim detainment centre.
Blokowa: (also Blokova) (G) The female supervisor of a block of barracks in a concentration or extermination camp. Sztubowa were assistants to the blokowas.
Boxberg: Likely refers to a municipality in Saxony.
Breitenbrunn: Likely refers to a town in Saxony, Germany.
Brunau: A municipality in the district of Saxony in Eastern Germany.
Buchenwald: (G) Death camp in Germany where 43,045 people died.
Budapest: The capital city of Hungary.
Chelmno: (P) Death camp in Poland where 320,000 Jews were gassed.
Cracow: City in Southern Poland.
Csepel: District of Budapest, Hungary.
Dachau: (G) Concentration camp in Germany where mainly political prisoners were interned.
Dortmund: City in Western Germany.
Dresden: City in Eastern Germany.
Ebensee: A town in Austria and former site of the camp codenamed "Zement" and part of the Mauthausen complex.
Einsatzgruppen: (G) Mobile execution units of the Nazi Security Police (SD) in Eastern Europe. These Einsatzgruppen comprised the units:
Einsatzgruppe A (Baltic countries): Einsatzkommandos 2, 3 & Sonderkommandos 1a, 1b.
Einsatzgruppe B (White Russia): Einsatzkommandos 8, 9 & Sonderkommandos 7a, 7b & 'Vorkommando Moskau' (November 1941).
Einsatzgruppe C (Northern and Middle Ukraine): Einsatzkommandos 5, 6 & Sonderkommandos 10a, 10b.
Einsatzgruppe D (Bessarabia, Caucasia, Southern Ukraine): Einsatzkommandos 11a, 11b, 12 & Sonderkommandos 10a, 10b.
Enns: City in Austria.
Erfurt: City in central Germany.
Essen: City in Western Germany.
Gelsenkirchen: A city in Western Germany.

Gyarmat: Village near Gyor in Hungary.

Gyor: Town in Hungary.

Haftling: (G) Prisoners forced by the SS to brutalize Jews in the camps.

Halle: City in Eastern Germany.

Kalocsa: Town in Southern Hungary.

Kapos: (G) Camp inmates appointed by the SS to supervise kommandos. Kapos were often drawn from the ranks of German criminals.

Karlsbad: An administrative area in the district of Karlsruhe in Germany.

Kassa: (H) Town in Eastern Slovakia.

Kaufering: A municipality in the district of Landsberg in Germany. During World War II, a sub-camp of Dachau was located there.

Kiskunhalas: Town south of Budapest in Hungary.

Kisvarda: Town in Eastern Hungary.

Koleda: (P) Village in South-west Poland.

Kommando: (G) A work gang comprised of camp inmates.

Locse: (G) Town in Eastern Slovakia.

Lublin: City in Poland.

Maramaros: County in Eastern Hungary.

Mauthausen: (G) Death camp in Upper Austria where at least 110,000 people died.

Meissen: City in Eastern Germany.

Miskolc: City in Hungary.

Nagykanizsa: Town near Lake Balaton in Hungary.

Nyirjespuszta: Town in Northern Hungary.

Obecse: Town and municipality in the district of Vojvodina in Serbia.

Oberwiesenthal: Town in Eastern Germany.

Radebeul: Town in Saxony in Germany.

Ravensbruck: (G) Largest and earliest major concentration camp for women founded in May 1939 in Mecklenburg, Germany. A killing installation operated there from January to April 1945.

Salzburg: City in Austria.

Sommerda: Town near Erfurt in central Germany.

Spremberg: City in Eastern Germany.

Stollberg: Town in Eastern Germany.

Szeged: City in Southeastern Hungary.

Szered: City in Hungary.

Turkheim: A municipality in the district of Unterallgau in Germany.

Ujpest: A district in Budapest.

Ungvar: (H) City in Western Ukraine.

Vienna: Capital city of Austria.

Wolfsberg: Possibly refers to the sub-camp of the Natzweiler-Struthof concentration camp in Germany.

Testimony One. Testimony of Ms A. B.

Recorded on October 10, 1945 in the National Centre for the Welfare of Deportees, Budapest VII. District, Bethlen Gabor square 2.

Name: A. B.
Place of Birth: Szered

Occupation: Housewife

A. B. was taken from the Szered ghetto to the following camps:

Auschwitz	April 15, 1942-January 2, 1945
Ravensbrück	about 2 weeks
Neustadt-Cleve	about 3 months

A. B. recounts the following:

I was taken from Szered to Auschwitz on April 14 1942. There were about 2000 Jews living in Szered. I was the only fifteen-year-old child in the whole transport, in which there were about 1000 people. The others, among them my parents, were taken to Lublin where they were executed. During the trip, we did not get any food or drink. We arrived in Auschwitz on April 17. Lagerführer-Hauptsturmführer Schwartz was waiting for us upon our arrival. I saw the writing above the gate "Arbeit macht frei!" We entered the Lager, where Schreiberin (the most likely translation from the German is 'clerks'), Blockowa (female warders) and some SS women were already expecting us. They took our luggage and took us to the baths. There they gave us Russian uniforms ridden with lice, and some men's underwear and wooden shoes. We could not recognize each other, we did not even feel like women, but rather we looked like animals in those ugly shoes and ill-fitting men's uniforms. After the baths, we were taken to the Blocks. Old women were taken to block no.10. Between blocks, 10 and 11 there was the men's lager and there was a wall. At this wall, people were executed. We witnessed this every day. Not only men were shot dead, but women too, and political prisoners from Cracow. The next day we were woken at 4 in the morning and were made to stand on the Zählappell (The place where roll call was taken). It was terrible. We had to wait 4-5 hours while they counted us. We were very weak and depressed, and did not want to go to work. However, the German Kapos and Häftlings beat people until they stood in work-Kolonnen (columns). I was crying for my parents all the time but later on, I was happy that they were not here to see the horrors. The composition of the Kommandos differed: there were those who were taken for road construction or sewerage work; there were those who were taken to the forest to chop down trees or to work with wood; those taken to Birkenau where they demolished houses; or for agricultural work. The method of assignment into these Kommandos was according to the following: there was a table, around the table sat the Rapportführer and some Aufseherin (warders) who chose people for each Kommando. When the choice was made, those leaving for work had to go out through the gate. It was terrible having to see old women having to march like soldiers. At the gate there were 200 SS men standing with vicious dogs. Every Kommando had 4-5 guards. We had to march out barefoot, holding our wooden shoes in our hands. Behind the lager (camp), there was a beautiful park and the crematorium was set up behind it. Naturally, it was not possible to leave the camp without women seeing their husbands, sisters their brothers etc. There was such shouting and crying there everyday that in the end the SS prohibited us from looking at each other. Men had to look to the right, women to the left. The trip to the workplace took 1-2 hours. One of the kommandos had the job of re-building the road. Poor old women had to do this barefoot. To illustrate what this meant I only have to say that in April there was still snow in Auschwitz. The Aufseherin (warders) beat the old women and the SS just laughed at it. Guards stood at every 100 meters and watched to see that nobody stopped working. In the meantime, the SS were amusing themselves by inciting dogs to attack the women, with the result that every day badly mauled women were brought back to the lager. They worked with fantastically cruel methods. For example, they were ordered to bring back a quota of dead to the lager every day. Whoever could produce enough dead would get extra free days. Following this, corpses were brought in every day from the workplace. The victims were killed by dogs, beaten to death or shot dead. They even used tricks. For example, they chased the women to forbidden areas and there they shot them dead for trying to escape. In Birkenau women had to demolish houses. There they erected a wooden bar so that the wall would fall between the worker and the bar. The task was to demolish the wall with the bar but the falling wall often struck the women dead. In Birkenau, there were 1000 women in the Kommando, but they did other work as well apart from demolishing houses. For example, they had to carry bricks and many were beaten to death there too. If someone needed to go to the toilet, they first had to ask permission from the Aufseherin or the SS. If permission was granted then she could go, if not then the unfortunate woman would have to manage anyway as best as she could. At noon, we had a break. Then everybody had to take his or her shoes and plate and march back to the lager. There in heavy snow lunch was distributed. Daily it was carrot soup, cooked in water without salt. After lunch there was marching again. We had to continue work in the afternoon until 5.30. After marching back to the lager there was the evening Zählappell. This lasted from about 9 till 10. During Zählappell there had to be quiet and calm. Meanwhile the SS and the Aufseherin would say things like we were going to stand there until we turned black. Many people fainted during Zählapell, especially the older women. Our kapos were German Häftlings: murderers, political prisoners, burglars and other doubtful characters. It is worth mentioning that among the prisoners in the lager were some who were courageous. There was for example Szombatos sect members who were told that if they signed a document that they would leave the sect then they would be freed. Not one of them was prepared to betray their conscience and free themselves at that price. They were not only proud but also very good people. After Zählappell we were sent back to the block and were given dinner, which consisted of a quarter of a slice of bread, one spoonful of jam, or one fiftieth of a part of margarine, or two dekagrams of meat. After dinner, there was "Lagerruhe" (the time when the camp rested). Everybody had to go to bed. In the barrack, there were three storey beds with hay mattresses infested with fleas and lice, so we did not sleep well at night but instead scratched ourselves bloody. In the meantime newer and newer transports arrived so there were more and more young people. When there were more than 100 of us, they started to work us too. The first week they took us to the forest, but they did not care that we were young and could not work like the older ones; the SS beat us just as violently as they beat the others. Then we were taken to an onion field, where we could eat onions, as many as we could, but we were not allowed to take any with us to the lager. However, once I took some in under my blouse. The Aufseherin body-searched me and found them. She was then suspicious of everybody, had a better look at the others and found onions on 6 other girls. This was still not enough. The Rottenführer came and search us as well, but found nothing. We then marched toward the lager. On the way, however, we met Lagerkommandant Schwartz and of course, he was immediately told about our "sin", so we had to turn back. They took us to a glasshouse where they searched us again. This time they were not only looking for onions but for anything. They took our photos and other objects we were not allowed to keep on us. Then it was my turn. They immediately told me what I had done was sabotage, and I would hang for it. Nothing happened for three days. On the third day my number and the numbers of the six other girls who had hidden onions was called out at the Apell. They stood us next to the fence.

We had to stand there motionless for 5 hours. After 5 hours, we had to go back to the Lagerführerin, but thank God, nothing happened. She said that she did not want another case like this or else we would be punished more. For three months after this, I was with this kommando, and then I was put into the Effektenkommando. There we had a nasty Schaarführer. One day, for example, he chose 10 men and told them he would perform "Mittagspause" with them. (This bastards name was Wiegleb). They took them to a warehouse full of lice-ridden clothes. There they had to dress up in furs and put on gasmasks and run for an hour, then lie down, run some more and lie down. In the meantime, they were flogged until they collapsed. He did the same with women as well as men. The first gas chambers were erected in July 1942. We were told that the old women were going to go to "Altersheim". A black car came for them, took them away, but it came back soon with their underwear, glasses and clothes. We heard only later on that they had been executed, although we did not know how. This had been executed by Lagerkommandant Schwartz and the Aufseherin Frau Langersfeld. Later on Frau Langersfeld also became a Häftling, because it became known that she had been stealing from the Effektenkammer. Then the first Slovakian transports arrived and they were immediately sent to be gassed. At that time, we still did not know what that involved. Later on, so many men were brought in that the whole camp became a men's camp and we had to move over to Birkenau. At the time of our move, there was a big selection. The sick and the weak were left behind to be gassed and we were taken over to Birkenau. There were low buildings there where Russian prisoners of war used to be kept, but who were later executed. We stood in a queue and marched into a courtyard where there was a huge pool of water. Our Aufseherin wanted to boast in front of the SS and she sent many women through this water. it turned out that formerly it had been a moor where many women had been drowned. In the camp, there was no water or lighting and the barracks looked terrible. We had no blankets or hay so we slept on bricks or planks of wood. In the dark, we could feel rats jumping on us. The wood itself was full of lice and we immediately became lice-ridden. Meanwhile a well had been dug for the sick. This was immediately discovered. It was a terrible sight to see thirsty people pushing each other around the water. Many people fell in and drowned. There was no toilet, they only dug some trenches. Of course, the wet ground soaked by human excrement was very slippery and people fell into these trenches. If someone needed to go to the toilet, they had to go before leaving the camp. If they could not finish by the time we had to stand in the queue, or were not quick enough the Aufseherin would push them into the trenches. In a couple of weeks, malaria and typhus epidemics broke out. The malaria caused a fever of 40 degrees but everybody was still taken out to work. Therefore, every day dead bodies were brought back to the camp, people who had died of malaria. Then the selection process was restarted. Oberaufseherin Drechsler and Mandel carried this out. By this time, we knew about the existence of the gas chambers. According to my estimates about 3-4000 women a day were sent to the gas. Nobody dared to appear sick because they were afraid of being sent to the gas. Eventually even the Aufseherin became lice-ridden. There was a terrible selection on the December 13th. I will always remember this day. They woke us up at 2.30a.m. in addition, made us stand in the meadow just as we had stood at the beginning of the first transportation. From my transport, there were only six women left. We stood there all day. Eventually at 6p.m., they let us back into the barrack. There Frau Drechsler, Aufseherin Wolkenrath, Lagerkommandant Schwartz and Oberaufseherin Frau Mandel were waiting for us. We had to jump over a one-meter wide trench. Those who succeeded would be left alive; those who did not were immediately taken away. Naturally, the malaria and Typhus had left many women weak and unable to jump. They were all sent to the gas. On that horrible day of the 25-30,000 women, only 4,000 were left alive. All of the others were taken away by cars. I can still hear the screams of these poor women. They were even then still 2,000 short for the "death-transport", so they randomly chose another 2,000 people and took them too. One of my girlfriends died in this random way. For those of us remaining the Aufseherin gave a speech. She said that if we keep ourselves clean they would not harm us, however if we became lice-ridden we would have the same fate as the others. Therefore, we had to keep clean from then on. Without water! The next few days were "Entläusung". First people, then dishes, rags and hay-beds were thrown out of the barracks. We were then sent into the sauna where our hair was cut, a process, which was repeated every two months from then on. Three women cut our hair. In the same time, these women were making good business with the Häftlings who gave them bread and other foodstuffs for letting them watch us naked. After this, we went to a steam bath where there was a staircase. In the middle stood a huge fireplace. It was so hot we thought we were going to suffocate. The Aufseherin Frau Lotte Claus, a big black woman was seated in there. We had to sit on the hot steps. Of course, those suffering from heart problems could not stand the heat. Meanwhile Frau Claus was beating us with a hot fire poker. From the hot steam, we had to go straight to cold showers. There were dirt and lice so we had become lice-ridden. The old clothes were put into the gas and we were given civilian clothes but without underwear or shoes. You can imagine how cold we were in the civilian clothes when we had been in the relatively warm uniforms. Until everybody had finished we had to wait there in the frost without food or drink. After the delousing, we were taken back to the blocks. It was very cold, the blocks had no roofs, but it had small windows. So not only the cold air came in but also the rain. Later on latrines were made, but these were not useable and everybody used the barrack floor instead. As a punishment we had to take the excrement out, which caused even more dirt. There were times when we used our cups, and whether we could rinse them or not, we had to eat from them. As a result, the whole block was sent to the gas. Later on, they built better latrines, which suited their purpose a little better. Everybody had a blanket, which was not enough, so we stole them off each other at night. The clever ones slept with the blanket between their teeth so they could feel if someone was pulling it off. The sick wanted to stay in the blocks, which they could do. However there were surprise selections for the gas, and then they were also taken. On day, a Strafcommando was brought in consisting of old Jews. The dogs were incited to attack them. That was a terrible sight. We saw men stark naked in winter standing in the Apell. I have to say a couple more words about the Blockows. They were all ordered to treat us very badly. Naturally, they did that according to their own nature. There were better and worse ones, but some had a particularly cruel streak in them. We were so hungry, we ate grass. It was in March 1943 that we had potato in the lager for the first time. We did not talk of anything else all day besides this event. It was a Sunday. Of course, everybody was pushing to the front of the queue, because they did not want to be left out. There was a terrible fight. Eventually the food truck arrived and it turned out there was no potato, only potato skin. The Effektenkommand was doubled, because more and more transports arrived. The first Hungarian transports arrived as well. Then we moved from Lager A to Lager B. There were men there too but they moved them out. New Blockaelteste and Schreiberin came and the Effektenkammer had to be moved out to Brezsinka too. The old women did not want to go out to Zählapell, because it was very cold. Of course, they realized that some people were missing and these were later found hidden in the hay-beds. Then came Unterschaarführer Tauber. He beat everybody who had been caught and immediately took them to block no.25, from where they were taken to the gas. We heard their screams and shouts from that block all the time. There were dead every day at the electric fence too, those who had committed suicide. The Russians were approaching on the 18. Jan. 1945 and they wanted to execute the Solderkadert of Auschwitz, but this did not happen, as there was no time. 500-1000 people were taken away in a transport. The sick were left there and we thought they were going to be blown up, but there was no time for that either. The retreat was so urgent, we marched all night. At dawn, we stopped at a barn. During the march of course people were constantly shot. They kept telling us if we did not hurry, we would end up like "those down there". "Down there" meant people who lay shot through the brain. It was a horrific sight. There was a cold wind blowing and it was very slippery. Old women were begging and crying to be shot in the head, because they could not carry themselves further. A desire of theirs was fulfilled; they were shot in the head. We marched two days and two nights, and then we were put into wagons in Losbau. The Russians were behind us all the time, so we were rushed even more. We were put into open coal wagons. In front of the wagons, they selected the strong and the weak once again. The weak were shot dead in front of our eyes. We traveled through Berlin for a week and selections were made during this time. Eventually we arrived in Ravensbruck. We stood there all evening, when eventually at midnight they put us into a Jugendlager. After a week, we were taken to the Stammlager then they put us, 2-3000 people, into smaller Lagers. Those old women still alive were put in the Jugendlager, and were not given food for days on end, and eventually died of hunger, or were executed with injections. Together with 4000 people, I went on a transport to Neustadt-Cleve. There 3500 of us worked in a plane factory in day and night shifts. It was terribly cold. The work was so hard that there were daily injuries amongst the girls. I and ten others were put in the Leichenkommando. 5-6 people died daily of tuberculosis and hunger. In the first month of our stay, we received one tenth of a loaf of bread, and at first some soup everyday, and later on every three days. Our task was to put three corpses in a coffin, take them to the forest, dig a grave and throw them in. There were daily body searches and then they took whatever was left of our things. The hunger was unbearable, if we had had to stay for two more weeks we would surely have died. Eventually on May 5th, the Americans arrived and freed us. The SS had already fled and we were waiting to see what was going to happen. The big question was if we were going to be blown up or be freed. Luckily, it was the second. First, the Americans came and later on, the Russians replaced them. They had a good look at the lager, but did not like what they saw as we were in a terrible state. People were so weak they could not stand up, and we were full of lice. The Americans started to rehabilitate us and they kept us there for 1-2 months before we set out for home via Czechoslovakia. At the moment, I am living with my uncle in Budapest, as my parents were unfortunately executed in Lublin.

Recorded by Lazar Gyorgy.

Testimony two. Testimony of Ms C. D.

Recorded in Budapest, on 14th Sept. 1945 in the National Centre for the Welfare of the Deportees. (VII. Bethlen Gabor Square 2)

Name:	C. D.
Place of birth:	Obecse
Occupation:	Physical education teacher

C. D. was taken from the Bekescsaba Tobacco Factory ghetto to the following camps:

Auschwitz	June 29 1944- September 22 1944
Bergenbelsen	September 25 1944- October 23 1944
Markkleberg	October 27 1944- April 13 1945
Radebeul	May 5 1945-May 16 1945

C. D. recounts the following:

Around 2500 Jews lived in Bekescsaba, mainly well-off traders, factory owners and lateiners. My father was a bank manager there; we lived in our own house in very good material circumstances. I was teaching in Szekelyudvarhely in the Teacher Training College, and that is where I was on 19. March 1944. I had Aryan papers, so I could travel to Budapest, from where I traveled to Bekescsaba for the Easter holidays. After the arrival of the Germans, my father was daily insulted even by the citizens. Generally, they behaved very nastily; they drew different signs on the walls.

However, we could not hold anything against The Lord Mayor, Gyula Janossy. Mr. Lukacs was the Chief of Police, he was also a friend of the Jews and as such, he was soon removed. We were put in the ghetto by the end of April. The ghetto comprised the streets around the synagogue. Often there were round ups and one night the police apprehended me. They did not want to believe that I lived with my parents. They thought I was an escapee and took me to the police station. There they checked to see whether I was registered, and after finding the registration card, they let me return home. We had quite a decent flat in the ghetto, where the whole family lived together. My father used to go into the bank until the last day with the permission of the Lord Mayor. The members of the Jewish Council, Dr. Revesz, and Dr. Sebestyen etc. behaved quite decently. The women were taken out to do agricultural work, but only if they volunteered. Later on, this was stopped by the county high sheriff. The ghetto windows opening onto the street were plastered up. The gates were constantly locked and adorned with the sign: "Jewish House". Many people escaped from the ghetto. I wanted to escape too but because of my parents, I rejected my plan. As I recall there were, at this time only natural deaths in the ghetto. There were daily house searches for jewelry and food. There were 2500 of us in the city ghetto for four weeks. We were then taken over to the tobacco factory next to the railway station. We were put into dirty barracks, where there were constant tortures and beatings. SS interrogations were carried out regularly. Mr. Deutsch, the director of the Hubertus Factory was beaten to death. Mainly the wealthier, respectable men were called in and interrogated as to the whereabouts of buried jewelry and they were made to unearth their buried clothes. I was apprehended because of a letter that had been written to me by a Christian girlfriend of mine. She advised me to dye my hair blond. They took me into the cell for interrogations, and a hairdresser had to examine my hair to see if it was dyed or not. She found it to be the natural color. The SS let me go after this on the condition that I would not attempt to escape or help anyone escape or else they would shoot me in front of my mother. For this reason, my mother had two heart-attacks. There were daily searches here too; papers were confiscated, photos torn. Once one of the SS brought 3 kilos of cherries into the ghetto, threw it amongst the hungry little Jewish children and watched happily, as they scratched each other in their fight for the cherries. I was a nurse in the ghetto hospital and saw many attempted suicides, the majority of which ended in death. Amongst others, the director of the Pajor Sanatorium of Budapest died there too. He poisoned himself, his one and half year old son and his wife with morphine. The father and the little boy died, whilst the mother recovered. We came together to Auschwitz.

In the tobacco factory ghetto, there were 4000 people together with the Jews from Bekes County. The women were made to do all sorts of useless jobs, while the SS commandant walked around with a baton. SS police were keeping order in the ghetto; Jewish police were looking after the internal order. On the 24th of June, they put me in a transport. The whole ghetto was cleaned out and everybody put in the wagons. Straight before this, there was a big search. Nurses from the Red Cross searched the women, and very thoroughly too. We took many things with ourselves, as the detective looking after it at the time was a good acquaintance of my father. The others could take 2 sets of underwear, 2 pairs of shoes, 2 dresses, bed cloths and food for two weeks. 86 people were put in one very small wagon. We were given water upon departure. As a nurse, I was allowed to get off for some water on the way. WC buckets were provided as well. On leaving, we were given enough bread too. Everything was arranged by the Jewish Council. Some reckoned it was about swapping prisoners, but the pessimists thought we were being taken to die. We went toward Kassa where we could see we were being taken to Poland, and we knew then, nothing good was waiting for us. In Kassa the police escorting us were changed to SS. From our wagon nobody escaped. My father was the "wagon leader" he told me that we arrived in full numbers. On the way the SS were constantly asking for leather wallets, leather belts, fountain pens etc. They said we were being taken to work, we would be paid for it, and the families could stay together. After five days we arrived in Auschwitz-Birkenau at 10 a.m. We were taken off the wagons by Polish boys dressed in stripy suits and the men were immediately separated from us. The luggage had to be left in the wagons. I was standing in front of an SS officer together with my mother and younger sister and he immediately sorted us. The aim of the selection was to separate families and it was done based on similar features. This was my perception but others said so too. My sister was put in my group. My mother cried out after us, my sister went over to her and thus they found themselves on the side from which nobody ever returned. On our arrival we immediately saw the electric fences; you can imagine how this effected us. Then we were taken to a disinfection room, where they cut our hair, shaved us, took away all our clothing and gave us one piece of summer dress instead. We were then escorted by armed guards in to Lager no.3. There were 1500 of us in a block. This was a prison camp, there were no beds, no toilets, no plumbing. We were lying on the floor on top of each other without blankets. We were in this Lager for 3 months, we did not really do proper work, but we carried heavy dishes. We were constantly cold; we had to kneel for hours on the appels. We slept a little; the rooms were so crowded we could hardly move. The food: One quarter bread, in the morning black coffee or tea, dry stew for lunch that was often inedible, rarely some margarine or a small slice of salami, a teaspoonful of jam, possibly 1 dekagram of tinned meat. In August I was take to the hospital with typhoid. Here Dr.Mengele put me in the transition camp together with the dead and dying, saying I was unable to work. There a woman doctor friend of mine from Szeged (Dr. Klara Nagy) swapped me for a corpse, after Mengele had selected me, so the numbers were matching and Mengele did not look for me. He was a wonderfully handsome man, and was always walking around nicely dressed up. We thought he was in love with Klara Nagy. He checked out the toilets very thoroughly, generally it was clean in the lager, thanks to him. Once we went to the disinfecting room toward the crematoria. An SS officer was standing at its fence with a gun in his hand; we were not even allowed to look in its direction. Through the live hedge we saw people moving about. Later in the Bordicsev Lager I met a Jewish boy, who had worked in the crematoria. He told me that the building of the crematoria looked like a bath house, where the gas was let into the rooms through the shower heads. First people were given soap and towels, there was music, they were playing the

Donauwaltzer and at every tenth act there, in the hall of the bath one person was shot dead. The corpses were taken out by a pulley. The Jewish doctors had to take the gold teeth out of the corpses and eventually these were put in the crematoria. The roads were made with human ashes. Jewish haftlings occasionally found small human bones. Often there were punishments at the appel. Sometimes these lasted for hours, kneeling with big rocks in the hand. We had to do different exercises with these stones, like frog leaps etc. During the appel nobody was allowed to go to the toilet. All the women had diarrhea and they needed to do it, for which they got heavy beatings. Often we were standing in heavy rain with our bare heads and were not allowed to wear scarves. There was no regular work in the prison camp, so we were not tattooed. In September almost every day there were selections. We had to march naked in front of Dr. Mengele and the soldiers. Normally he was looking at the stomachs. Those with hunger-flattened stomachs were not put into the work transports. I was thrown out at the first selection, but one week later at the next I was eventually put into a work transport. We were taken over to Lager A, about 4500 of us, where we had to stand for 12 hours on a row. There they bathed us , I was given a dress suitable for a 12-year-old girl, wooden shoes, underwear (this was the first) We also received some bread, about 4 dekagram of margarine, 2 pieces of cheese and then were put into a wagon. There were 70 for a wagon. On the stations we were escorted to the toilet by the SS. After 4 days of traveling we arrived in Bergenbelsen. Here we lived in (alltek)? we slept on the floor on hay and had two woolen blankets. This was the first place where we got separate dishes for eating, which was very pleasant after Auschwitz. We could have a proper bath; we were given soap and towels. There were no beatings here, appel was only once a week, and we did not work regularly. Though the food was edible, it was very little. Later on we were given stripy coats. A month later they took these away, gave us winter coats, and with these we were taken to Markleberg, next to Leipzig. The trip was four days, 70 in a wagon, and we had enough food for the trip. On arrival we found a tidy, clean work lager, where there had been German workers previously. Clean beds, toilets and a bath-hall with a fountain. For a month I was working with the Baukommando, we had to push 75 kg wheelbarrows; the workday was 8 hour long. At work we were terribly beaten by the Schaarfuhrer. At the beginning we were given one third of a bread for the day, tea for breakfast, 1 liter of edible soup for lunch, in the evening carrot soup (carrots for animals) some margarine or marmalade. After the Baukommando I got into the Junkers airplane factory, I was given an overall, there was no clothing under it, and I spent the winter in a wooden barrack. The workday was 12 hours long day and nightshifts. We had German bosses. The leadership of the factory was generally sympathetic to the haftlings. They accused the lagerführer of the punishments like shavings etc. and occasionally the bosses gave us some food. We worked together with German civilians, but we were not allowed to get in touch with them. We were constantly watched by the Aufseherins, and they were watching the workers too. If they saw someone talking to the Germans, they immediately told the Oberschaarführer, whose name was Qunittel. Once one of the haftlings received a scarf from one of her bosses. It was forbidden to wear scarves, so they interrogated her as to where the scarf had come from. Qunittel reported the German worker, and the girl's growing hair was shaved in the middle. Then on the Sunday zehlappel they stood her aside and we had to march in front of her. Following this she was shaved again. If somebody wanted to look a bit more human, she was punished. A girl from Kassa was sentenced to four days bunker on bread and water for buying cigarettes for soup. We worked in the factory for four months, where we made airplane components. One day the order came to empty the factory as the Americans were advancing. That very night, on the 13th of April, we were (kihajtott) in rows of fives. We did not get bread, only carrots for the trip. We marched with the SS for two days. Two of my friends collapsed from hunger and tiredness. I managed to escape with two others into the forest. They shot at us, one of my girlfriends died, but two of us were not hit. We continued and joined an Aryan Polish transport where we lied that we were Aryans as well and came to Germany voluntarily. From here we walked into Meisen (the porcelain factory was intact). There I met a Serbian war prisoner who told me not to go on walking with such a weight loss (I was 42 kilos then), but wait for the Russians. My girlfriend and I stayed there for a week, and on the 18th April the Russians reached the outskirts of Meissen. Naturally there were heavy bombings, we were amongst fire and explosions, but the main thing was we had enough to eat. From here we went on with a German man, who took us to Radebeul II and then to Dresden where we reported to the Germans, because at that time the Germans still controlled the city. We told them the same story, that we were Aryans. We were wearing Hitlerjugend uniforms because our dresses had been torn apart during the trip and our German escort had given us these uniforms. Naturally our escort did not know that we were Jews either. The German police supported us wholeheartedly, and they were very happy as they had not seen Hungarian girls before. They gave us food tickets and took us to the lager for foreigners where they gave us separate rooms and good food. There we have to know a Hungarian family who took us in. (She was the younger sister of Gyorgy Endresz the pilot.) We stayed there until the Russians arrived on May 16. Then we confessed that we were Jews. We could see our hosts did not like it too much, so we left. The Russians provided us with the 12 room villa of the Nazi leaders of Radebeul. By then there were three of us. We found lots of clothes and valuable things, which we sold upon our return and lived off the proceeds. From Radebeul the Russians took us to Csernovitz by bus and train, and from there to Bordiscev and Kiev. I worked there as a nurse for the Russians and I was given food and clothing. There I lived like a human being again. They took me to their dances, to the cinema and were very kind to me. Russian officers brought 78 Hungarian Jewish deportees from various lagers. 400 Arrow Cross and Schwabians also arrived with them too. We stepped into the country through the island of Maramaros at Satoraljauhely. At the stations we were received by Jews with food and bread. We were very happy all the way home although we intentionally did not want to think about what awaited us. This is how we arrived in Budapest. My future plans: As I did not find my parents or sister, I am alone. I would like to find a position in the College for Physical Education. The testimony was recorded by C. D. (by her own hand).

Testimony three. Testimony of Ms E. F.

Recorded in Budapest on 4 October 1945 in the Office of the National Centre for the Welfare of the Deportees, Bp. Bethlen Gabor ter.2.

Name:	E. F.
Place of birth:	Budapest
Occupation:	Home duties

E. F. was taken to the following German camps:

Auschwitz	August 10, 1944- December 20, 1944.
Bergen-Belsen	December 23, 1944- January 22, 1945.
Markleberg	January 25, 1945- March 13, 1945.

Dresden   April 15, 1945.

E. F. recounts the following:

On the April 2, 1944 I went to register in the "KEOK" because my father was a Polish citizen. I was arrested there by the police and taken to Rökkszilárd street in a prisoner's truck. We arrived in the evening, and were sent to the courtyard. They took people in groups into the gymnasium to register. When it was my turn I registered too. They immediately took all my money and food coupons and then took us upstairs. This is when I got the first terrible shock. There was a boy of about 14 years of age bound to the bars of the staircase, his arms pulled up behind his back. The poor child had attempted to escape and was captured. He was probably already dead because he had been there since morning. We were put into an empty classroom, where I sat down in the corner. Later on when more people arrived, I gave my place to an older woman. I spent the night awake on the corridor. I was there for 10 days, and then I was taken to Csepel with the first transport, where I received an office job. I had to censor the incoming and outgoing letters of the detained Jews. I did this for two months. One morning the gate suddenly opened and many police on bicycles came in. They surrounded the camp and immediately gave orders for us to pack. When we were finished they searched everybody and took away our nicest and most valuable possessions. Previously we had been allowed to take these with us. Then they took us to the boat station, and that night we arrived in Pünkösdfürdö. From there we had to walk to the brick-factory in Budakász. Upon our arrival our first impressions were terrible. We could see huge windowless buildings and little children standing around looking terribly pale. We received neither food nor water. At night people started to scream out of fear as if they were mad. Some of us did not get a place inside so we had to sleep outside on the bricks. The SS were constantly controlling the cleanliness of the camp, and if they pointed to a piece of paper we had to pick it up and eat it, as there was nowhere to throw it. This is how we lived until July the sixth. In the meantime people were constantly being taken away in transports. I was constantly hiding so they would take me later but eventually I was taken in the last but one transport. 8oth of us were put into wagons, together with the elderly and children. We were escorted to Kassá by the police where the SS took over. Before the SS arrived the police performed one last search to see who had their watches, money or other valuables still with them, and these they took away. When I wanted to get off to get some water, one of the officers took his sword out and said he would cut off my head immediately if I did not get back in. Our train then left for Slovakia. On the way the SS searched us and took away our food. Once we stopped at night, it was very dark and the SS were walking on top of the wagons. I heard a hissing noise and thought they were letting some gas into the wagons. Then I realized someone had opened a valve on the engine. Before we arrived in Poland from Slovakia, we stopped in a tunnel. There was total darkness for about 5 minutes, and we thought we were going to die there. It was terrible in the wagon, and we hardly had any air. Eventually we arrived in Auschwitz at 3 p.m. on July the tenth. At that time I was still with my brother, sister-in-law and a cousin. On the station I saw men dressed in stripy outfits, who did not say a word as it was forbidden to talk. They herded us out of the wagons and took our remaining belongings away. We had nothing else left but the clothes we were wearing. The men were separated from us, and I held onto my sister-in-law tightly, so that at least she would stay with me. In the meantime we reached the gate of the lager. I saw a very nice looking SS man come from the opposite direction. When he saw me holding on tight to my sister-in-law, he motioned for me to go to the right, and her to the left. He did not even take his hand out of his pocket. I walked on numb, not even realizing what this meant. Then for the first time they made us stand in rows of five. We walked 1 kilometer amongst electric fences to the bathhouse. When we arrived we had to undress and stand naked in front of the SS and Slovakian girls. Then one of the SS came and gave a speech. We were standing there ashamed; everything had been taken away from us. The SS said:"Do not be afraid, if you work you will get fed". Then we went into another room, where they completely shaved us and poured some liquid on our heads that ran down my face and burnt my skin. We could keep the shoes but unfortunately I had a good pair of walking boots, and one of the Aufseherin fancied them. She took them from me. Then we got into the bath where we had to stand under a shower, but we were given neither soap, nor towels. After showering we went out one by one and we were given one torn dress. This was our whole wardrobe. I did not get shoes. Nor did I get underwear. This is how we got into Lager C, where for 4 days I was lying in dirt and mud, as there was hardly enough space to even lie down. Around 2 a.m. there was loud shouting "Zählappel, alles hinaus". We did not know what this meant, we thought they were crazy. They chased us out into the night with sticks and dog whips. It was terribly cold and the rags we were wearing did not warm us. They made us stand in rows of five, but apart, so that we could not warm each other. We had to stand there like this until 11 a.m. the next day. We were frozen blue, and barely alive. After this they brought a liquid called soup in big barrels. It was made of dirty potato skins, pieces of wood and grass. They put this soup in 5-6 liter-pots from which we had to drink, one after the other. Needless to say none of us could drink it. We lived there like this for 4 days. After 4 days the Lageralte came and started to select us. Those he liked were put in a different row, and were told they were bring taken to agricultural work. We were very happy because we knew if we worked we would be treated better. After this we had to get undressed again and were ashamed. We had to march in front of Dr. Mengele (the handsome man) holding our right arms above our heads. Then we set out for the other Lager in rows of five. We were constantly being taken among electric fences. We arrived in Lager B and there we were put to work. I was put in the "Esskommando"; my job was to carry the food from one block to the other. This was a rather difficult job. Six of us carried a barrel. Here the Appel started at 2a.m. and lasted until 8 in the morning. After that the Kommandos could leave, the order "Antreten" was given and everybody had to go to work. The other poor people had to stand on there. At 8 a.m. an Aufseherin arrived and counted us. There were several Esskommandos and we worked in shifts. Once I was very hungry but it was my girl-friend's shift, not mine. I had a little cup and she and the others let me dip it in the barrel. Unfortunately the Blokkführer saw me and took me to Block 2. The Schreibstube was there. He took the stamp from the desk, heated it up and pushed it into the skin of my neck. The mark it left is still there. After that he nonchalantly started to smoke and asked me if I was still hungry and pushed his cigarette into my arm. I could not stand the pain any more and fainted. He poured water on me after which my wound remained infected for months. I did not want to go to the Revierre (police station)? because from there no-body returned. For a sip of water we gave our daily bread, but water was so bad here, that it caused diarrhea. I had diarrhea for five months, but we were not allowed to use the toi-let. We would have dirtied it. Sometimes I had to go out 5-6 times a night but by then I was so weak I could not hold it back. Luckily at night there was water -it was closed dur-ing the day- so I could wash myself. This is how it went for five months. The weather was difficult, during the day it was 40 degrees and at night freezing. The strong sun was burning our heads and I got sunstroke. My head swelled up, my eyes were bulging and I was lying in the sand for days without help. Once during the Apell I could not stand up any more and sat down in the dirt for a little while. The Blokkältesterin shouted "Achtung", and I jumped up immediately, because this meant the arrival of the Blokkführer. He then walked between the rows and once I realized that he was standing behind me. He started to move the whip in his hands, and then beat me on my head, back and neck, until I bled. I did not know why I received these beatings. He went on walking, stopped behind an other girl, and gave her the same treatment. He repeated this with several girls and we were wondering why we received the beatings. Then we realized that our dresses had become dirty when we had sat down and unfortunately we forgot to dust them when we stood up. This is what our life was like in Auschwitz and Birkenau. One nice day, the 20th of December, I was chosen for a transport and about 2000 of us was taken to Bergen-Belsen. On the way we had two SS soldiers in every wagon. When the SS man took out his newspaper we secretly had a look and realized that the Szálasi government was in office in Hungary. This depressed us terribly because we were already hoping for freedom. On arriving in Bergen-Belsen we were pleasantly surprised, because there everybody was eating from there own plates, which was a big thing. We received two blankets per person and we were put in tents. We did not have to work here at all. Apell was only every second or third day and this was heaven. Living in the tent was not pleasant because it was terribly cold and we were lying on the ground. Compared with Auschwitz the food was quite good here. This was a so called rest lager, from where the transports were sent to work. One day there was selection and I was put into a transport too. We arrived in Markleberg in 3 days. There they took us to a huge factory, where we learned airplanes were being manufactured. There we were treated more humanely. We were given overalls, underwear and finally I managed to get some shoes here. Our Lagerführer was such a terrible man that we trembled even when hearing his name. His name was Alois Knittel and he was in the German SS. One day I did not get food and I reported it to one of the Aufseherin, who then reported to the Oberschaarführer that I was a troublemaker and did not want to work. As a punishment I was shaved again, for the second time. It was very uncomfortable to go to the factory and stand behind the machine. We were working together with civilians and I was very ashamed of myself. Naturally I was not allowed to put a scarf on my head, as this was forbidden. At the beginning we worked 8 hours in the factory, and then when we arrived back at the lager we had to continue with 'Baukommand', which meant digging in the garden or shoveling sand in the quarry. When we dug out the sand we took it away in wheelbarrows and filled in the roads. We had to work in snow and rain and sometimes it was so cold the shovel froze to our hands. Later on we worked 12 hours per day in the factory though happily this meant that we no longer had to work in the Baukommando. The factory operated both day and night shifts. We made airplane screws and clocks. I reckon very few good planes were made in that factory but in spite of that they were satisfied with us and said that the Hungarian girls were hard working. Once I was given a piece of bread from one of the German Vorarbeiter (foreman). I was unlucky and the Aufseherin saw it. (We were not allowed to accept anything or talk to anybody in the factory as we were Jewish Häftlings, meaning we were the bottom of humanity). In the evening she reported the action to the Oberschaarführer. When we got back from the factory they called me out of the line. I already knew what was going to happen and was terribly afraid. The Oberschaarführer called me into the office and started to ask if I had received bread before. He also asked how I dared to accept it when I knew I was not allowed to accept anything. Then he asked sarcastically if I was hungry. "Don't you get enough to eat?" he said. "800 mls of soup for lunch and one sixth of a bread for dinner is enough to keep you alive. If you ate more you would be wasting food". At the end he was talking venomously like a snake. My punishment was to be locked in a bunker for 24 hours. This was a one person guard bunker, a round building of about 3 m high. They locked me in there naked for 24 hours without a thing. I was almost dead when I got out and had to go to the factory. That night nobody worked in the factory, everyone was talking about what had happened to me. I was standing next to the heater all night unable to move. Even my boss did not mind, he felt sorry for me even though he was German. This is how we lived until the 13th of March. On the 11th of March we did not go to the factory and there was huge excitement in the Lager. We already knew what it meant if the factory stopped. It would probably only be a question of days or hours before we would be freed. Suddenly they were shouting Zählappel. We went out to the yard and knew that something was going to happen. The Lagerführer took a chair and stood on it. It was terrible to see this man, a real soldier broken, and having to admit defeat. We hoped everything he had done to us would happen to him. It was very quiet and when he started to talk his voice was very weak with no life or strength in it. He said: "Unfortunately I have to go away now, you will remain at the factory, and from now on you do not have to march between SS soldiers. Aren't you happy that freedom has arrived?" He could not continue because we started to scream and shout with happiness. At this moment an SS soldier came running and called the Lagerführer to the phone. We knew that this signaled trouble. It was then that we thought he might have been playing a practical joke on us. In five minutes though the entire Lager was ordered to leave. Later on we got to know from one of the Schwabian SS who could speak Hungarian, that we should have been given a piece of bread and margarine per person for the trip. However we never received this food. We left at night without a bite of food to eat. Our pathetic group dragged itself through towns and villages. We ate grass and roots on the way. We were on the march all the time, escaping from the Americans- us Jews. I was able to keep this up for 5 nights and days after which my feet would not take me any further. One of my girlfriends had to stop to go to the toilet on the roadside and I (it was probably a good move, but probably I was crazy) threw myself under an 8 wheeled SS truck. The car braked, my leg broke, my nose and mouth were bleeding and I fell on the ground. The SS driver got out, started to swear at me, kicked me several times and then left. I stayed on the ground and my girlfriend dragged me down into a ditch. In the meantime the transport passed on. Slowly it became dark. Some distance away my girlfriend discovered a barn, and dragged me there, because I could not walk. We hid there. We were wondering what to do if found. We had overalls on and a coat, although my hair was shaved, our arms were tattooed and we had no papers. If we were found we would be shot. Morning came and we were terribly afraid. Then we heard steps- fear grabbed our hearts - and we believed that our suffering was still not over. There was a German peasant standing in front of us - the owner of the barn- and his first words were, why did we not put hay under ourselves. When he said this, we started to cry. My girlfriend immediately told him what happened to me. She told him we were Dutch Christian girls, who came to Germany voluntarily and I had wanted to commit suicide because I could not go on without food. We lived there in the barn for a week. The old man occasionally brought us some warm soup, and when I could stand up we left to look for work. Before leaving we washed the stripes out of our clothes and tried to hide all suspicious signs. I put a scarf around my head and we thought if anybody asked why I did not have hair then we would say I had had typhoid and lost my hair. The place we were hiding was called Meisen. When fit we climbed a hill to where the village was. I had terrible pain in my leg. We got a job with one of the peasants. They were very frightened, because the Russians were very close. The peasants employed every foreigner as a way of insuring themselves. Our peasant got to like us a lot, he could see we were not like other agricultural servants. We planted potato for him, hoed and I even ploughed for him. When the Russians were very close, the boss packed his most valuable belongings onto his cart and gave the key to his house to me. He said: "I say goodbye to you, you are a good girl. I trust you with my belongings. When the Russians come tell them I was good to you. If I come back and find you here I will give you some reward". He left and we stayed there together with servants who were angry with us, because now everything was in our hands. They had been there for a long time and we had only arrived some days earlier. The next day the Russian troops arrived. We were naturally very happy to see them as they represented freedom. All the suffering and horror was over. I gave them the keys, so they could eat and drink and use whatever they needed. The very next day we left for home in the direction of Dresden. We went into the Lager in Dresden, where they were organizing transports from there. After three days we left together with some Italians and Romanians. We arrived in Spremberg where we spent 4 months and were well treated. It was there that I finally succeeded in getting myself together a little. Together with the Italian transport we were taken to the American zone of occupation. We stayed in the American Lager in Hammerau for a month and we were looked after really well. There our daily menu consisted of the following: sweet coffee in the morning, at 11 a.m. a liter of milk per person, for lunch meat or liver soup, fried meat, potato and salad, for dinner a stew, salami, butter and half a loaf of bread. We could drink as much beer as we wanted. We were given 20 nice cigarettes a week and sometimes chocolate and oranges. From here we went on to Salzburg with the Hungarian transport where we stayed for 3 days and from there we went to the Hungarian border over a period of 4 days and then on to Budapest. My plan for the future: I am going to get married soon.

Testimony recorded by E. F. (in her own hand).

Testimony four. Testimony of Dr. G. H.

Recorded at DEGOB (Asylum of the National Committee for the Welfare of Deportees), Dózsa György street 27, Budapest XIV District, on 6th August 1945.

Name:	G. H.
Place of birth:	Munkács (Munkachevo, Ruthenia).
Profession:	lawyer

G. H. was taken from the Munkács ghetto to the following camps:

Auschwitz	May 20, 1944- May 23, 1944.
Dihernfurth	May 26, 1944- September 20, 1944.
Fünfteichen	September 21, 1944- January 3, 1945.
Wolfsberg	January 5, 1945- February 15, 1945.
Brunau	February 18, 1945- February 26, 1945.
Ebensee	March 3, 1945- May 5, 1945.

G. H. recounts the following:

The Jews who had lived in Münkacs and in the neighboring settlements and were by that time concentrated in the city of Münkacs, my place of birth and permanent residence, were deported in fact, not from the ghetto but from a brickyard where gradually some

10,000 Jews were collected as even the ones resident in Münkacs had been taken there. This took place in the following way: At six o'clock in the morning Hungarian gendarmes, Hungarian special constables and SS men broke into the ghetto, ran into the houses and drove the Jews out of their houses. Almost nobody could take any personal belongings, a maximum of a few things already packed but otherwise everything had to be left behind. In the streets were special constables, who, by the way, did not belong to the local police of Munkács but were dispatched there from other towns of the province. They were armed with heavy sticks and rained blows on the Jews, making no distinction between men, women and children. Not even elderly people or nursing mothers with infants at their breasts were spared. A lot of men were hit so hard on the head that they remained lying in a pool of blood. We were forced so brutally to hurry that even the few people who had managed to take along some personal belongings threw their packs away so as not to expose themselves to further corporal punishment. They could see for themselves what happened to those who were not able to get along: those poor people were hit so hard that they gasped their last gasp. Numerous people were killed this way during the short distance of some two kilometers from the ghetto to the brickyard, among them Géza Schönfeld, a wholesaler dealing in bicycles, gramophones and motor parts, and the accountant Márton Weiss. All the way to the brickyard we literally waded in blood, and I daresay that never during the whole period of my deportation in Germany did I witness scenes as terrible as those. For instance, the following episode took place before my eyes: on the road lay an un-weaned baby whose mother seemed to have fainted or been killed. A twenty year old woman I knew and whose name was Anna Grünberger, wanted to attend to the baby but an SS man went up to her, and stopped her from this act of mercy with several strokes of a stick and stamped on the child's head with his boot. The conditions were not better during our stay in the brickyard either. Abuse and corporal punishment were daily routine. The most brutal character was a special constable from Sárospatak named Németi, who invented the following method to torture Jews: Every morning he had all the men between the ages of eighteen and sixty line up and do gymnastic exercises (endless crouching and duck-walking etc.). In the meantime, he made them sit on the ground and hit them on the head with a heavy club, very often so hard that they fell senseless. One day the rabbis were called. Fifteen of the rabbis obeyed this command and when they were all gathered they were forced to sign a piece of paper saying that the Jews use Christian blood to make their Passover bread. The rabbis at first refused to sign this monstrosity but finally were forced by way of strokes and torture to do so. Then they were carried off and the following day physicians were sent to see them. A terrible scene confronted the doctors: the fifteen rabbis stood buried up to their necks in sewerage sludge and pig's excrement. Their bodies were smeared with clotted blood and most of them were unconscious, already beyond help. Nevertheless, the physicians were ordered to attend to the miserable men and make them fit for transport. As transport was immanent the rabbis were also to be sent along. The doctors did their best and all fifteen of the rabbis were indeed loaded into the goods train although they were still in a sad way. As was to be expected none of them survived the journey to Auschwitz after being so terribly tortured....One of the favorite pastimes of the SS people was to beat young men and women until they bled and rolled about in great pain and then force them to have sexual intercourse with each other. Anna Grünberger, already mentioned, was tied, together with her fiancé József Kocsis, a Christian man permanently resident in Nyiregyháza, to a horse, which was then made to gallop hauling the couple along for several kilometers. The young man suffered this punishment after he was accused of hiding his bride. Women were tied up in the most impossible contorted positions or turned upside down and forced to sing Hungarian folk songs until they fainted. Many young men were beaten to death. If they fell unconscious they would be brought to again and beaten until they finally gave up the ghost. One of the victims of this brutality was a good friend of mine, Fischer the fancy goods dealer from Munkács. The commander of the camp, Márton Zöldi, an ex-Hungarian gendarme officer was the instigator of these horrible crimes and in most cases explicitly authorized them. He had played an active part in the pogroms against Jews and Serbs in Novisad in January 1942 and had been sentenced to death by a Hungarian military court. However, Zöldi had managed to escape custody, fleeing to Germany whence he returned to Budapest after the occupation of Hungary as an Oberscharführer in the SS. This bastard was now in command of the concentration camp in which there were over 10,000 Jews in the brickyard of Munkács! It would take many volumes of paper to list all the crimes and describe all the monstrosities committed by Zöldi's assistants and by his authority. The abovementioned cases are only random examples of the immeasurable and indescribable suffering of the Jews concentrated in the brickyard at Munkács prior to their deportation. It is no surprise therefore, that many of us were happy to be deported as any place was considered better than in the clutches of the bloodhound, Zöldi. When I was deported to Auschwitz I had my family (wife and son) with me. Two days later we reached Auschwitz where my wife and son were immediately separated from me after alighting from the wagon. I have neither seen nor heard of any news of them since that time. I was firmly determined to escape from Auschwitz as I believed that life there with its nerve wracking inactivity, endless lining up to be counted, disciplinary punishments and hunger would soon kill me. However I did not know how I could escape. Then I had a stroke of luck. On the third day of my stay in Auschwitz, skilled workers were recruited for a labor camp. I presented myself without a moments thought, as a joiner. I was placed into a group of 500 workers and we were transported to Dihernfurth. Dihernfurth lies close to Brelau Wroclaw and we were employed at a building site. It turned out that I did not have to think twice when presenting myself as a joiner in order to become a member of the labor group as nobody inquired as to whether or not I was a skilled worker. All that mattered was to be able to carry a 50kg bag of cement or some similar heavy weight from one place to another, since this was the job I was assigned. I had to move rather quickly under that weight otherwise I was beaten, in the first instance by the SS men who took the matter seriously. And what punishment the SS failed to exercise was made up for by the Kapos, who were in no way lacking in brutality compared to the SS, although they too were captives, albeit Christian Poles. We found the job difficult not only because we were unaccustomed to it and lacking the necessary physical strength but also because our provisions were poor and insufficient. Consequently, the work, coupled with insufficient nutrition soon claimed it first victims. Of my friends, the engineer Benedek Sebok, the bank clerk Artur Gottesmann and József Fenyves, a clerk and son of a lawyer, all from Munkács, died in Dihernfurth. I survived there for almost four months when on the 20th of September all Jewish convicts were ordered to be transported to Fünfteichen. This place was also close to Breslau and once again we were employed on a building site where I worked as a carpenter. The work was very hard here too though we did not suffer as much from hunger as in Dihernfurth because the food was not only more nourishing but also increased in quantity. In addition, the treatment, although stringent enough was also a bit more humane. At the same time, there was another factor that added to our suffering, the cold weather. Our clothes covered us without keeping us warm. Unfortunately the winter in Silesia was especially severe that year. On January 3rd I was moved from Fünfteichen to Wolfsberg together with some other workers. Wolfsberg was an all Jewish camp holding 3,500 people. Even the senior convicts in charge of the individual blocks and the Kapos were Jewish though exclusively of Polish origin. They treated us very strictly. We worked in a tunnel in two shifts. There was two weeks in the day shift then two weeks on night duty. There was no break in the daily shift of twelve hours. On top of the hard work the food if it could be called that was extremely bad and meager. The worst thing, however, was the treatment, the ultimate goal of which, as with the work and the food, was to kill us. The situation was so bad that convicts tried to commit suicide whenever possible. The fact that most attempts failed was attributed to one young man, whose name I cannot remember, who hung himself. Thereafter, the sentry duty was reinforced and from that time on no one else was able to successfully commit suicide. If taken ill you could be taken to hospital but there was no medicine and few medical instruments and operations were sometimes performed using a pocket knife. At least twenty convicts died every day in the camp at Wolfsberg. Eventually the whole camp would probably have been liquidated in this way had the Russians not pressed on to Wolfsberg so rapidly. The camp was evacuated at the last moment when we could hear the roar of Russian guns. We were forced to march for two days without bread or water. We then received only 150 grams of bread as provisions for the next two days. People became weaker and weaker with someone collapsing at almost every step. The number of dead grew so rapidly that we no longer even glanced at them. How could we have when 300 to 400 people died before our eyes during the three or four days we were marching? We finally stopped at Brunau, a Sudeten German provincial town eight kilometers from the Czechoslovakian border. We were driven into a barn large enough for 1,000 to 1,500 people although there were more than 3,000 of us and it was certain that we had to all fit in together. Inside there was a bitter fight for room, which ended in a fearful mess with the winners, gaining no more than the defeated. Finally we "settled in" as well as we could. Because of the awfully cramped conditions by the following morning more than 50 convicts had suffocated. We spent eight days in this horrible barn, which resembled a mass crypt much more than a place of accommodation. Every 48 hours we were given about 100 grams of horse meat but no bread. At the end of this time we were again loaded into wagons and transported through Czechoslovakia to Ebensee. We spent the journey in open wagons and it easy to guess what this means in February wearing a minimum of clothing. We were terribly cold during the six days of the journey suffering also from hunger and thirst. Provisions were limited to some 200 to 250 grams of bread and even that was distributed only every other day. We suffered most from thirst however as we were given absolutely no water and were not allowed to eat any snow on the journey. When some of the more daring of us managed to smuggle some snow into the wagon (at the risk of their life) each of us would trade our most valuable treasure i.e. the small allowance of bread, in order to quench our terrible thirst. On March 3rd we finally reached our destination of Ebensee. Once again our numbers had been further reduced as many had froze to death. Right after our arrival at Ebensee we again risked freezing to death. On our arrival we were told that we had to be immediately disinfected. We were duly led to the place of disinfection but only small groups were let in at any one time. The rest of us had to wait outside until our turn came. This waiting took two days and a night spent lying in the snow. Not even the ill, of which there was more than enough, were given any cover. Many froze to death right there on the first day. By the time the procedure of disinfection was completed the open area in front of the disinfection chamber was literally covered with dead bodies. More than half of those who had survived the journey to Ebensee had perished from the extreme cold in front of the chamber. Among those who died there were my friends Dr. György Szalai, a lawyer from Kassa (Kosice) and Dr. Dezso Fuchs, a lawyer from Beregszász (Berehovo). Those still alive were put up in a special block, where we spent ten days in quarantine. At this time the remaining Jews were divided into three groups: fit for hard work, fit for easy work and unfit for work. The latter group went to block 26. The senior man of the block was a Christian Pole who treated them so cruelly that they soon died. Undoubtedly he was instructed to systematically kill those who were unfit for work as this method was even cheaper than gas. In addition, really the efforts of the senior man of the block were crowned with success as at least fifty people died per day in block 26. In none of the deportation camps where I had so far been was anti-Semitism as strong as in Ebensee. The Jewish captives were meticulously separated from the Christian ones, including those who were sick, there being an area for Christian sick people and another special area designated for the Jewish sick. Being put up there in the Jewish sick area was equivalent to a death sentence as people were left completely unattended or treated in such a way that they would soon die. After selection everybody was closely examined for gold teeth. One day they found a gold tooth in the pocket of a man from Brod (next to Ilosva) called Goldstein, who had deliberately pulled out one of his teeth to trade for some food. The poor fellow was first beaten until he bled and then hung. The same happened to a young man from Ökörmezo- from memory his name was Weiss- who had committed the same 'crime'. In contrast to senior man I, who behaved relatively fairly, senior man II of the camp, an Austrian named Lorenz, was a virtual bastard. Lorenz, an ex hardened criminal, was a cruel monster who day after day invented new kinds of brutality with which to torture us. One day he could not find his pencil and immediately accused the Jewish captives of having stolen it. As a punishment he picked out eighty of us to stand completely nude in the open where we were administered eight to ten strokes on our exhausted bodies. At that time there were 12,000 captives in the camp, of which 4,000 were Jewish, the rest being mostly Christian Poles, Frenchman and Russians. Had they even wanted to, the Jews would not have been able to use any facility, the writing-room or elsewhere because, as I have already mentioned there prevailed an especially strong anti-Semitism in Ebensee, stronger than in any previous camp. Later I was assigned to work in a tunnel, blasting rocks, carrying stones and placing concrete, that is to say the heaviest jobs possible. The treatment was very strict and the SS men who supervised us drove us to work quicker and harder and immediately hit us if the tempo of the work slowed. The food was insufficient and not just in relation to the labor performed. We received 150 grams of bread and some soup, which was nothing more than warm water with potato peels floating in it. That was all we were given for the whole day! Every day many captives fell to the ground exhausted from the work never to rise again. The furnaces worked continuously as there were at least two hundred corpses to be cremated each day. The bodies were delivered there both from the work-sites and from the blocks where the senior block men, almost always "Reichsdeutsch" and professional criminals, seemed to excel in being able to supply the furnaces with as much fuel as was possible. On the day of our liberation, May 5th, 1945, we were all called to line up and the commander of the camp, an SS Obersturmführer told us that the Americans would soon arrive and we should go into the tunnel and remain there as he "could not take any responsibility for our safety". We had, however, been warned by our foreman that we could expect worse to come before liberation and that it was possible that we would be concentrated in the tunnel to be killed by machine gun. The Czech foreman thus advised us not to obey such a command. It seemed that we could run such a risk as the liberating troops would not be far away. It was also the case that for some days we had noticed the unmistakable signs of confusion in the camp. The SS had become somewhat irresolute and did not hurry to execute orders given to them. As a consequence we answered in chorus to the commander's address that we would not go into the tunnel and that he should not worry about us. In a few hours time Ebensee was occupied by the American troops. I have lost, in addition to my wife and son, my mother, three brothers, two sisters, a brother-in-law and a niece and am the only one still alive from a family of ten.

G. H.

Testimony recorded by Otto Rauch.

Testimony five. Testimony of Dr. I. J.

From the National Jewish Faith and Historical Collection
Budapest Sip Street 12.

Recorded in Balassagyarmat, on 18th November, 1945.

Name:	I. J.
Place of birth:	Balassagyarmat.
Occupation:	Doctor

I. J. was taken from the Balassagyarmat ghetto to the following camps:

Auschwitz:	14.6.1944-4.7.1944
Gelsenkirchen:	14.7.1944-11.9.1944
Sömmerda:	12.9.1944-4.4.1945
Altenburg:	12.4.1945-16.4.1945

I. J. recounts the following:

I worked in the psychiatry department of the Maria Valeria Public Hospital in Balassagyarmat until 4.4. 1944. I was told by the director of the Hospital, that on the order of the deputy sub-prefect Sándor Nógrádi Horváth, I should hand in my application for retirement. I received my salary up until 30th April, but during this time I was not required to serve the hospital. However I was asked to introduce the service to my incumbent. Thus I was still visiting the hospital until 30th of April. After the 30th of April I had to move into the ghetto, from where I could only leave in the evening with permission. To heal Christians was very difficult even with the requirement coming from the Christian. Once I was called to a Christian patient. He had to ask a separate permission from the Balassagyarmat police, to allow me to go and examine the patient. The person named Simon, a tobacco seller, on arriving to the police station was asked very nastily: "You have very funny taste to have your wife examined by a Jewish doctor!" The permit said the following: "I allow the "Jewish" Dr. Erzsebet Schenk Jewish doctor to leave the 'Jewish' ghetto for one hour on the request of Simon tobacco seller, to examine her patient. The Jewish doctor may only leave with an armed escort together with the relative of the patient. This relative must return this written permit within the hour. Miklós police scribe." The Christians had mixed feelings towards us, some of them disputed these rules, but the majority were happy with the separation of the Jews. A lot of them were very curious and wanted, for differing reasons, to get into the ghetto. There were many times when I had to go to the hospital with a separate permission, now without armed escort, with the yellow star on my breast. People looked at me as if I was a curious breed of animal. After the ruling about the compulsory display of the yellow star, the director of the hospital, Dr Kenessey, decided that it was not necessary for the Jewish doctors to wear the star in the hospital, only after leaving its walls. However deputy sub-prefect Horváth changed this and made it compulsory to wear the yellow star on our white gowns, and even in the theatre. After we had moved into the city ghetto, some police arrived from the Miskolc secret service and moved into 15. Kossuth Lajos Street and set up their office (their killing fields). It was here that almost all the Jews were taken in smaller groups. First Jews were interrogated, then with physical torture were forced to reveal where they had hidden their valuables. Naturally the majority of these tortured people had no valuables at all. My sister, Mrs. Istvan Kovács, who had been supported by her parents because her husband had only 150 'pengö', was tortured for two days. They did not want to let her go, wanting to know where she had hidden her gold, which she never even had. (After deportation both she and her little son's lives ended in the gas chambers of Auschwitz). These tortures did not stop even after our deportation to Nyirjespuszta. The gendarmes came in daily in the morning and at noon and took people in groups to the house in Kossuth Street. They brought them back in the evening on carts and in cars, because they were unable to walk as a result of the beatings. I examined a lot of them and in a lot of cases I found serious internal wounds. There were two cases when the patients died in the train during their transport to Germany as a result of the gendarmes' batons. One of them was a 68-year-old man from Gyarmat, named Adler . I can not remember the name of the other man, I think he was from Szokolya, he was 52 and suffered from tabes doralis. His thighbone got broken when he got beaten and as a result of that his blood vessel clotted and he died. The lawyer Dr. Ferenc Hajdu was beaten so hard that he began to bleed from the kidney. He was taken to Auschwitz already very ill, but alive, only to end his life in the gas chamber. After our move to the ghetto the assistant to the county doctor, Dr. Károly Furia, decided that the ghetto should set up its own hospital with a surgery, a birthing room, and a theatre, with adequate medical and nursing staff. However this plan was never realized and remained unfinished when on the 5th of June we were taken to Nyirjespuszta from the city ghetto. The transportation proceeded in cars and on foot. On the streets there were a lot of people standing and watching us with interest. There could be seen no traces of good or bad intentions on their faces, only curiosity. Even before we left the looting of the Jewish flats in the ghetto had started. They took food, movable objects etc. We could see these items being taken away from the derelict houses, and I personally witnessed one of the gendarmes go into a flat, open the wardrobe, and stuff his pocket full of cigarettes handkerchiefs and women's silk stockings. Unfortunately I do not know his name or address. In Nyirjespuszta we were put up in a tobacco barn, 1800 of us. The locals were in one barn and the people from the surrounding areas were in the other. There was no health equipment, no water or proper toilets. We had to walk 3 kilometers for water to the nearest animal well. Bathing facilities were the worst possible, because the owner did not want to let us take water from the same well for bathing, as he was afraid the water would run out. Those who wanted to bath had to walk daily to the fish lake, which was even further. There was nothing done about medicine, tape, or a separate room where patients suspected of a contagious illness could be separated. While we were at Nyirjespuszta there were two births. One of them was delivered in the dust of the barn, but mother and daughter were healthy and arrived in Auschwitz to end up in the gas chamber. The other birth occurred- after my very strong intervention in a room of a small close by peasant house. During our stay a 60-year-old woman poisoned herself with an unknown drug, and though I immediately reported it, by the time the ambulance took her to hospital she had died. The ghetto was transported in two lots. The first transport left on the 10th of June, the other on the 12th. Each transport consisted of 1800 people. The Jewish patients of the Balassagyarmat hospital and of the mental department left with the second transport, together with the new mother with her one-hour-old baby. On the morning of the 10th. of June the commander of the gendarmes said that those who still had some belongings in the city ghetto could go in and get them. We were told to get into groups and with gendarme escort we would be able to go back to our flats in the ghetto and get what we had left there. By 12 o'clock there was a big group made up of people wanting to go into the city. After an hour's wait the commander sent the crowd back saying nobody could go today. Instead we were to wait until the following day. Soon after the inhabitants of the ghetto were called together in the yard and were read the order of deportation. In this order there was no mention of Germany, only that the whole group and their families would be taken for work and would be placed in camps where the health and comfort facilities would be much better compared with the current situation. We were told what we were allowed to take with us: food for four days,1 small pillow,and 1 blanket, 1 change of underwear, 2 dresses and 1 coat. This package should be prepared very quickly, because the trucks would come to take us to the Balassagyarmat train station very soon. The first group with its small packages was put on the carts at 2 p.m. and the last ones left at 6 p.m. When I got to the station the wagons were already full but the new arrivals were still being squeezed into these full wagons. 80-90 people were put into one wagon. When a wagon was declared full the gendarmes jumped up, kicked and squeezed people into smaller and smaller places. We were not given toilet buckets, but one of us sacrificed his bathing dish in our wagon. We were given one bucket of fresh water per wagon. However in the next wagon the bucket was kicked out by a rail worker and director of the deportations at the train station, named Pongrác, who said: " the Jews do not need that much water". Whilst still at the station I was called to a patient, an elderly woman who was dying. I went to the gendarme captain (named Bretány) and asked him to let the woman be taken off the train, as she would die within minutes. Laughing, he answered with the question "would you be so cruel as to leave one of your fellow Jews out of this fun?" I turned to another officer but he turned me down with a wave of his hand. The woman died at the next station, but she traveled with us in the locked wagon through to Auschwitz. In the summer heat, her corpse began to turn green and was only removed after our arrival. We left Gyarmat on route to Aszód at 7.30. Before departure our wagon doors were sealed and only through the barred windows could we get a little fresh air. The wagon I traveled in was under my supervision, as there were a lot of old people and children, some 89 people, in this wagon. The air was foul but the gendarme would not open the door even once in 24 hours of begging. The only time we got some fresh air was when I indicated an emergency. This happened twice on route to Kassa, once for a birth, and once in the event of a stroke, which ended in the death of the patient. We arrived in Kassa on the third day of our trip. Here the SS took over our train. At Kassa we were given fresh water more regularly than had been the case with the Hungarian gendarmes. The SS opened the door, the next morning, gave us toilet buckets, which the Hungarians had not done, and if we stayed longer at a station we were allowed to renew our fresh water. I do not know of anybody who would have escaped from the transport. We were told both in Gyarmat and in Kassa that if anyone should escape, the whole wagon would be killed, so nobody dared to think of escaping. In Kassa the gendarmes did not want to part from us without any 'memories', so they stole our last valuables. For example I still had my winter coat then (I do not know how it had previously escaped their attention) . I was sitting on it and one of the gendarmes tore it out from under me so viciously that I almost fell out of the wagon together with the coat. One of my fellows had to hold me by my arm. The gendarme said " This is going to be very good for my wife, it is very light." There were a few lighters, torches, pencils, cigarettes, all were taken away. They searched the suitcases again saying they were looking for cigarettes, but if those were not found , handkerchiefs, towels, soaps, perfumes were good enough too. We arrived in the station of Auschwitz-Birkenau on the night of 14th of June. We were not let out immediately, but had to wait until dawn. At first light Mengele's pen separated wife from husband, mother from child, children from their parents, sibling from sibling, in the provision of ammunition for the Auschwitz death factory. I myself did not see the selection that day as immediately after the opening of the wagon door I was taken off and sent to an already selected group going to the bath. I did not want to be separated from my loved ones . First an SS women pushed me, but when I did not want to obey her, an SS obersturmführer stepped up and very politely asked me to go with them. He said it really did not matter to me who I was going with , as I was going to receive a two room flat, where one room would be the surgery, and I could live in the other with my family. I was very naive and without any further hesitation and even feeling some happiness I went to the bath so I would soon be ready to rejoin my family again. After a long wait in the bath those from Balassagyarmat who had been chosen for life arrived. Neither my parents nor my younger siblings or my three-and-a half-year-old cousin were in this group. When I asked an acquaintance where they were, she said she was not sure, but she thought they had been taken somewhere in trucks. On arrival to the block I went to a Polish Jewish woman, who was putting us into rows of five and told her there must have been a mistake because I had been told by an SS officer at the station that as a doctor I would be put in a separate flat together with my family. She started to laugh loudly and said "I should never believe a word the Germans say anymore, as these are lies." She also told me that if my family is not here, you will never see them again". Unfortunately she was right, I never saw them again. Before arriving at the block we were forced to bath. We had to strip naked in a room in which there were men walking about. Our hair and all body hair was shaved, then they washed us with a disinfectant. Afterwards we had to wash under the shower. We did not have any towels, wet and naked we were herded out to the courtyard. From there we had to go to the cloths storeroom, about a 100 feet away, where everyone was given one dress but no underwear. The majority were allowed to keep their shoes. We had to go to the courtyard and stand in rows of five, and then we were put to Block 4 of Lager B. We received no food or drink that day. That afternoon people from Miskolc and Győr were brought in. In barracks fit for 5-600 people there were 1350 people. Naturally there was not enough space to lie down. At 2 a.m. we were woken up and made to stand in the yard on Zehlappel . From 2 at night until 9 in the morning, when the sun was high above us, we stood there. As cold as it was at night, it was as hot already in the morning at 9. A lot fainted from tiredness and hunger. At 9 o'clock we were given a type of semolina, and an hour after they brought sour tea, which would have been good to quench our thirst, had it been enough for everybody, and everyone could have at least have 100 mls. However there was not enough for everyone, and only those who could push themselves to the thermos or those standing close by could get some. The SS woman said that if we were quiet we would be given some drinking water soon, but we should not drink a lot, because the drinking water was polluted. At noon 20 buckets of water were brought for 1350 people deprived of fluids for two days. Now, like animals they attacked the buckets, nothing could hold them back, not the dog whips of the SS women, nor the wooden sticks of the Polish and Slovakian Jewish girls. Naturally most of the water was wasted this way. After this luxury we could squat, lie in whatever position in front of the block. There were no bathing place or bathing dish of course and the toilet was very primitive consisting only of a deep trench with a delicate piece of wood on the side. However, even this primitive toilet we were not always allowed to use. There were days that we were forbidden to use it. Those who used this toilet on those days when it was forbidden were badly beaten by the Polish or Slovakian blokkältests guarding us. These girls themselves were so terribly afraid, that it was no wonder they behaved like animals in this state of mind. Naturally there were some exceptions, but not "Baby", the blokkältest of barrack 4, or "Anny", the sub-blokkältest. Next morning I could already see that no allowances would be made for the sick. There was one particular patient whom the blokkältste (block leader) woke and drove out to appel. As she did not want to and could not go out, the block leader beat her. I went up to her and said that this person had high fever. Though I was unable to take her temperature I could see that the woman had a high temperature from her condition. The block leader shouted at me, saying it was not my business and the patient should immediately go out to the queue. I reported the case to the Jewish girl from Besztercebánya, who was the lagerkapo (chief inmate appointed by the SS), but she informed me, that you should not fall ill here, because the sick are eliminated. For two weeks after our arrival we did not have to work at all. At 2 a.m. we were woken and had to stand in the yard for long hours in all weather. From the third day on we received coffee or tea in the morning, dörgemüze (?) for lunch and at 4 p.m. there was 'bread time'. We were given 500 grams of bread for two days with kvargli (cheese), margarine, horse-salami, tinned meat or a spoonful of marmalade. It was not unusual for some of these ingredients to be omitted. There were a very few dishes so 30-40 of us were eating from one dish. At six we were herded into the barracks to squat until the 2 a.m. wake-up-call. Sometimes we had to start the appel at 12 midnight. On the second day I was given the job of Block doctor, which was the saddest and most depressing job of my life. Naturally I was not given any equipment, bandages or medicines. My real job was to try to console my fellows and tell them to hang in there as we surely would soon be free. Sadly we had to wait a year for that! SS women came almost every day to select the weak from among us. They asked who had some problem, they said they would take them to the surgery. They took these unfortunates to the so called surgery, which was nothing else but the gas chamber followed by the crematorium. Once a fat, bowlegged bulldog-faced SS woman came into the barrack and said the pregnant women should put their hands up and report- because as she said pregnant women should not be in a crowded place like this, they need more comfort, they would be put into birthing homes, where they would receive milk, milk coffee , white bread or sweet bread for breakfast. We had 11 pregnant women in this block and 3 of them believed the German rather than their fellow inmates who wanted to dissuade them from reporting . These 3 pregnant women, 2 patients of coma diabetes, a psychiatric patient, and 3 women suffering from TB volunteered to be taken to hospital and were collected by this SS woman. The SS woman asked who the block doctor was. After making myself known she told me to go along too. She gathered some more victims from the other blocks in the 1st block of the B Lager. There were 11 more people, other 'volunteered' patients, some pregnant women, 8 women from my block, and another doctor named Edith Fodor. Together we set out for the "surgery". We traveled a long way , about 60kms [This is as written in the original transcription but seems incorrect]. We were told it was the C Lager. There we went toward a red-brick building with tall chimneys. We were told this was the "surgery". It was all chimneys, all the chimneys were smoking and behind the building I saw a big fire. We were not taken close enough to the building for me to be able to tell what sort of a fire it was. On the way we met Dr. Mengele, and we heard him abusing the SS woman for not bringing enough 'patients'. After this the patients were taken over by SS soldiers and men in stripy suits. They definitely did not look like doctors or nurses. Then we were ordered to turn back and were told we would be shot in the head if we turned back. I was curious and not afraid of death. I looked back and I saw one of the patients being put into a big linen bag and an other bag was standing beside it already full. The mouth of that bag was zipped up and it was rolled toward the crematorium like a barrel, but we could not hear any screaming from it. Then their belongings and blankets were brought back to me to be returned to the lager. On the way back we passed in front of a bath building which was a short distance, about 150-200 steps from the crematorium. On its door there was a sign in several languages, in French, English, German, Czech, Polish , Cyrillic letters and in Hungarian. It said: "Disinfection, be careful that your shoes, towel and soap are not stolen or swapped. At that time I did not know yet what this " Disinfectant" we were passing by was. In a few days I was unfortunately assigned to escort some of my fellow inmates to the so called "surgery", This time the door to this bath building was open. It did not seem to differ at all from other disinfection facilities except that it had a thickly padded door with a rubber strip around it . Inside there was a railing, which were in fact empty railings, with holes resembling showers. Through these holes poured in the quickly killing gas that was provided by the I.G. Farbenindustrie. I was told this by a group of men in stripy suits working around the gas chamber. They asked us :"Do you know what this is? The gas chamber." I asked the Polish girls in our escort and they said the same too. I did not come to this area again. However I was in a grass-cleaning-team on the railway station on the 29th June, when a transport train arrived. Dr. Mengele was standing waiting for the train. I heard someone ask him where the occupants were to be held as there were at that moment no empty barracks. I heard him answer: "Alles in Gas". I think it was a group arriving from the 'Great Plain', because from one of the wagons somebody asked if we knew anyone from Kiskunhalas or Kalocsa. At the end of June I was given a thermometer and a stethoscope. Around this time a real surgery was established in our lager. It also had an additional room with a few beds, for less critical patients. If the doctor recognized scarlet fever, diphtheria, or typhoid, the patient was able to remain for 24 hours. This hospital was called the 'revier'. Then a car came and these poor people were taken away naked to be eliminated. A few of those with scarlet fever were hidden in the barrack and actually recovered. Some of the häftlings I was acquainted with in Auschwitz tried to help by hiding patients and providing extra food. This situation lasted only a few weeks however, as the häftlings became selfish. It was not that they did not care for their fellow inmates but as conditions worsened it became a question of their own survival. They even informed on their own inmates if it was a matter of their own survival. Sometimes I was horrified to see a child stealing food, soap or a towel from their mother or one sibling stealing from another sibling. On the 3d of July I was summoned to the revier by Dr. Mengele. He said I was to go immediately to Lager A. I was not allowed to say good-bye, I could not go back to the block any more. An SS woman escorted me to lager A. where I was first of all taken to the revier. I was questioned about my qualifications and where I used to work. They said I was to leave with the transport immediately. First I was taken to the bath, where I bathed, received a grey linen dress, trousers, shirt and a pair of wooden shoes. I was then taken into block 9 and loaded into a wagon together with people from Máramaros, Bereg, County Ung, and Nagykanizsa. I left Auschwitz on the 4th July at noon, together with 2002 people, 2000 workers and 2 doctors. Immediately on entering the wagons we were somewhat relieved to see that the soldiers looking after us, apart from the officer, all belonged to the Wermacht, who proceeded to treat us in a more humane manner. There were two soldiers in every wagon and most were invalids from the previous war. Our wagons were open during the whole trip and we received fresh water at every station. They allowed us to wash. Before leaving Auschwitz we were given 1 kg of bread, 5 dkg of horse salami and 10dkg of margarine. At the bigger stations in the mornings we were given a bucket of hot black coffee. There were 50 people in the wagons and in the evenings our escorts made sure everybody had a turn lying down. Our escorts sometimes distributed food amongst us from their own supply, some cubes of sugar if nothing else. Once they had some beer and gave everybody a glassful. They said: "Aber niemanden sagen und erzählen davon!" (No-one should tell anyone about this) Our two escorts, oberfeldwebel Hinze and Heller the 'rechnungsfhürer' of the lager gave us cigarettes. After a 10-day journey- sometimes we had to wait a whole day for example in Dresden, Halle and Dortmund- we arrived in the station of Gelsenkirchen, from where we had to walk 5 kilometers to the Gelsenberg artificial fuel factory, which was in ruins. From Dortmond to Gelsenkirchen all we could see were ruins, huge water pipelines and fuel barrels broken on both sides of the train line. It was raining and we were very cold in our light clothing. It is already summer at home around this time. At the side of the fuel factory we were shown a sandy site for our camp. We arrived earlier than expected so there were no barracks or food waiting for us. Moreover the Todt association, who were our employers, were quite unhappy to receive us as they were expecting men. We arrived at about 3-4 o'clock, and by 6 our tents were standing. Next to the tents there were two huge bathing rooms with cement basins and showers. The toilets were not ready yet although two trenches dug for that purpose. The next day this problem was satisfactorily resolved. There were 500 people to a tent sleeping on three-story beds. For the patients a separate tent was built with rooms separated by wooden planks. There were 2 rooms for contagious patients, one normal room, one surgery, and a little room for two doctors and a nurse. There was a three-storey bed there and a little cupboard in which we kept the medicines and bandages. The SS officer here handed us over to a SS obersturmführer named Edmund Dittrich, who was the commander of this work lager till the day of our freedom. He was a drunken man of over 60 years, but not a bad one. He was very surprised on the first day to see our very few belongings. The häftlings were wearing one thin linen dress, while some of them did not even have underwear. Dittrich gave everybody two blankets, a plate, a cup, a spoon and fork. I still do not know why they gave us forks when the only food we received was soup and boiled potatoes. To start with the lager was completely without medicines and bandages for the first week. This was not the fault of the commander , but the central SS kommando was slow to send the allowed amount of medicine for us. Later on even if our medicine supply was not the best, we always received the most necessary things, even if we had to fight for it every month. The workers were cleaning up the ruins, which was a very difficult job for young girls. The majority of the workers were between 15-30 years of age, though there were about 40-50 women of around 50 years of age. Many of these used to go out to work, but the majority did internal jobs. The wakeup call was at 5 in the morning, at 6 we had to line up and by 6.30-7 everybody would arrive at their designated place of work. The workday was 8 hours long, with half an hour lunch. Lunch was delivered by cars to those working further away. Some of us, for example, unloaded cement and bricks arriving from Holland and Belgium on the shore of the river Ruhr. Amongst these workers sunburn on the legs, arms, neck and face was very common. These wounds would heal very slowly because of the lack of vitamins and there were some cases where treatment lasted for half a year. Food supply : Before work bitter black coffee without sugar, at lunch a soup, sometimes with potato, sometimes with cabbage and potato, on Sundays pasta soup with potato. In the evenings we received our bread ammunition, which was 500 grams per day. There was margarine, salami or a spoonful of jam, or sugar, cheese, or some tinned beef. These alternated every second day. Occasionally we received potato in its jacket, 5 pieces per person. At the beginning the sick received semolina cooked in half milk and half water instead of the soup, but later on they stopped this practice. The health standards were quite satisfactory-compared with other lagers-, we did not have serious epidemics here or later in Sömmerda. However we had a lot of cases of "ruh and furunkolozis" despite the possibilities for cleaning, and treatments. There were only a limited numbers of tick cases and there were two disinfections for that. There was not one case of " flecktiphoid" during the whole year. We had five cases of typhoid, but these could be put in the Gelsenkirche Marie Hospital in time. After discharge of these five patients and the disinfection of the lager we had no more typhoid cases. Two out of those five died in the hospital, the other three went home healthy. We were totally segregated from the civilians, however the girls worked together with Belgian, Dutch, French workers, who sometimes gave them food, handkerchiefs, scarves, soap, occasionally a bottle of beer. At the workplace Todt workers were guarding us, the majority of whom were friendly towards us. However those who were openly friendly could get into trouble, because there were some SA people who were watching the behavior of the citizens. In the third week of our stay there we were given SS women as guards in addition to the Wermacht soldiers. Altogether there were 4 guard women and 100 guard men. The number of the women grew and that of the men decreased, so by the time we left Gelsenkirchen, we had 20 women and 50 men guards. In July in Gelsenkirchen we had a birth too in the lager. The birth itself did not happen in the lager, because within the circumstances there with the lack of underwear etc it could not have been done. The commander of the camp had the woman taken to hospital, from where she was sent back to us after 10 days. The newborn was a very underdeveloped prematurely born baby, we could give him only very little food, sometimes some mother's milk mixed with water. Once a Todt foreman saw the child and one morning we found a little package in front of the tent. In it there were 2 milk bottles, 3 dummies, 2 little shirts and one naval bandage. I have certain knowledge that this package was put there by a Todt foreman for the baby. In order not to have any more births in the camp the commander had all the women of the lager examined and ordered the pregnant ones to be taken to the concentration camp. he wanted to have the mother and baby taken away a well and ordered me and the other doctor to destroy the baby. Naturally we were not prepared to carry out this order, because doctors have to heal and not to take lives knowingly. He did not force the issue any more, however the next day an SS woman took the child from us, and we never saw the little one again. The mother stayed in our lager, was working again after 2 weeks and in my knowledge she returned home healthy. I would like to recount another episode as well. In August I took 9 patients to the Horst hospital with the escort of an SS woman guard. As we crossed a street there was an old woman coming from the opposite direction, carrying a tray full of baked fruit bread. When she saw us she took it off her head and gave some to each of us. The guard told her she was not allowed to do that. However she did not take a notice of this, but told her not to be so cruel, could she not see how hungry these poor women were, and God would give her more instead of this. The SS woman did not report this event in the lager, I know that for sure. The woman in question was called Maria Reich. On an other occasion I saw here kneel in front of a sick häftling and helped her do up her shoes. This woman was later on replaced. In our lager there were no political movements, the workers received news from other workers in the workplace and in turn we received updates on the war from them. On the 8th of September we were badly bombed, and 300 of our people died. The wounded were taken to surrounding hospitals where both the nurses and doctors were trying to save these unfortunates to the best of their knowledge. Lots of them were saved not only to live but to be able to become useful members of the society too. I especially have to mention the name of two doctors, Dr. Bertran the head surgeon of the Horst hospital and Dr. Eugen Gäng, who tried to heal and look after our häftlings with the upper most altruism, and succeeded in saving some of them from the terrible fate of the lager by keeping them in the hospital as long as they possibly could. They did not even let them go at the order of the Gestapo, only when time came to evacuate the hospital. Then they let them go with blankets, clothing and food, however the Gelsenkirchen Gestapo confiscated some of the blankets and foodstuff when they were taken back to the lager. We only saw these people again in Sömmerda. On the 11th of September, when one bombing was followed by another, we were taken to Sömmerda, where we got to within a day. When still in Gelsenkirchen 500 people were taken away to Essen, and we lost 300 people during the bombing. From amongst those there were about 30 wounded who could be transported, so 1250 people left for Sömmerda. There we lived in wooden barracks, with full comfort, running water in the bath and toilets. On of the barracks was named furnished as revier. The work here was physically easier because they were working in the munitions factory, but mentally more difficult, and the workday was longer too. 12 hours was the official workday with 1-1.5 hours brake, but the workplace was far and it took 14-15 hours to get home again , to get to their food and to be able to rest. There were two shifts, a day and a night shift. There we only received 300 grams of bread per day until February, then 200 gr. till March and from then on only 120 grams. There was soup every day made of turnip, once a week carrot and potato and occasionally so called flour soup. Sometimes on Sundays the whole lager received milk soup, which was a terrible, most of the time burnt , inedible meal. For dinner we received 5 pieces of potato per person. The majority of the workers were very diligent and the Germans were very satisfied, with the exception of two girls who always sabotaged work. One of them caused 3000 Marks damage by braking a machine, which took a week to repair. the other one broke a machine too. These girls were severely punished, they were put outside in the cold for the whole day, their hair was shaved and an SS called Otto Reinhardt beat them so they fainted. Still they could not be persuaded to work for them. In my knowledge a brief was sent to Berlin about these two saboteurs. In the lager they were put to work in the hoffkommando and were told every day that the order was being waited on from Berlin when to transport them to lager where they would be killed. We were asked to provide doctor's opinion about their health and naturally we said both were mental cases. The two girl arrived home safely at the end, one of them was from Máramaros county, the other from the area of Ungvár. In Sömmerda the majority of the people were very hostile towards us. It was the case, for example that doctors did not want to refer our patients to surgery, saying : "Jews can die". I am unable to name one doctor in the Sömmerda hospital who behaved humanely toward our patients. They were so hostile and unfriendly that even our SS guard found it too much and reported it to the commandant. However I have to mention a dentist in Sömmerda by the name of Wagner, who attended to some of the häftling's teeth, and who was always very friendly toward us. Often he carried out work on our teeth without being paid by the munitions factory. The majority of our guards who came with us from Auschwitz stayed with us till we were freed. First they belonged to the Wermacht then to the SS but deep down they did not change. Hartmann, Scheilen, Rudolf Wolf were good to us from the beginning. There were four very cruel and sadistic guards in the camp who beat the häftlings even for the smallest mistakes. These were taught by Otto Reinhard how to deal with häftlings. Hans Künzler was a young SS, a university student who spoke quite good English, there was the economics officer and two other SS officers.(one of whom was called Müller and I do not know the other's name). These two

were transferred away from us. In April the environs of Sömmerda were heavily bom-
barded by the Allies especially Erfurt, 30 kilometers from us and every night the airport
of Köleda, 10 kilometers from us. The planes going to attack Berlin-Marburg-Breslau and
Leipzig flew above us every day. On the 3d April the order arrived with Himmler's signa-
ture to empty the lager, and us to be terminated at Köleda airport. We got to know about
this order and went straight to the commander of the camp . He told us that yes, we were
going to leave toward Köleda the next day, but we would not be hurt as he did not even
have machine guns only one gun, so everybody could not get a bullet. Anyway he had
been a soldier for seven years, but never killed anyone and he would not do it now either,
especially that the Americans were only 30 kilometers from us. On the evening of the 3rd
we heard a huge blast and only got to know the next day that the Germans blew up the
munitions factory. As soon as the situation changed, the people became more friendly, so
when we left Sömmerda on the 4th on foot both the workers and the civilians behaved in
a friendly way. We left in the direction of Köleda at 3 p.m. on the 4th of April. The sick
and weak followed us by truck, overtook us in Köleda and went straight to Altenburg. After 8 days of marching we arrived there too. Those who could not walk on the way were
dragged along by ropes tied to their waists by the SS soldiers. It was very slow to walk
like this, so those unable to walk were put on trucks and followed us. In Altenburg we
could see the difference between our guards and the guards there. Ours were much more
humane, than those of that lager and the lager commandant was very unsatisfied with us,
as according to him we were extremely unruly. He did not have much chance to work on
us, because on the 5th of April the American troops arrived in the vicinity of Altenburg.
Our lager was emptied in a great hurry and sent on toward Glachau. Our people stayed
with us, however the ones from Altenburg went on with the escort of the commander of
the lager, and we never met them again. These were Christian and Jewish Poles, and Jewish girls from different areas of Hungary, Jewish men from the areas of Máramaros and
Munkács. We set out to be accommodated in Karlsbad but they did not succeed in escorting us there as the American and Russian troops were already pouring in from all sides by
then. We were on the Erzgebirge, Stollberg, Gemsgrün, Breitenbrunn, Stolzenheim, Boxberg road. The following morning after leaving Altenburg we found ourselves in the middle of a battle. About 4 kilometers behind our back the American tanks were shooting the
Glachau factory and railway station, and the Germans were defending themselves. From
10 a.m. till 6 p.m. 206 people out of the 1246 were lying in the ditch waiting for the battle
to finish. We lost one person, the rest were OK. The SS and several of our häftlings ran
away here but the Gestapo caught them and took them to a village next to Glachau, called
Meran. We could not find our escort , so I went together with another person till Stollberg, where we met an older woman from our group. She told us that the majority our
group had been put into a prison, and then we were taken there too. By then our numbers
were down to 600, as hundreds escaped on the way or went in other directions. 200 of
them stayed in Glachau. From Stollberg we proceeded in the direction I mentioned before. On the way the SS took care of our accommodation and food, but it got less day by
day. After Hütmersgrün , from the 27th of April we hardly received any bread, 500 grams
a day, sometimes clear soup and sometimes a piece of potato. We arrived in Boxgrün on
the 5th of May, already only 220 of us, as in every village on the way we had left 30-50
people. By now the SS did not escort us, they were happy if our numbers were smaller.
From here on there were hardly any atrocities. An SS soldier called Müller still tried to
keep up his authority by slapping some people, but he got told off by the commander. We
were supposed to continue with the SS escort on the 8th of May at 5 a.m. We arrived at
our point of collection, but the SS said that Germany had surrendered and that we were

now free and that we did not have to be afraid of them any more as they themselves would be imprisoned soon. They wished us well after freeing us. As far as I know the SS guarding us fell into American hands about12 kilometers from Boxgrün, at a place called Oberwiesenthal. We waited in Boxgrün for two days for our saviors to come, but neither American, nor Russian or English troops arrived, so we set out towards Prague. Originally we intended to go to Karlsbad, as there was a collection point for foreigners, but we heard that there was such a crowd there, that they were unable to provide any additional food and shelter, so we set out in the opposite direction, to Kaden. Naturally the behavior of German civilians changed immensely. Those who previously did not want to give us any food or accommodation, now begged us to stay with them. The German civilians provided us with everything from cooked meals to cube sugar and cakes. All we asked for was a horse cart, first that was refused by the bürgermeister, but after our strong demand ,and also after having promised we would send it back to its owner, he gave it to us. To Kaden we rode on the cart, and then sent the cart back as promised to its owner. From Kaden we went on to Prague by train. 17 of us arrived in Prague, because some of the others had gone to Karlsbad from Boxgrün, and some had stayed there and arrived in Prague within a week or two. I can hardly find words to describe the generosity of the Czech people on our arrival in Prague. They really spoilt us. They received us with love and were very helpful in offices, restaurants, hotels. We did not have to wait around a lot in offices, because they had employed enough people to be able to cope with the distribution of identifications and food coupons. There were 10-15 public soup kitchens. The only rude people were the two officers of the "Clothing Action" in the Lecarsky Dome, because I could not speak any Slavic languages. As I was crossing Vaclavszky Namnest in my very ragged cloths, an old men came up to me, and though I could not understand what he was saying, I could see he was not satisfied with my clothes, because he desperately pointed to my shoes and dress and than waved me to follow him. He lived close by on the Narodni Tida, he took me to his flat and there talked to his wife. She told me in German that he had invited me to their place to try on some of her clothes, and shoes. She gave me a summer dress and a pair of brown shoes. Unfortunately I did not experience the same kindness and helpfulness in Budapest on the Bethlen Tér, where even though I was very poorly dressed I did not get any clothes. The 1500 Pengö help was not enough to buy clothing for myself. My future plans: If I was younger I would realize my old dream to go to Palestine. Unfortunately this dream of mine can not come true now because of my age. Recorded by: Margit Oblath. Dr. I. J., Doctor, by her own hand.

Testimony six. Testimony of Mrs K. L. & Mrs M. N.

Recorded in the office of DEGOB (National council of supporting of deportees), Budapest, Bethlen Square 2.

Name:	K. L.
Place of birth:	Budapest
Occupation:	Housewife

Name:	M. N.
Place of birth:	Budapest
Occupation:	Hairdresser

K. L. and M. N. were taken from where they had been detained at the Budakalász brick factory to the following camps:

Auschwitz	July.8. 1944-Dec.6.1944
Bergen-Belsen	Dec.10.1944-Jan15.1945
Markleberg	Jan.18-April. 1945

Mrs K. L. & M. N. recount the following:

We worked in a military factory in Ujpest. At the beginning of July gendarmes came in and took the Jewish girls over to the nearby tennis court. There in front of town officials and police officers they completely undressed and took everything from us. Afterwards they took us to the Budakalász brick factory. The situation was worse there than any other time during the deportation period. László Endre came to have a look and was satisfied with the circumstances of the Jews there. At that time there was a huge summer storm and people wanted to put bricks on the ground to lie on. This was not allowed, we were forced to lie in the mud. People fell into the latrine daily, though nothing was done to prevent these accidents. Those who were well known or wealthy were identified by their names and taken away. They were returned some time later half beaten to death. If Germans came into the factory, everybody had to stand up and there had to be dead silence. Those who did not notice the entry of Germans were beaten with a dog whip. A week later we were put into wagons. In our carriage there were 85 people. We were given neither water nor a bucket for use as a toilet. I had nothing to eat during the trip so that I would not need to relieve myself. The children cried and there were sick people among us. In Kassa the Germans took over. A German officer came in and gave his word that families would not be separated, we would work and the elderly could look after the young. He said all this only to prevent us from escaping. It was evening when we arrived in Auschwitz. On the station they immediately separated the able-bodied from the sick, old and young. This happened so quickly that members of the families did not even have time to say good-bye. We were somewhat numb from the trip, the excitement and the volume of traffic of the station. They led us to the bath where they made us undress naked in front of the men and took everything from us. The owners of very good shoes were rid of those and were given wooden clogs, which immediately hurt their feet. They shaved us everywhere, then we had a hot shower, but were not given towels. We had to stand for hours wet in a cold room, while we were distributed our stripy rags instead of our cloths. We were given neither underwear nor stockings. That day we received neither water nor food. I was taken to a block without a roof, it only had some bars instead of the roof. There were 1500 of us in the block, we could not sit or lie down because it had been raining for 9 days and the block was covered with mud . We could only stand and if we got very tired we would lean to the wall. The wake-up call was at 2.30 a.m. From 3 a.m. -9 a.m. we were standing the 'appell'. It was always terribly cold at dawn. There was appell in winter in rain snow, frost. If we were punished we had to kneel with our arms up. If you put your had down you were beaten with the dog whip by the SS. There were some who fainted during the appell. Those were poured cold water on and then had to continue standing there. There were serious sunburns on the bald heads. Our ammunition was black coffee in the morning and evening, and thick soup with one sixth of a piece of bread for lunch. It sounds strange but we used to measure bread with a measuring tape, because we had to divide a loaf into 6 later to 8 pieces. People were watching the procedure with great angst and they could have killed for 1 millimeter of bread. People went totally wild, the instinct of survival ruled, and the poor häftlings became rough and selfish. The sick were taken to hospital, where they were treated by häftling doctors. It was a nicely furbished hospital, with medication. Then Dr. Mengele appeared, had a look at the sick and sent 80% to the gas chamber. Initially it took 2-3 minutes to die of the gas. However later on when the gas was running out or they put a smaller amount in, people suffered for 10 minutes. Dr. Mengele and his escort watched their suffering from the outside. To my knowledge they did not leave anybody under the age of 12 alive, except twins. These children however had a good life. Blood was taken from them every day. This was their only ordeal. With different experiments Mengele wanted to achieve the result that German women would give birth to twins. Food was served in a big dish for 50 people. The clever ones could get some sort of a little cup, but those without had to drink from the dish one after the other. This way there were a lot of mouth diseases, and it happened in our block that the mouth of some girls swell up, they could not eat and they died of hunger. The most usual motifs of Auschwitz life apart from the appels were the selections. It happened in the open air, we had to march in front of Mengele stark naked. He did not only select the sick and the very thin, but he was very unexpected in his choices and his reasons. There was incredible excitement and those who could hid somewhere and did not attend these selections. One day I was selected to a work transport, I was bathed, given clean clothing and after four days of travel I got to Bergen-Belsen. Initially we lived in tents, there was hay on the floor and we slept on it. On arrival we received two blankets and a bowl, which was a big thing for us. We did not do any work , but suffered badly of cold and hunger. The daily ration was terribly small and we could not get any extra here. We received 150-200 grams of bread and half a liter of cabbage soup was the daily warm meal. That was the time when the rain started , everything got muddy in the tent as well and it was terribly cold. The basins were outside and naturally so were the latrines as well. We needed a lot of willpower to go out, but later we did not even have the strength, because we became extremely weak, every step felt like an excursion, and we thought twice even before moving. A windstorm swept the tents away and we were put into wooden barracks. There were beds there 3 above each other, so close that we could not sit only lie there. Two of us slept on a 3.5 m. bed. It was pitch dark in the barracks, and when we were very cold and weak, we lay in there for days. At the beginning of December there was a great excitement, Mengele was coming for a visit. As there were no gas chambers here nobody hid. Again we were put into transports. We were given spring coats -in the coldest winter- and after 3 days of traveling we arrived in Markkleberg. The camp was in the outskirts of Leipzig. The Junkers Motorwerke was located here, producing the V.1 and V.2. On arrival they took our coats and instead they gave us grey overalls, which we were not allowed to take off, not even in the warm workshop. The new arrivals were not put in the factory because they had relatively more strength. We had to do earthworks with picks and shovel in the fiercest cold. We were standing in icy water and both my legs froze. Later on we had to clean the lager. The block was wet and we were not allowed to light fires. The treatment was cruel, they beat us. We were afraid of the holidays, because they thought of some amusement for themselves at our cost. There was appell at 8 a.m. Everybody had to undress in front of the SS and if they found you with an extra piece of warm clothing apart from what they had given, they would lock you up in a dark bunker for the night without a blanket with only bread and water. You had to work during the day and then back in the bunker for the night. Shaving was another big punishment as well. Not because we were vain, but because our heads got very cold if we were cold. Once I heard one SS say: "To Hell with these Jewish women, I do everything so they would get sick, but they are still healthy". Later on we worked in the factory. We had to work 12 hours a day. We worked on huge heavy machinery, standing all day, so that lost a lot of weight, until we were skin and bone. Our daily food ration was half a liter of soup and 500 grams of bread. Twice a week 20 grams of margarine. When the Americans were nearing the Lagerführer called us and told us they had to go but that they would leave us there, we would be free. The factory staff would be responsible for us until the Americans arrived. We were unbelievably happy, some started to cry. However they did this to make us suffer a bit more, because after a few minutes they withdrew their promise and said we had to go too. The disappointment was unbearable. I could not stand it any longer. Eight of us girls agreed and cut the electric fence around the lager and in the upheaval we escaped. Our entire ration was three carrots. We went on for 5 days without eating or drinking, amongst the heaviest bombing. I must mention that Wehrmacht soldiers helped us through the German front. We told them we were Dutch. Eventually we met the Americans and we were freed. Recorded by: Klára Vincze. Mrs K. L. and Mrs M. N.

Testimony seven. Testimony of Mrs O. P. & Ms Q. R.

Recorded on the 10 October 1945 in the office of DEGOB, Budapest, Bethlen Gabor square 2.

Name:	O. P.
Place of birth:	Löcse
Occupation:	Housewife

Name:	Q. R.
Place of Birth:	Löcse
Occupation:	Clerk

O. P. and Q. R. were taken from the ghetto in Kisvárda to the following camps:

Auschwitz	3.6.1944-24.10.1944
Kaufrering	27.10.1944-10.3.1945
Türkheim	10.3. 1945-27.4.1945

Mrs O. P. and Q. R. recount the following:

At home in Kisvárda we had a timber mill, 2 houses and a cement factory. We were living very well. There were about 4,000 Jews in Kisvárda before the arrival of the Germans. Generally these people lived off commerce, production etc. They lived in good circumstances. The anti-Jewish policies started with the wearing of the yellow star. Ten days later it was announced that Jews were not allowed to leave their flats. The town clerk, Csenyánszky was not anti-Semitic, rather he was good toward us. Around the 15th of April they the establishment of the ghetto was announced. The following happened: three streets were taken for this purpose, non-Jews were moved out and we were moved in. The conditions were cramped. The Jews from the surrounding areas were also brought in bringing the total in the ghetto to around 700. We were guarded by camp police and 'Jewish police'. Even the men were restricted to the ghetto and could not leave to work. There was no postal service and we were not allowed to have contact with non-Jewish civilians. There were constant body searches. Some wealthy, well known men were taken away daily, interrogated and beaten. We were told we would be taken to the Dunántul (an area west of the Danube). Non-Jewish civilians generally behaved cowardly, or at best were merely passive. There were also those who seemed happy with our sad fate. Three Jews succeeded in escaping from the ghetto in exchange for 100,000 Pengö. However it was as if money was of no help as they were betrayed and we met these three in Auschwitz a couple of weeks later. A 100% disabled war veteran called Grünvald was accused of hiding his jewels and was beaten to death. The Jewish Council: Jozsef Kain (now an American citizen), Dr. Sándor Katona lawyer, Miklos Fischer, generally did not behave incorrectly, however could achieve nothing. Not long after the transports started. There were two transports, 3500 people each. We left with the second. Before getting into the wagons the gendarmes took every possible thing away from us. We left on the 1st of June, 77 people in a wagon. We were not given water, only later in Kassa, in exchange for cigarettes from the police. There were some deaths on the train, not in our wagon, and I do not know of any escapes. An old woman was put into the wagon, she was in agony already. In Kassa the Germans who took us over told us everything would be all right, we would have enough food as well. We arrived in Birkenau on the evening of the 3 of June, we had to leave the luggage in the wagons, and stand in queues of 5. We hardly realized that the men were taken away from us we could not even say God be with you. Then they selected the old and the young and stood them at one side and those who could work on the other side. After partitioning the men a truck arrived and drove straight into our queue. There was panic, we fell on the mountain of luggage, and by the time we got up, we could not find our loved ones. We stood there on the street of the lager at night for 3-4 hours. We saw two huge chimneys from the distance spitting fire and smoke, it was a peculiarly horrible sight in the night. There was a wagon full of people suffering from 'sarlach'(illness) tied to our wagon, because the Jewish doctors thought if they had the wagon of the sick and their relatives tied to ours, they would save the whole lot. Unfortunately this did not happen, in fact this was our first disadvantage, as it got reported to the Germans on our arrival. We saw then as they put the two wagons on trucks and took them away immediately. When we were taken to the disinfecting rooms, we heard their shouting in front of the crematorium. About 20 minutes after the leaving of the trucks we heard their death cry. We asked one of the SS what that meant, he answered: "Ich höre nicht, ich habe Vatte in der Ohr". After this we were taken into the disinfecting rooms, there we put all our clothes in front of us on the ground, with only our shoes in our hands, and than stark naked we had to march in front of the SS line. We were horded into another room where they shaved us completely while constantly hitting us shouting and calling us names. After this we had a bath, we were given trousers, shirts, they were dirty, full of holes, everything was like rags, even the summer clothes were ragged. After we came out of the bath we stood outside in heavy rain, but nobody came for us. If we dared to move the SS bastards hit us. We stood there in the rain until 7 in the morning, when they came to get us. The blockälteste took us into block No. 29 in C lager. There were 1200 of us, 13 of us on a bed with two ragged blankets. The appels started at 2.30 a.m. and lasted till 6.30-7.a.m. There was kneeling from day to day, we were constantly punished and there was appell again in the afternoon. We received a little cold liquid for breakfast, one cup for five women, and carrot soup for lunch full of rubbish and bromine, so we were in a constant daze all day long. Suffering was ever present, hunger, the appells, we even had to fight to get to the taps to wash. If we washed our only clothes, there was nothing to put on, our shoes rotted off our feet, but we could not get another pair, we had to walk barefoot. In the best of cases we could get wooden shoes. Six weeks later we got into lager B. Dr. Mengele came in, sat in the middle of the room and directed us to the left and to the right. This is how he decided on life and death. Those going to the right went to the workers' blocks, and those to the left remained in block C. These unfortunates had not much hope in staying alive. The chimneys of the crematorium constantly poured fire and flames. They were very busy around that time, the gipsy and Czech lager were exterminated then, along with the men's hospital. We were warned for God's sake not to report sick, but the majority did not believe in this. It was our general observation that the pessimists stayed alive. The Hungarian Jews were almost stupidly optimistic, they did not believe for example in the crematorium. Later this changed. There was different "news" going around, for example that the Hungarian Jews will be taken home, the gendarmes will come and escort us home. A lot of people believed in this impossible tale. The end of the war was always believed to be about two weeks away. The pessimists tried to get into a position where they did not have to starve as much as the others. Our luck was that after 6 weeks we were transferred to Lager B, where the good thing was the existence of more beds and even blankets. There was about 600 of us in the barrack, later on when mass transports arrived, the situation deteriorated again. The food was no more here but at least edible. However we could get into the barracks only after the appell. We were told we were workers now and we had to train ourselves. They beat us here as well. After about a month they tattooed us. It was a huge thing that we could stay together all the way through. We had to think of all sorts of things to be able to stay together. They already wanted to separate us in the C Lager, but somehow we always succeeded in avoiding it. At the end of September Q. R. came down with scarlet fever. The doctor realized and put me in the hospital. I had to be there for two weeks, and we were constantly expecting Dr.Mengele. After 5 days I thought it better to deny my temperature, and my mother was constantly begging them to let me out. So somehow, still feverish I managed to get out of the hospital. I was lucky, a week later there was a huge selection and there were hardly any patients left in there. If I had stayed I would not be telling this story now. During this time my mother was almost put into a workers' transport. Two weeks later both of us were chosen for a transport. A civilian German factory owner came to ask for workers, and we were happy to get out of there. Mengele appeared in the bath and chose me into the transport but not my mother. I acted as I had not realized the direction he was pointing me to and my mother was coming after me. Mengele called me back and hit me so hard I fell on the floor. He called the SS women and the bitches hit me with sticks or with their boots wherever they could get me. When they tired of beating me, Mengele told them to throw me in the corner, where there were already about 40 people. We stood there for a while. Then he shouted at us "Hinein in die Gazkammer!". They pushed us into a small gas chamber, which they used to disinfect blankets in. I was desperate, I heard shouting: "We are still young, we want to live!". I looked around, we were in a small room, there were two doors opposite each other, and they did not have keys on the inside. It was almost pitch dark, on one of the doors there was a small window. There were two big holes in the ceiling, with taps, I could see they let the gas in through these. They opened one of the taps, the SS women herded us out, we were screaming, and they explained they had locked us in there only to stop us escaping after the transport, but those who panic "der soll etwas erleben!". They pushed us back, locked the doors behind us. We were there for about another 3/4 of an hour. Some were still shouting, but the majority relaxed a bit. when they let us out they took our details. I wanted to go back, but they realized I escaped again so they caught me and beat me until blood was oozing out of my mouth and nose. I was extremely desperate that they were taking my mother away from me. It was a very good transport, but still I stepped out of the line, and then met my mother in the Lager again. We stayed there until the end of October. Then eventually both of us succeeded in getting into a work transport. It happened that when putting the transport together it was already dusk and Mengele did not see my (O. P.'s) white hair. We were put into wagons, 800 women and about 1000 men. There were 52 of us in the wagon, we had food and we received a dress and a coat, but we were still not allowed to put scarves on our heads so we covered them with socks. After 3 days of traveling we arrived in Kaufering, where initially we were put in Lager 4. We were there for a couple of weeks, they did not make us work, apparently to be able to recover a bit. The treatment was un-comparably better than in Auschwitz, there was more food too, more soup and bread, occasionally we were even given some sugar. Then 60 of us were put into barrack 3. Here we were the first women transport, we got the best jobs possible in a camp. I myself, Q. R., became a nurse in the revier, O. P. became a Putzfrau in an SS barrack. The most terrible thing was that everything was full of ticks. The walls were wooden, we did not receive any wood for heating, and we were always cold. We were lying on hay, the snow would fall in, in the mornings we would wake up on a blanket of ice. We were here till the 10th of March, then we were put in a transport again and sent to Türkheim. Only 30 of us went, but we already found a lot of women häftlings there. The Türkheim lager wanted women for the earthworks, this is how we got here. We had to work with picks and wheelbarrows, collecting wood in the forest. We worked 12 hours a day. The food was less here, 2 slices of bread, 30 dgms of soup. This was all and even this we received very irregularly. We often went hungry but were unable to complain of our treatment. When the front was nearing, two transports were taken to Dachau. There was a big upheaval by then, nobody worked, there were no appells, and it was possible to escape. At that time we both were in the revier, Q. R. as a nurse, O. P. pretended to be sick with the knowledge of the Jewish doctor. We did not know how far the Americans were then. When the transports left, we got out and hid for two days. After two days, an SS doctor came by car to take away the sick. We thought it better not to stay there any longer, so four of us escaped to the forest. The SS guards were not too strict any more, they more or less let us through the gate. We walked to the vicinity of the third village we came to. There we hid for 24 hours. We were right on the front, there was the most horrible air battle going on above us. 24 hours later heard that the tanks went into the camp, and the SS escaped into the forest. They told us that the Americans had arrived. It was 28 April. We wandered around Bavaria until we arrived in Augsburg and registered there. We were there for 6 weeks, there were no trains, so we received a room in the school where there were some Hungarians living. We tried to get home from here at the end of June, but only got as far as Enns. The Russians did not let us through; the borders were closed, so we stayed in Salzburg until we left for home. We lived in a private house and were fed from a restaurant that catered for the political häftlings. We came home from there with a Hungarian transport. The Americans escorted us to Vienna; from there we took the Vienna express to Budapest. Our future plans: We shall stay in Pest for now. We would like to get employment here. Recorded by: Margit Obláth. O. P. and Q. R.

BIBLIOGRAPHY

Ancel, Jean (ed.). *Bibliography of the Jews in Romania*, (Diaspora Research Institute: Tel Aviv University, 1989).

Angier, Carole. 'The Evil of Banality', *The New Statesman and Society*, 5 Nov. 1993, pp.41-43.

Arad, Yitzak & Gutman, Yitzak & Margaliot, Andre. *Documents on the Holocaust*, (Oxford: Yad Vashem & Pergamon Press, 1987).

Arendt, Hannah. *Sur L'antisemitisme*, (Paris: Sueil, 1984).

Arendt, Hannah. *Eichmann in Jerusalem*, (London: Penguin Books, 1977).

Bartov Omer (ed.). *The Holocaust's Origins, Implementation, Aftermath*, (London: Routledge, 2000).

Bauman, Zygmunt. *Modernity and the Holocaust*, (Cambridge: Polity Press, 1989).

Bauer, Yehudi. 'The Place of the Holocaust in Contemporary History', *Journal of Contempoary Jewry*, 1984, pp. 246-265.

Bernstein, Michael. 'Against Comfort', *The Times Literary Supplement*, May 5, 1995, p.10.

Bernstein, Richard. *The New Constellation: The Ethical-Political Horizons of Modernity/Postmodernity*, (Cambridge: Polity Press, 1990).

Blanchot, Maurice. 'Thinking the Apocalypse: A Letter from Maurice Blanchot to Catherine David', *Critical Inquiry*, Winter 1989, pp.475-480.

Blanchot, Maurice. *The Writing of Disaster*, (Lincoln: The University of Nebraska Press, 1986).

Borowski, Tadeusz. *This Way for the Gas, Ladies and Gentlemen*, (New York: Penguin, 1976).

Braham, Randolph. *The Politics of Genocide in Hungary*, (New York: Colombia   University Press, 1981).

Braham, Randolph. *The Holocaust in Hungary*, (New York: East European Monographs, 2002).

Breitman, Richard. *The Architect of Genocide: Himmler and the Final Solution*, (New York: Knopf, 1991).

Browning, Christopher R. *Nazi Policy, Jewish Workers, German Killers*, (Cambridge: Cambridge University Press, 2000).

Browning, Christopher R. *Ordinary Men: Reserve Police Battalion 101 and the Final Solution in Poland*, (New York: Harper Collins, 1993).

Burrin, Philippe. *Hitler and the Jews, the Genesis of the Holocaust*, Patsy Southgate (trans.), (London: Edward Arnold, 1994).

Calhoun, Cheshire. 'Moral Failure', in Card, Claudia., *On Feminist Ethics and Politics*, (Lawrence: The University of Kansas Press, 1999), pp.81-99.

Calhoun, Cheshire. 'Standing for Something', *Journal of Philosophy*, vol. 92, no.5, 1995, pp.235-261.

Card, Claudia. *The Unnatural Lottery: Character and Moral Luck*, (Philadelphia: Temple University Press, 1996).

Card, Claudia. 'Living with Evils', in Haber, J & Halfon, M (eds.), *Norms and Values: Essays on the Work of Virginia Held*, (Lanham: Rowman & Littlefield, 1998), pp.125-139.

Caroll, David. 'Foreword', in Lyotard, Jean-Francois., *Heidegger and "the jews"*, (Minneapolis: The University of Minneapolis, 1990).

Clendinnen, Inga. *Reading the Holocaust*, (Melbourne: The Text Publishing Company, 1998).

Critchley, Simon. *The Ethics of Deconstruction: Derrida and Levinas*, (Oxford: Blackwell, 1992).

Davison, Donald. 'Paradoxes of Irrationality' in Wollheim, R. & Hopkins, J. (eds.), *Philosophical Essays on Freud*, (Cambridge: Cambridge University Press, 1982), pp.289-305.

Dawidowicz, Lucy. *The Holocaust and the Historians*, (Cambridge: Harvard University Press, 1981).

Derrida, Jacques. 'Heidegger's Silence', in Neske, G & Kettering, E., (eds.), *Martin Heidegger and National Socialism*, (New York: Paragon House, 1990), pp.145-149.

Derrida, Jacques. *Of Spirit, Heidegger and the Question*, (Chicago: The University of Chicago Press, 1991).

Donagan, Alan. 'Consistency in Rationalist Moral Systems', *Journal of Philosophy*, vol. 81, 1984, pp.291-309.

Edelheit, Abraham & Edelheit, Hershel. *History of the Holocaust*, (Boulder: Westview Press, 1994).

Emery, Jean. *At the Mind's Limits*, (New York: Schocken, 1986).

Evans, R. J. *In Hitler's Shadow: West German Historians and the Attempt to Escape from the Nazi Past*, (New York: Pantheon, 1989).

Ezorsky, Gertrude. 'Hannah Arendt's view of Totalitarianism and the Holocaust',   *Philosophical Forum*, vol. xvi, nos. 1-2, 1985, pp.63-81.

Fenelon, Fania. *Playing for Time*, (New York: Atheneum, 1977).

Fink, Ida. *A Scrap of Time and Other Stories*, (New York: Schocken Books, 1989).

Frankl, Victor. *Mans Search for Meaning*, (Washington: Washington Square Press, 1997).

Freud, Sigmund. 'The Unconscious', vol. 14 of *The Standard Edition of the Complete Psychological*, (London: Hogarth Press, 1978).

Freidlander, Saul. 'Introduction' in Burrin, Philippe. *Hitler and the Jews, the Genesis of the Holocaust*, (London: Edward Arnold, 1994).

Friedlander, Saul. *Memory, History and the Extermination of the Jews in Europe*, (Bloomington: Indiana University Press, 1993).

Gaita, Raimond. 'Remembering the Holocaust: Absolute Value and the Nature of Evil', *Quadrant*, December 1995, p.15.

Geras, Norman. 'Richard Rorty and the Righteous among the Nations', *Journal Of Applied Philosophy*, vol. 12, 1986, pp.152-173.

Gilbert, Martin. *The Holocaust: The Jewish Tragedy*, (London: Fontana Press, 1987).

Goldhagen, Daniel. *Hitler's Willing Executioners: Ordinary Germans and the Holocaust*, (New York: Vintage Books, 1997).

Griffin, Roger. *Fascism*, (Oxford: Oxford University Press, 1995).

Gowans, Christopher. *Innocence Lost: An Examination of Inescapable Moral Wrongdoing*, (New York: Oxford University Press, 1994).

Gross, Jan. *Neighbours: The Destruction of the Jewish Community in Jedwabne, Poland*, (Princeton: Princeton University Press, 2001).

Gurewitsch, Bran. *Mothers, Sisters, Resisters*, (London: University of Alabama Press, 1998).

Haas, Peter. *Morality After Auschwitz: The Radical Challenge of the Nazi Ethic*, (Philadelphia: Fortress Press, 1988).

Habermas, Jurgen. 'More Humility, Fewer Illusions- A talk between Adam Michnik and Jurgen Habermas', *The New York Review of Books*, March 21, 1994, p.25.

Hartman, Geoffrey. 'Shoah and Intellectual Witness', *Partisan Review*, vol.65, 1988, pp.39-48.

Hartman, Geoffrey. 'Judging Paul de Man', *Minor Prophecies: The Literary Essay in the Culture Wars*, (Cambridge: Harvard University Press, 1991).

Hilberg, Raul. *Destruction of the European Jews*, (New York: Holmes & Meier   Publishers, 1985).

Hilberg, Raul. *Perpetrators, Victims and Bystanders*, (New York: Harper Perennial, 1993).

Hillesum, Etty. *Letters From Westerbork*, (New York: Pantheon Books, 1986).

Jaspers, Karl. *The Question of German Guilt*, (Fordham: Fordham University Press, 2002).

Kant, Immanuel. *Critique of the Power of Judgment*, (Cambridge: Cambridge University Press, 2002).

Kant, Immanuel. *Groundwork of the Metaphysic of Morals*, (New York: Harper & Row, 1964).

Karacs, Imre. 'Poland apologises 60 years after Nazi massacre', *The Daily Yomiuri*, Sept. 2001, p.15.

Klee, Ernst, Dressen, Willi & Riess, Volker. *"The Good Old Days": The Holocaust as seen by its Perpetrators and Bystanders*, (New York: The Free Press, 1991).

Kolmar, Gertrud. *Dark Soliloquy: The Selected Poems of Gertrud Kolmar*, (New York: The Seabury Press, 1975).

Krall, Hannah, Stasinska, Joanna & Weschler, Lawrence (eds.). *Shielding the Flame*, (New York: Henry Holt, 1986).

Kren, G & Rappoport, L. *The Holocaust and the Crisis of Human Behaviour*, (New York: Holmes & Meier, 1980).

LaCapra, Dominick *History, Theory, Trauma: Representing the Holocaust*, (London: Cornell University Press, 1994).

Lackey, Douglas P. 'Extraordinary Evil or Common Malevolence: Evaluating the Jewish Holocaust' in Almond, Brenda & Hill, Donald. (eds.), *Applied Philosophy, Morals and Metaphysics in Contemporary Debates*, (London: Routledge, 1991), pp.132-158.

Lacoue-Labarthe, Philippe. *Heidegger, Politics and Art*, (Oxford: Basil Blackwell, 1990).

Lang, Berel. 'The Concept of Genocide', *The Philosophical Forum*, vol. XVI, nos. 1-2, 1984-85, pp.1-18.

Lang, Berel, *Act and Idea in the Nazi Genocide*, (Chicago: The University of Chicago Press, 1991).

Langer, Lawrence. *Holocaust Testimonies: The Ruins of Memory*, (New Haven: Yale University Press, 1991).

Langer, Lawrence. *Admitting the Holocaust*, (Oxford: Oxford University Press, 1995).

Lanzmann, Claude. *Shoah: An Oral History of the Holocaust*, (New York: Pantheon Books, 1985).

Lebor, Adam & Boyes Roger. *Surviving Hitler: Corruption and Compromise in the Third Reich*, (London: Simon & Schuster Inc., 2002).

Lesser, A. 'The Holocaust: Moral and Political Lessons', *Journal of Applied Philosophy*, vol. 12, 1986, pp.142-168.

Levi, Primo. *If This Is a Man & The Truce*, Stuart Wolf (trans.), (London: Abacus, 1987).

Levin, Nora. *The Holocaust: The Destruction of European Jewry 1939-45*, (New York: Ty Crowell Company, 1973).

Levinas, Emmanuel. 'As If Consenting to Horror', *Critical Inquiry*, Winter 1989, pp.485-488.

Lifton, Robert Jay. *The Nazi Doctors: Medical Killing and the Psychology of Genocide*, (New York: Basic Books, 1986.)

Linden, Ruth. *Making Stories, Making Selves, Feminist Reflections on the Holocaust*, (Colombia: Colombia State University Press, 1993).

Lyotard, Jean-Francois. *Heidegger and "the jews"*, (Minneapolis: The University of Minneapolis Press, 1990).

Mackie, J. *The Miracle of Theism: Arguments for and against the Existence of God*, (Oxford: Clarendon Press, 1982).

Marrus, Michael. *The Holocaust in History*, (London: Penguin Books, 1987).

McIntyre, Alison. 'Is Akratic Action always Irrational' in Flannigan, O. & Rorty, A. (eds.), *Identity, Character and Morality*, (Cambridge: MIT Press, 1990), pp.379-400.

Midgley, Mary. *Wickedness*, (London: Routledge & Kegan Paul, 1985).

Milchman, Alan & Rosenberg, Alan. *Martin Heidegger and the Holocaust*, (New Jersey: Humanities Press, 1996).

Milgram, Stanley. *Obedience to Authority*, (New York: Harper and Row, 1974).

Modras, Ronald. *The Catholic Church and Anti-Semitism in Poland, 1933-1939*, (London: Harwood Academic Publishers, 1994).

Nagel, Thomas. *Mortal Questions*, (Cambridge: Cambridge University Press, 1979).

Nussbaum, Martha. *The Fragility of Goodness*, (Cambridge: Cambridge University Press, 1986).

Ott, Hugo, *Martin Heidegger: A Political Life*, (London: Harper Collins, 1993).

Padfield, Peter. *Himmler: Reichsfuhrer SS*, (London: Macmillan, 1990).

Paulsson, Gunnar S. *Secret City, The Hidden Jews of Warsaw*, (New Haven: Yale University Press, 2002).

Pick, Daniel. *Faces of Degeneration: A European Disorder*, (Cambridge: Cambridge University Press, 1993).

dePres, Terence. *The Survivor*, (New York: Oxford University Press, 1976).

Rawls, John. *A Theory of Justice*, (London: Oxford University Press, 1973).

Rittner, Carole & Roth, John (eds.). *Different Voices: Women and the Holocaust*, (New York: Paragon House, 1993).

Rorty, Amelie. *Mind in Action*, (Boston: Beacon Press, 1988).

Rosenberg, Alan & Myers, Gerald (eds.). *Echoes from the Holocaust: Philosophical Reflections on a Dark Time*, (Philadelphia: Temple University Press, 1988).

Roth, John. 'On Losing Trust in the World' in Rosenberg, Alan & Myers, Gerald. *Echoes from the Holocaust: Philosophical Reflections on a Dark Time*, (Philadelphia: Temple University Press, 1988), pp.163-180.

Rubenstein, Richard & Roth, John. *Approaches to Auschwitz: The Holocaust and its Legacy*, (New York: John Knox Press, 1987).

Sartre, Jean-Paul. 'Existentialism is a Humanism' in Solomon, Robert (ed.), *Existentialism*, (New York: The Modern Library, 1974), pp.196-204.

Scott, Joan. 'The Evidence of Experience', in Chandler, James & Davidson, Arnold & Harootunian, Harold (eds.). *Questions of Evidence: Proof, Practice and Persuasion across the Disciplines*, (Chicago: The University of Chicago Press, 1994), pp.363-387.

Sereny, Gitta. *Albert Speer: His Battle with the Truth*, (London: Macmillan, 1995).

Sereny, Gitta. *Into that Darkness, From Mercy Killing to Mass Murder*, (London: Pimlico, 1995).

Shklar, Judith. *The Faces of Injustice*, (London: Yale University Press, 1990).

Sinnot-Armstrong, W. 'Moral Realisms and Moral Dilemmas', *Journal of Philosophy*, vol. 81, 1984, pp.263-276.

Smiley, Marion. *Moral Responsibility and the Boundaries of Community: Power and Accountability from a Pragmatic Point of View*, (Chicago: The University of Chicago, 1992).

Statman, Daniel (ed.). *Moral Luck*, (New York: State University of New York Press, 1993).

Steiner, Jean. *Treblinka*, (London: Weidenfield & Nicholson, 1967).

Thompson, E. P.*The Making of the English Working Class*, (London: Peter Smith Publishers, 1999).

Thompson, E. P. *The Poverty of Theory and Other Essays*, (London: Merlin Press, 1978).

Todorov, Tzvetan. *Facing the Extreme: Moral Life in the Concentration Camps*, (New York: Henry Holt, 1996).

Todorov, Tzvetan. *The Fragility of Goodness: Why Bulgaria's Jews Survived the Holocaust*, (New York: Princeton University Press, 2000).

Walker, Margaret. *Moral Understandings: A Feminist Study in Ethics*, (London: Routledge, 1998).

Wiesel, Eli. 'Does the Holocaust Lie Beyond the Reach of Art?', *The New York Times*, April 17, 1983, p.23.

Williams, Bernard. *Moral Luck*, (Cambridge: Cambridge University Press, 1981).

Wilson, J, Harel, Zev & Kahana, Eva (eds.). *Human Adaptation to Extreme Stress*, (New York: Plenum Press, 1988).

Zimmerman, Michael. 'Luck in Responsibility' in Statman, Daniel (ed.), *Moral Luck*, (New York: State University of New York Press, 1993), pp.218-244.

Zucotti, Susan. *The Italians and the Holocaust: Persecution, Rescue and Survival*, (Lin-

coln: The University of Nebraska Press, 1987).
Zvie Bar-On, A. 'Measuring Responsibility', *The Philosophical Forum*, vol. XVI, nos. 1-
    2, 1984-85, pp. 95-110.

INDEX

A

Akrasia, 105-107
Alternative morality, question of an, 136-137
Amery, J., 65
Ancel, J., 88
Anti-Semitism, 138
Arad, I., 124, 131-132
Arendt, H., 29-31
Arrow Cross Party, 145
Auschwitz, 156, 162-163, 164, 175

B

Bardon, K., 95
Bauman, Z., 15, 116, 141-143, 146
Beauvoir, S., 44
Bernstein, M., 160
Bertran, 164-165
Blanchot, M., 17
Bomba, A., 180-181
Borowi, C., 78-81, 134
Borowski, T., 66
Boyes, R., 75
Braham, R., 88, 145
Breitman, R., 124
Bretany., 175
Browning, C., 13-14, 19-29, 31-35, 53-54, 105, 108-110, 170, 184
Burrin, P., 2-3, 15, 112, 116, 123-125, 146

Bystander behaviour, 73, 76, 94, 129-135

C

Card, C., 64, 185
Carroll, D., 185
Choice-less choice, concept of, 181
Circumstances, role of, 64, 103
Claus, L., 175
Clendinnen, I., 35-36, 171, 173-174
Cohen, E., 174
Collective responsibility, 85-86

D

Davidson, D., 106, 106
Deutschkron, I., 177-178
De Pres, 64
Derrida, J., 15, 116
Dewey, J., 1
Diner, D., 9
Donagan, A., 48
Dostoevsky, F., 107
Dressen, W., 129-135, 137
Dr. G. H., 174-177
Dr. I. J. 164-165, 166-167, 175-177

E

Edelheit, A., 136
Edelheit, H., 136
Edelman, M., 63
Eichmann, A., 30-31, 116-117, 145
Evans, R., 152
Evil, problem of, 8, 39
Ezorsky, G., 30-31

F

Fenelon, F., 66-67
Fink, I., 158-159, 173-174, 178-179

Finkelsztajn, M., 93
Foot, P., 48
Frank, H., 52
Frankl, V., 65
Franz, K., 45
Freud, F., 107
Friedlander, S., 124, 129

G

Gaita, R., 161-162
Gang, E., 164-165
Gens, 182
Geras, N., 5, 82
Gilbert, M., 88, 141, 162
Globocnik, O., 21, 58
Goldhagen, D. J., 27
Goscicki, W., 95
Gowans, C., 12, 43, 46-55, 104, 160
Griffin, R., 127
Gross, J., 88, 93-95

H

Haas, P., 15, 112, 116, 119, 140-141, 143-146
Habermas, J., 84-85
Hartman, G., 16-17, 75
Heidegger, M., 116-117
Heydrich, R., 132, 135
Hilberg, R., 3, 6-7, 88, 122, 141
Hillesum, E., 74, 156-157
Himmler, H., 21, 124-129, 131, 136
Hitler, A., 1, 21, 145
Hoess, R., 173
Holocaust testimonies, 17, 145, 147-148, 155-157, 179
Horowitz, F. G., 10
Horthy, M., 145
Hungary, an account of the Holocaust in, 145

I

Individual responsibility, 92

J

Jaspers, K., 85-88
Judgment, as an element of moral life, 42

K

Kaltenbrunner, E., 135
Kant, I., 51, 100-101, 116
Karacs, I., 80
Kierkegaard, S., 154
Klee, E., 129-135, 137
Kolmar, G., 157

L

LaCapra, D., 61-62, 154
Lackey, D., 40
Lang, B., 15,116-122, 125-127, 131, 146
Langer, L., 11, 16, 154-162
Lanzmann, C., 76, 81, 122
LeBor, A., 75
Lengyel, O., 179-180
Lesser, A. H., 84
Levi, P., 43, 173
Levinas, E., 157
Lifton, R., 58
Lifzyc, P., 63-65
Linden, R., 4
Lorenz., 175
Luck in moral experience, 15, 97, 163
Lytoard, J. F., 1, 156, 159

M

Mackie, J. L., 120
Marcus, R. B., 48

Marrus, M., 165
McIntyre, A., 109-110
Melville, H., 49
Mengele, J., 170-173, 178, 183
Midgley, M., 40-43, 55-57, 139-140
Milchman, A., 9
Milgram, S., 34
Modras, R., 82-83
Moral agency, an account of, 53
Moral complexity, 2-3, 6, 8-9, 32, 39-40,
116, 143, 145-146, 154, 179
Moral enormity, 8-9, 12, 32, 40, 145
Moral dilemma, 55
Moral luck, 99-112
Moral tragedy, 155
Moral trauma, 153
Moral wrongdoing, 46
Ms A. B., 163, 168-169, 173, 175
Ms C. D., 165, 169, 171
Ms E. F., 163-164, 168, 171, 183
Mrs K. L. & Mrs M. N., 168-169, 172-173
Mrs O. P. & Ms Q. R., 163, 167, 169-170, 172
Myers, G., 10

N

Nagel, T., 99-102, 104
Nemeti., 176
Nietzsche, F., 107
Nussbaum, M., 104

O

Ott, H., 116
Ordinary virtue, 63, 179

P

Padfield, P., 124-125, 128, 136-137
Paulsson, G., 68-69
Perpetrator behaviour, 22-29, Philosophy and the Holocaust, 10
Pick, D., 51-52
Plato, 111

Polish Catholic Church and the Holo-
caust, 83
Pongrac., 175
Practices of responsibility, 45

R

Ramotowski, B., 94
Rawls, J., 47
Reich, M., 164
Responsibility, an account of, 12, 14,
39-40, 43-46, 49-50, 77, 90-93, 112,
181
Responsibility, to self and others, 62
Riess, V., 129-135, 137
Rittner, C., 157
Rorty, A., 106-109
Rorty, R., 5
Rosenberg, A., 9, 10
Roth, J. K., 60, 157
Rubenstein, R., 141

S

Sartre, J. P., 8, 90-91
Scott, J. W., 152-153
Secrecy, issue of, 131-139
Seeskin, K., 11
Sereny, G., 57-61, 135-136
Shklar, J., 89-90
Sinnot-Armstrong, W., 48
Speer, A., 135-136
Stangl, P., 57-62
Stangl, T., 58-62
Statman, D., 104
Steiner, J. F., 44-45
Stier, W., 76-77

T

Tännsjö, T., 48
Tauber, M., 137-138
Testimonies, importance of, 151-162

Todorov, T., 43, 62-66, 68, 88, 179,
184

V

Virtue, expressed as caring, 66-69
Virtue, expressed as dignity, 66-69

W

Walker, M., 42-43, 45-46, 79, 154, 179,
184
Williams, B., 99
Wolff, K., 131

Z

Zabecki, F., 77-78
Zimmerman, M., 102-103
Zöldi, M., 174, 176-177
Zuccotti, S., 88
Zvie Bar-On, A., 86- 88

About the Author

Marc Fellman works in the area of research governance at the University of Notre Dame Australia. Dr Fellman's most recent work is 'The Case for Moral Complexity' in Tabensky, Pedro. *Judging and Understanding: Essays on Freewill, Narrative, Meaning and the Ethical Limits of Condemnation,* (Hampshire: Ashgate, 2006).